LASAGNA

The Man Behind the Mask

**Ronald Cross
and
Hélène Sévigny**

Talonbooks   Vancouver   1994

Published with the assistance of the Canada Council

Talonbooks
201 - 1019 East Cordova
Vancouver, British Columbia
Canada   V6A 1M8

Typeset in Times, and printed and bound in Canada by Quality Color Press Inc.

First Printing: June 1994

An earlier version of *Lasagne: L'homme derrière le masque* was first published by Les Éditions Sedes Ltée., Saint Lambert, Québec in 1993.

Canadian Cataloguing in Publication Data

Sévigny, Hélène.
    Lasagna : the man behind the mask

        Translation of: Lasagne : l'homme derrière le masque.
        Includes bibliographical references.
        ISBN 0-88922-348-3

        1. Cross, Ronald, 1957- 2. Quebec (Province)—History—
Native Crisis, 1990.* 3. Mohawk Indians—Claims.
4. Mohawk Indians—Biography. 5. Indians of North America—Quebec
(Province)—Biography. I. Cross, Ronald. II. Title.
E99.M8C7613 1994   971.4'04'092   C94-910502-3

To the Mohawk People

All that has been done was done for our children and for future generations of the Mohawk people. I hope that our children and grandchildren will never have to suffer the same problems we have, and that we have succeeded in bettering their futures.

I truly hope our children will respect us for this as we respect our ancestors for all the sacrifices they have made for us.

—Ronald Cross

CONTENTS

ACKNOWLEDGMENTS

I first wish to thank all our supporters, Native and non-Native. Thank you for standing by us through a very difficult crisis. Without your help and support it would be almost impossible to achieve justice, something which Native and minority people have rarely seen in a society where governments tend to forget that all people are equal and, as such, all are entitled to basic human rights.

My thanks to my family, especially my wife and my mother, who stood by me through some very hard times. I love you both with all my heart.

Thanks especially to my "Treatment Centre" family, who helped put a missing piece back into my heart. I will keep your memory for all eternity.

To my brothers at the barricades: We put everything on the line for the Mohawk Nation and we will never be forgotten. Nor will our brothers Tom Paul ("The General") and Tadd Diabo ("the Toadster"), who have finally found peace and happiness with their people. Your spirits will forever live on with your Native brothers and sisters.

I would like to give my thanks to my friend Jimmy McComber and his family for helping me through a very difficult time in my life. I have always felt like a part of the family.

A special thanks to Owen Young and Julio Peris, who defended us from the heart and who stood by us through thick or thin no matter what the consequences. Whatever the outcome, I know of no one who could have done a better job.

Finally, I especially want to thank Hélène Sévigny for giving me the opportunity to express my feelings, my disappointments, my happiness and the TRUTH about the Oka Crisis, which I will never be able to forget. To her also, my appreciation for letting me share with the world my understanding of the struggle of the Native people.

In spite of my youth, I have learned much during these past few years. I understand the feelings of my elders much better now.

—RONALD CROSS

I wish to thank: Eric Desbiens, for his involvement in the translation of this book and his interview with Shaney Komulainen, on behalf of Les Éditions Sedes; Francine Dufresne, for the photographs and her interview with attorney Julio Peris, on behalf of Les Éditions Sedes; Mr. Julio Peris, attorney-at-law, for agreeing to read and comment on my manuscript; and Ronald Cross, who allowed me to enter his life, who opened his heart to me, and made me discover the man behind the mask.

—HÉLÈNE SÉVIGNY

PUBLISHER'S PREFACE

In early 1993, Talonbooks received an offer from Les Éditions Sedes for the English language rights to Hélène Sévigny's *Lasagne: L'Homme Derrière le Masque*. It turned out to be a fascinating biography of Ronald Cross, the most notorious of the Warrior heroes of the "Oka Crisis" of 1990, which was about to be published in Quebec. We replied immediately, expressing our interest, subject to the author's agreement that we be permitted to completely re-edit the book for the English language market. We felt that Sévigny's biography was both too reliant on, and too directed at, the Quebec market, and the book required the addition of a great deal more background information on the history, traditions and customs of the Mohawk Nation and the Iroquois Confederacy in order for the events at Oka [Kahnesatake], and Ronald Cross' role in those events, to be comprehensible to readers in the wider English-language market. We also wanted permission to update the book to cover the events that continue to unfold from that historic summer of 1990. Sedes agreed, and our reworking of the book began.

This concern for a wider context for the story was of particular importance to us because, of course, neither the Mohawk Nation nor the Iroquois Confederacy recognize the Canada/USA international boundary: They consider themselves to be sovereign peoples whose territory encompasses a large portion of what is now known as southeastern Canada and the northeastern United States of America. In February of 1994, with our reworking of the original translation done, I travelled to Montreal to meet with Hélène Sévigny, who introduced me to Ronald Cross in his home in Kahnawake. There, much to my delight, he generously provided me with all of the answers I had been seeking on the history of his people, and on the profound cultural and spiritual changes the events at Oka had initiated in his own life.

I wish to thank Ronald Cross, Hélène Sévigny and Julio Peris for all their kind and generous assistance in allowing me to make this book a reality. Any and all differences between this book and *Lasagne: L'Homme Derrière le Masque* are, of course, my sole responsibility, as are any errors or omissions this new material may contain.

KARL H. SIEGLER
Vancouver, June 1994

INTRODUCTION

In the tiny room reserved for lawyers and their clients, more precisely in room number 6 to which I have been assigned, I sit and wait for the most notorious of the Mohawk Warriors, Ronald Cross, a.k.a. Lasagna. In a few moments I will be facing the man whom the print and visual media have branded a fierce and remorseless killer. I am nervous.

In spite of myself, I am assailed by a whirlwind of thoughts as ludicrous as they are agonizing. Why am I here? What am I *doing* here? My legal and literary careers were not eventful enough as they were?

As the media have told us, the Warriors are supposed to be Mafia killers, most of whom have been in Vietnam. As the name the popular media have given them would seem to imply, they have presumably been born and bred for battle and most are believed to have criminal records. Some, we are told, are wanted by the American police. Many of their own Native people, it has been reported, are wary of them and are unhappy to see them in their midst.

By the racket of the heavy doors slamming behind me in this prison corridor I realize that I am now involved, for better or for worse. For a moment I think I can still leave. I could just turn around, write him a note that I changed my mind or that I was needed elsewhere. If I were smart, that's what I could do. But something prevents me from doing this: It's never been my nature to run away.

I feel at home in this place. I have come here before, to Parthenais detention centre. Each time I get this indescribable feeling, as of some inner void, as if life did not exist beyond these walls. Then, suddenly, a creaking gate, an oath, and I'm reminded that there is indeed life, of a kind, within this place.

Prisons have souls. Sad souls, certainly, but also something reminiscent of monasteries, where the slightest sound is pregnant with intent. An opened door, footsteps in the hall, an iron grill that clangs shut—then the meeting. Your client looks at you with eyes filled with hope, with expectations, with naïveté. Yes, I miss that time of my life when I represented first this one, then that one, borne aloft by my daring, my enthusiasm, my fire, and even my madness at believing in impossible causes. I enjoyed being told: "You'll never win this one." Those were the key words, the *magic* words that made me charge ahead.

But this sentimental mood quickly fades, and in spite of myself, my terrifying thoughts return. "What if he decides to strangle me, just for the fun of it? Last night I did not sleep a wink, seeing over and over in my mind that searing video image: Lasagna staring down—or, depending on your point of view, glaring at—the soldier. Time crawls along while I wait for him to arrive. And what if *he's* the one who ducks out of this encounter? Did he change his mind? Does he still want to see me?

Suddenly, someone shouts, "Door number 6." Too late now. I'm trapped. In a moment, I will raise my eyes and there before me will stand "the killer."

HÉLÈNE SÉVIGNY

THE FIRST ENCOUNTERS

I had imagined him as being big and tough, cruel, arrogant, contemptuous and—insulting. A sort of character from a horror movie who defied you with his sadistic eyes. A rebel. Obstinate, hard-headed....

But everything about him is calm. His walk, his voice—even the way he smokes. For a minute I have my doubts: I don't recognize the man who went eye-to-eye with the soldier. What if they've sent me the wrong prisoner—that trick had been pulled on me once in Bordeaux prison.

I imagine it must be frustrating for a celebrity who has been featured on the cover of *Maclean's* not to be recognized immediately, but I ask him anyway: "Are you Ronald Cross?"

"Yes," he replies simply and slowly. "And you're Hélène Sévigny?"

How does he know how to pronounce my name correctly?

"Yes," I answer.

And so the conversation gets calmly under way. It's regrettable that the Parthenais authorities refused to allow us to use a tape recorder. I know that we never behave exactly the same way twice—that, depending on the circumstances, events can make us feel nostalgic or blissful. Held at Parthenais for six months now, Ronald Cross—as is the case with everyone else to whom this happens—will never again express himself the same way once he's freed. I would have liked to retain the memory of his voice, listen to it again and again, so as not to misrepresent his story with my personal impressions and my emotions—so as not to betray his story while transcribing. To be very sure that the nostalgia which I thought I detected in him wasn't a figment of *my* imagination.*

For this expanded English edition, the substantial additional material provided by Ronald Cross was gathered in a session of taped interviews conducted by Karl Siegler in Kahnawake, in February, 1994.

I'd visited many prisoners before. They are almost invariably nervous, upset. For his part, Ronald Cross—a.k.a. Lasagna—told me his story in a detached tone of voice—almost neutral. As if he were telling someone else's story or describing a boring movie. As if he didn't want to flare up. Or as if he were smart enough to know that rebels are not taken seriously.

I admit to having done everything I could to provoke him. Lawyers need to know how far a client can be pushed. They need to be aware of the client's level of aggression, his contradictions, his excesses and his impulsiveness, all of which can often defeat him on the stand. The accused must pass his own lawyer's cross-examination or he will never survive the ultimate test of the witness box. Once in court is not the time to discover you are representing a lunatic or a suicidal case, waiting to drag you along with him in his fall.

He was so calm that I felt the need to push him to his limits just to see if he were putting me on. I risked asking questions which, had he really been a killer, would have meant disaster. He remained impassive throughout. Phlegmatic. And I was almost sorry for being so insolent because it had not brought me anything. I wanted to trigger a loss of control in him to convince myself that he could not be so gentle and patient.

Without realizing it, I was trying to prove that everything the media had been saying about him had been right.

I especially wanted to see if he would stare me right in the eyes, the way he had allegedly done with the soldier. His stare was the only thing I thought I knew of him. Would *I* be capable of taking it? How are you supposed to look at someone like that? Straight in the eyes?

I asked him: "Some Mohawks have told the press that they didn't want your presence in this conflict, that you were part of the Mafia that wanted to take control of the reservation. How can you protect someone who rejects you? And how can you accept being jailed for having defended the claims of the Mohawks while your own people show you no gratitude?"

"Traditional Indians," he began, "are different."

Always with the same neutral tone and the same faraway look. It was like confronting Camus' *Stranger*. Without raising his voice, he flung all my questions right back at me, one by one.

I had trouble imagining that, just a few months before, he had projected an image of being such a violent man. Listening to him, I realized that often we project violence onto those we imagine to be our enemies.

14

The moment someone opposes our ambitions, our way of seeing things, and especially if he threatens our security, then he becomes our enemy. And from that moment on, everything this enemy says will be perceived as an aggression, even if he is only asking for his fair share. His power is magnified by our fear.

Did Ronald Cross really want to kill that soldier, or simply intimidate him because he was on Indian land and Cross wanted to drive him out?

Granted, we have all been well-indoctrinated by the media. Who could possibly imagine a peaceful Lasagna when our television sets said: "Fifteen of the Warriors behind these barricades... are actively sought by the New York office of the FBI for a variety of crimes committed in recent years" (Lamarche 112). Then other media immediately chimed in: "It is said that some individuals wanted by the FBI arrived in Montréal just days before the start of the Oka Crisis" (ibid.).

Slander and defamation. Who had a vested interest in spreading such lies? The White people—in order to sow dissension among the Indians? Or to convince pro-Indian Whites to switch sides? During a war, so many strategies are used. And what if it were the Indians themselves? Why not? Even this quickly, the Oka Crisis began to take on a different look.

As for Lasagna, sitting there before me, he had so many qualities fascinating to a writer: the absence of emotion, the cold but observant eyes—you cannot be born that way. It was as if right in the middle of a blank page a character suddenly sprang out to tell you his story.

How will I present him? As a hero of fate? A saviour? A Louis Riel figure? A gangster? Or a Mohawk pushed by fate and circumstance to the very heart of a revolt he had not wanted, but which he had long felt coming and which, years from now, will belong to legend and to history—with its usual freight of truth, lies and disparagement.

But for now, on this Thursday, 28 February, 1991, one single thought occupies his mind: His lawyer is suggesting that he plead guilty. He would only serve five years divided by three, which means twenty months—not a lot, but too much when you are not guilty. Lasagna refuses. For him, this would be a way of admitting he is a criminal. He does not want that. He *cannot* have that. All he did was defend his land, as would any good soldier under attack by an enemy. And for that people are dangling before him the prospect of a guilty plea. Guilty of what?

He explains his way of seeing the conflict, and it is easy to perceive that he never imagined—that he will never be *able* to imagine—how the defence of one's land can ever be interpreted as a criminal act. His people are in trouble; his duty is to help them. The White people want to take away this bit of land on which, centuries ago, they magnanimously allowed the Natives to stay. At first. And now they've changed their minds and decided to take it back. What could he do? Just look on, submit, give up yet one more time?

To this question I have no answer, but *he* does. Any Mohawk facing such a dilemma has the duty not only to protect his land but also to use any means necessary to defend it. To be a Mohawk, you have to understand this first great principle.

The original, terrifying image I had had of Lasagna dissolved little by little. Leaving him, I could not believe he had ever terrorized anybody. And yet, he was a symbol of all the violence of the Oka Crisis. But how had this violence come to be?

To some, Ronald Cross was born on July 11, 1990, along with the Oka Crisis. In their eyes he was the masked bandit wanted by the FBI and known by the code name "Lasagna." And, like all the other Warriors, his only wish and mission in life was to establish Mafia rule on Indian reservations.

Behind this description, that might make even Al Capone blush, was the truth that could very well disappoint those who imagine him mixed up in the crimes of the New York underworld. Ronald Cross is a Mohawk by birth, by heart and soul. The Oka Crisis was his first rebellion, his first consciousness-raising. It was on the day the rebellion broke out that he fully understood he was a Mohawk, and everything that came to mean to him. Since that day, his life has been spent discovering the magnitude of his people's oppression and paying with his freedom the price of having chosen to tell the entire world about the injustices suffered for centuries by North American Natives.

In the eyes of others, the public image of a rebel may be born on the day of a revolt, but the man himself was really born in different circumstances, and on another day. To better understand those we accuse, we must first discover everything about them. The media-created myth has gone on long enough. And though it might not please his persecutors, his story begins like that of any other well-raised North American child, as we shall see.

•

On my second visit, Cross is in the grip of despair. And while he talks about his life, beginning with his childhood in Brooklyn, I have but one question: Why is he, rather than another of the defenders of the Pines, in this jail? What have become of all the others?

It is not up to me to get him riled up against his own people. For the moment, I sense, he is at the point where he believes he will never get out of this jail. That is why there is so much nostalgia in his voice when he talks about his past. And I have to force myself to sit there and simply listen and take notes, when what I really want to do is scream at him that he is ruining his life. For a worthy cause, no doubt. But the others who defended the barricades resumed their normal lives after the crisis. Why should he pay more dearly than they? Besides, I think, is he so naïve to think that all this is furthering the Mohawk cause? He's been in jail, in utter silence, for six months and the whole world does not give a damn. Except for the Mohawks and some prison guards, no one knows what has become of his life. Even I had initially thought he was free, his incarceration had made so little noise. Why don't the Mohawks threaten to revive the crisis or to blow up the Mercier Bridge if the government doesn't release their hero? I would like to understand how they can let him rot here. And what about him? Is he even aware of how he has been suckered in this whole affair?

When he left the Kahnawake reservation at fourteen, Ronald Cross certainly didn't know he would be back there one day, dressed in the garb of a Warrior of the First Nations. But actually, I remember, he never really left the reservation. He had gone back there every weekend, to visit his mother and his son Ryan.

Does he miss his freedom, or New York?

His freedom, yes; New York, no. "It's a dangerous city," he says, "where I learned to survive." No: Real life for him is in Kahnawake, surrounded by his people. He will never again work the high steel in New York. That high-flying life is over.

A hero has no regrets, or at least he should not let them show. From the bottom of his cell, what does he think about, now that the best days of the autumn are over? How did his life take such a turn? In the heat of battle, amidst all the turmoil, when he decided to get involved in this affair, had he thought it would end like this? Did he think that his fate would be more dramatic than that of the others, or was it all just bad luck?

One thing is certain: In his narrow cell he has all the time in the world to review the events that led him there; to relive the Oka Crisis over and over again, step by step, and to ask himself where he made his big mistake. He is plagued by his memories of this crisis, the good and the bad. How could it be otherwise? The prisoner's solitude brings him back to his past, his childhood, and gives him time to think of his mother, his wife, his friends.

His silence, his smile, his apparent submissiveness—they all make me want to blow my top. People should not just accept their fates like that, I think to myself. In spite of myself I burst out: "You're in jail while the other Warriors are home. Are the Indians worth the sacrifice of your life?"

"I have no doubt that what we did was good," he answers. "I have no regrets. If we'd let the governments do as they wanted, we'd have nothing left now. Yes, the Indians are worth this sacrifice because it opened the eyes of the whole world, and it made people realize how the people of the First Nations are being treated."

He's heating up at last!

"Life at Oka and in Kahnawake is pretty comfortable, but the other Indian tribes live in poverty and are entirely dependent on their social security cheques. They're oppressed by the governments of Canada and the United States. Here we are, almost in the year 2000. We can send rockets up in space every other day, and meanwhile there are still people living in villages without electricity or water, without sewage systems, without schools, and who have no hope of economic prosperity.

Not so long ago, they were rich. They lived off the land, and the land took care of them. The Indians didn't abuse the land, they only took from it what they needed. The White man has poisoned the land and the water to the point where almost everything we eat or drink is laced with chemicals. Some places you can't go to hunt or fish anymore.

To me, this struggle is worth my life and I'll keep on fighting so that our children and the generations to come have their place in society. To retain what's ours and what is our due. To save what little we have left, by protecting the land from those who want to destroy it and who would do anything for a buck.

Money is the root of all evil, but one day it might not be of any use at all. Sooner or later the planet will be devastated. People will want to go back to the old way of life, but there won't be anything left!"

Who would have believed that the fate of humanity would be of any concern to Lasagna? That he could care about others, about those who will be here one day, after we are gone? Who will believe me when I say that Ronald Cross has a social and a humanitarian conscience? There is nothing left here of the "brutal warrior" of the Oka Crisis. And yet, in court, Ronald Cross refuses to take the stand. He has chosen to remain silent. He does not answer to the Crown's charges. Why such a strategy, such resignation? Has he so little confidence in White justice? I know he would get the jury's sympathy, if only he would talk to them the way he talks to me. But Ronald Cross remains silent, as if he had already accepted the fate that awaits him, thinking, "This is your justice, not mine."

He says nothing to reporters—or rather, nothing they don't already think they know. His private life, his feelings are of no concern to anyone but himself. And the myth about his rowdiness keeps getting around. He lets people talk, he lets people say what they want, he does not give a damn either way.

But he tells me everything. He goes beyond the answers I expect. He can talk for hours. Slowly. Intelligently. Wisely. The Indian cause has become his passion. I do not dare interrupt him, he is such a good history teacher. I listen to him and think that the Warrior is becoming a philosopher and that he might one day serve the Indian cause without taking up arms. But why does he persist in staying behind his walls? Is it because the terrifying image we have of him keeps out intruders?

But during those days in the Oka Pines, when he was armed and acting tough and arrogant, did he know then the risk he was taking? Did he expect an ending other than this one, or did he really think he could win?

"The risk of what was waiting for us at the end of the line didn't matter to us," Cross replies. "We knew there would be a price to pay, even though we didn't think it would go this far. We were convinced that an agreement would be reached with the governments before we lost control of the situation."

At Parthenais, the memories of Oka are still fresh. Between comments on the crisis, Cross sometimes digresses and talks about his incarceration. For example, he says that when he arrived here they took away his jacket because the word "Kahnawake" was written on it, which was seen as a possible incitement to trouble. He talked about it with his lawyer and he was given back his jacket. There were no more incidents. Here, no one bothers him any more.

•

At each of my subsequent visits, he arrives with documents and newspaper articles. He wants to know everything, learn everything, understand everything. Everything interests him. He reads everything he can find and devours it. From whodunits to Native history, everything captivates him. Legal stories and discussions of points of law. French instruction books, even—but those are hard, he admits. He has made a francophone friend here who doesn't speak a word of English. They make do with a dictionary.

The document he gives me today answers many questions I had asked previously or, rather, many attacks I had made previously. He has cut it out just for me: *"Natives Don't Pay Taxes? It's a Myth"* (Morrisseau n.p.).

The article deserves closer examination. With a touch of humour, the author asks the question: "If you ask a Canadian what special rights aboriginal people have, most would reply at the very least, 'Aboriginal people don't have to pay taxes'"—adding that he would like to be an Indian in order never to pay taxes again! But, Morrisseau goes on: "The only aboriginal people who are legally exempt from any tax are status Indians and they comprise less than half the aboriginal population. Taxation laws also make it difficult for status Indians to take advantage of this break as there are geographical limitations such as mile limits and delivery requirements. It's also very difficult for status Indians living off the reserve to exercise this right." Then he explains that just trying to convince a merchant to allow the tax exemption is in itself a problem. In the end, Indians have a right which most of them cannot exercise.

Another White myth has to do with the idea that Indians all benefit from special hunting and fishing privileges. So how do you explain the hundreds of Indians who are arrested every year for such violations?

Morrisseau brings up a final point: "And the so-called right to a free education is, in reality a farce. Actually it's more like a right to free assimilation as most schools across the country teach a standard curriculum that does not respect aboriginal people's language, culture and history." He concludes: "If aboriginal people get everything for free, why do they have nothing?"

We can wonder how Quebec francophones would react if anglophones forced them to go to English schools, cutting them off from their religion, their language and having the gall on top of it all to tell them that they were being treated extremely well: They were getting a free education.

20

Sitting comfortably at home near the fire, I read this article that Ronald Cross gave me and I have to admit that it not only answered the questions I had for him on this subject, but it is a bitter pill indeed.

Ronald Cross has the patience to wait for his victory. I still remember, during our first meeting, almost snarling at him: "By the way, what do you Indians like anyway, besides being supported by our government?" Impassive, he had asked me to define "being supported." Months went by, and I thought this old incident had been forgotten. Then one day he said he had clipped out an article—this one—he thought might interest me. Had I been in his place I would have have taken the opportunity to torment my victim, with reminders of that angry and all but forgotten statement. In the end, which of us is more "savage" than the other? But Ronald Cross is not like that. He has a strength very different from mine. He knows I am beginning to know. That is enough.

And I have reached the point where I tell myself that Ronald Cross is not in jail for nothing. In spite of the injustice of his being there at all, perhaps of all the Mohawks who were involved in the Oka Crisis he is the one who will benefit the most from this period of forced solitude. He has succeeded in organizing to the best of his abilities this sudden pause in his life. When he could see that there was nothing to do, he tried to make the best of it. Of course he does not like being here, and of course people should not be locked up on the pretext that it might do them some good. But he takes advantage of it to read, to learn, to document his and his people's history.

It is as if he has returned to being the good schoolboy, the top-of-the-class student at St. Theresa of Avila, and has suddenly awakened, wanting to make up for all that time lost working on the construction sites. Because, except for the fact that he earned a living at it, his intellectual curiosity was never satisfied climbing the skyscrapers of Manhattan.

●

Some days, a prisoner is not cooperative. Or else he sleeps right in your face, or acts restless as if he would prefer going on a twenty-kilometre bicycle ride.

Today he was doing everything possible to overcome his sleepiness. I put my documents back in my case because we were wasting our time. Everything about him was in slow motion and I told him he had probably not slept very well the previous night.

"No," he said, "I think it's the food."

"What food?"

He told me that the veteran inmates had told him to be wary of the food—that in order to gain the upper hand over so many violent prisoners, the authorities had little choice but to add some tranquillizing seasonings to the meal.

While I tried convincing him that any such practice would quickly become known to the public, the fact remained that he was apathetic. So we talked about his upcoming request for bail.

"It's the last time I'll see you," I told him. "In jail, I mean. The next time you'll be on the outside."

He grinned the sort of grin that might have meant: "If lawyers start gazing into crystal balls, we're not out of the woods!" And he said: "I don't know how many times my lawyers have tried getting me out of here, and it never works. I've been here six months."

"Well, this time will be the right time!"

And I gave him a thousand pieces of advice so that he would not end up back here the day following his release on bail. He smiled, perhaps because he felt sorry for me or perhaps because of hope, I could not tell.

In my head, it was all done: He was already free. I warned him that if I were a police officer and I disliked him, I would try to get him back in jail by very subtle means. "Everyone knows about your main weakness, alcohol." I told him. "It would be very easy to bribe an Indian to take you out drinking. With a White person you'd be on your guard. With another Indian you'd fall right into the trap. And, once drunk, you'd do something stupid which would bring you right back... in here!" He then swore to me that if his day of freedom arrived, no friend would take him out drinking.

Two days later he was granted bail. On Friday evening, March 15, 1991, he was freed. Everyone saw him on their television sets, smiling and relaxed. He was on all the networks and, the next day, in all the papers.

After he was let out on bail, he phoned me to set up a meeting, as we had previously agreed. And now here I am on this reservation for which Ronald Cross, and others, would give their lives.

A White Woman on the Reservation

When you are a White woman and you arrive in Kahnawake, that bit of land cut off from the rest of the world, you get a strange feeling. You are really not where you belong. Everything has been thought out and constructed to make you want to turn around and leave.

Signs saying "We Won't Forget" (the 1990 crisis, of course), remind you that to the Native people, vengeance is sweet. And, in spite of yourself, you start thinking of everything that Canadian history has taught you about the Iroquois so that, as brave as you thought you were, fear gets you in its grip. It is especially when you go deeper into the woods, leaving the main road, leaving "civilization," that you suddenly become aware of being cut off from all outside help. You are on foreign land, and here, no White person can come to your aid.

But of course there are many murderers among the White population. So how can I explain that here, among the Mohawks, and White man coming out of the woods would look like a saviour to me?

Admittedly, the previous evening some Whites who were driving through Mohawk territory were shot at—no one was hurt. "Stay home!" seemed to be the message behind this volley of shots. At least that is the impression I had when I heard of the incident on the news.

Quite sincerely and without wanting to hurt Ronald Cross' feelings, I would have preferred visiting him at Parthenais. But he is free now or, rather, he is out on bail—just as I had predicted during our last visit. I had a sort of premonition when I saw him enter the room.

The Mohawk standing guard at the entrance does not look very reassuring. The Mohawks have set themselves up like the army—they have put the biggest men in front. I was never so happy to show my lawyer's card and I was never in such a hurry to mention the name of my client. Ronald Cross, Lasagna, became the password. Finally—nothing more to fear.

When Ronald Cross arrives in his Jeep, my car doors remain locked and the key stays in the ignition in case I have to get out of there in a hurry. I must look scared since his first question is: "Would you mind telling me what or who you're so afraid of here? Indians don't hurt anybody. They're on duty at the entrance simply for surveillance purposes, that's all." I am made to understand that the Whites of the previous evening were drunk and had refused to identify themselves, thus creating the trouble that everyone had heard of.

I do not wish to pass judgment on that weekend "murder attempt" but the fact remains that, in his presence, my fear disappears and, in the hours that follow, I will be given a history lesson on the ways and laws of the Mohawks.

Still, as a White woman I feel strange walking around freely on this Mohawk land. In a split-second, the break with the white world is clean and sharp, almost brutal. And if this experience is upsetting to me, how much more so must it be when Indians come to visit us? Must we be surprised at how obstinately they cling to their traditions and their way of life? Just a little way away from Kahnawake, life rushes by at the breakneck pace of the digitized White world, surrounded by huge buildings of steel and concrete. Here, life has been partitioned from that. It's a sort of concentration camp that you can enter and exit at will. Walking in the middle of this reservation, I have trouble imagining that soon I will be back on the noisy highway, rushing home at high speed. Just a few hours will have come between the past and the present, between his way of life and mine.

How can someone who has lived in New York be happy here, hemmed in by this village of 5,000 inhabitants? But that is apparently *my* vision of Kahnawake, not his. Ronald Cross has known both worlds and he unhesitatingly chose to sink his roots back in here. He does not understand my obsession with New York. "We have everything we need here," he tells me over and over, as if to make me understand that he is not lacking for anything. And while he talks of what makes up the essence of his people, you feel that he really does belong here in Kahnawake.

Ronald Cross and Hélène Sévigny in the Pines in Kanehsatake. Photo by Francine Dufresne.

Ronald Cross in the Pines. Photo by Francine Dufresne.

Ronald Cross and the Mohawk Way

When the whole of the Western world was poised, in 1992, to celebrate Christopher Columbus' great discovery of the Americas, a proud people who had discovered it before he did—when it had truly been "empty of inhabitants"—felt robbed and ridiculed.

That is why today Lasagna greets me with a T-shirt that displays his humour and his state of mind. Out on bail once again, apparently "detoxed," Lasagna arrives at the Kahnawake reservation's checkpoint. He has that joyous look that I know so well. And yet, something does not sit right in his heart.

In spite of Lasagna's big smile, his T-shirt's logo "500 Years…It's Beginning To Piss Me Off!" stops me dead in my tracks. I had to be face to face with a Native North American to remember all of a sudden that Columbus did not invent America. At the very least, he got here in second place! And I feel as ashamed and as guilty as if I had just stolen someone's birthright.

Beyond the insult, there is all the contempt which this anniversary represented. It was like saying to the world that the Native people do not exist and never have. Because if, in our eyes, we granted these people the slightest importance, we would celebrate merely our *arrival* on this territory, not its discovery.

Celebrating Columbus means to deny blithely that the Indians already occupied North America before the arrival of the Great Conquistador. It is throwing in the faces of Natives what they are trying so hard to forget in order to live in peace.

"Columbus didn't discover America," Cross explains. "He came to America. And what's worse, he came to massacre the Indians!

"How can you celebrate Christopher Columbus?" he exclaims indignantly. "He killed as many people as Hitler. Is there a nation anywhere in this universe that would dare celebrate Hitler's birthday? So how can you celebrate Christopher Columbus?"

Suddenly he stops, as if realizing that it was not I who sponsored Columbus's caravel or fed his crew.

"Every nation has its country. Where is the Indians' country? All the Whites are Europeans. The French are from France, the English from England, the Italians from Italy, the Spanish from Spain, the Polish from Poland, the Russians from Russia. All those who are here come from elsewhere. But the Indians do not come from somewhere else. They were here. When Christopher Columbus arrived, the Indians were already here. What did he discover? A country already occupied by the Indians.

We were duped from the first day when we greeted Christopher Columbus on our land. Our ancestors were cheated and deceived by treaties and promises that have never been kept. We obeyed treaties that the Whites didn't respect. The Indians learned the hard way that the White man couldn't be trusted. He spoke with a forked tongue.

The Whites didn't understand our way of life and there was no place for us in their world. In short, we were on our land and we were in their way. They knew we didn't want to give away our lands and our territories. We've never surrendered to any government. We've never signed any documents whereby we accepted to give up our lands.

The only way they could rob us of what we owned was to exterminate the Indian Nations. They brought war and death with them. The White man taught us to hate him. He stole our country, our lands, killed our women and children, burned our villages and called us savages. How can we forget all these things when we're still being deceived today and nothing has changed?

We greeted the Europeans with open arms and we wanted to share our knowledge with them. They replied by giving us smallpox-infested blankets, hoping to kill our tribes this way and then to take our lands for themselves. They also massacred the buffalo herds. They almost succeeded in wiping them out and provoking famines among the Indian people. There are thousands of books written on this subject, but people only hear what they want to hear and read only what they want to read; and let's not forget that the government allows teachers to teach only what's approved by the government.

When the Europeans arrived a very long time ago, the Natives accepted to share their land with the Whites. Their goal was for Whites to live on their side and Indians on their own so that everyone would be happy without stepping on each other's feet. That was the first treaty. It was called the Two Row Wampum, and it was made with the Dutch who had come to settle in a place they called New Amsterdam. It was a trading alliance which said that the Indians wouldn't govern the Whites and the Whites wouldn't govern the Indians. This first treaty still exists, because when the British took over from the Dutch in that place and called it New York, they also agreed to abide by the law of the Two Row Wampum. In Canada we have the same kind of Wampum treaty. It was presented in Ottawa. It specified that Whites and Indians were to live side by side without interfering in each other's lives. Each would have its own form of government and its own way of life. The Whites accepted this. Everybody could have lived in freedom. You can see where this has gotten us!

The Whites don't want to understand our way of life or accept the fact that we're a Nation. It's like a Quebecer arriving in Germany and deciding that German laws aren't right.

Quebecers want to be recognized as a distinct nation. The Mohawks claim the same right. We are not Quebecers, we are Mohawks.

We don't want to be a part of the political debates concerning Quebec. We are a nation, just like Quebec. We have our own government and we have no need of another government to rule us. We have our own system and our own laws. We don't accept that there be another government above ours.

The Indians want to be responsible for running their own communities, just like your society is run by your government. But your government is trying to change our community to make it look like yours.

If the United States and Canada decide to go to war, that's their business. They can't forcibly draft us because the White war isn't our war. The only wars we're interested in are the ones that concern our people.

Now, we must adapt. There are cars, there's money. It takes money to do anything. Indians have to adapt to this new way of life, but it's not given to everyone to be able to integrate. There are many Indians who, unable to adapt, take to drinking because they feel useless. They just can't find a place in that type of society. Because they've been locked up on reservations, they feel they're good for nothing. They're isolated. They're on their reservation, they drink, they have kids. This attitude is now rooted in them. For many generations. Few of them have a chance to leave and make something of their lives.

The new generations have done the same thing as their parents. If their parents are alcoholics and on welfare, the kids do the same thing. Of course, there's poverty on the reservations, but it's not like that everywhere. The Indians aren't all alike. The Cree, for example, are well educated. They're one of the richest and best educated nations. They succeeded without having to sacrifice their traditions or their culture.

We have our doctors, our lawyers; we have our schools, our garages, our buses and our hospitals. We have all we need to be autonomous and a lot of Indians have become successful by studying."

In spite of its nameless streets, Kahnawake's social structure is well organized, with a hospital—the Kateri Medical Centre—and the Kateri School, where Mohawks can study till they reach high school level. High school classes are offered at the Kahnawake Survival School. These institutions were named in memory of Kateri Tekakwitha, who died in Kahnawake in 1680 at the age of twenty-four. There is also a church, a courthouse and the Longhouse, a long wooden building where the Mohawks meet to talk and make their decisions.

The Mohawks' spiritual counsellor, the late Louis Hall—a painter and a philosopher—was very modest, and he did not want people to give him any titles. It is true that an artist always reveals himself through his work. Louis Hall's paintings reproduce his Native universe. He lived right next to the Longhouse until he passed away in 1994.

"The Longhouse was established a long time ago, back when the Indians were the only people in the land. They too had territorial disputes. The land used by each tribe was sometimes contested by other tribes and so wars started. Then an Indian came along, he's a legendary figure called "the Peacekeeper," and he made a great peace. He brought together five Iroquois nations—the Mohawks, the Oneidas, the Onondagas, the Cayugas and the Senecas—to form the Longhouse. It's the Longhouse where the chiefs of each of these five nations would henceforth come and form their government. Later on, the Tuscaroras were admitted as the sixth Nation in the Iroquois Confederacy.

Painting by Louis Hall. Photo by Francine Dufresne.

The Longhouse is also the house of prayers. It's a sacred place where we pray to the Creator and thank him for everything he's given us to survive on the 'motherland.' Our ceremonies and our festivals are celebrated in the Longhouse.

Praying is considered as an act of generosity by the Indians. During the Oka Crisis, while we were in the trenches, we didn't pray for the Creator to punish the soldiers or for Him to wipe out the army and the White people, but rather for the White people to understand that our only goal was to save the land. We didn't ask for the death of those men, we just wanted that the Creator make them understand our situation and help them make the right decisions.

The Indians have also prayed for the Creator to guide the judge and jury in their decisions. They didn't pray for my release from prison, but rather to insure that the jury understood that the mission of the Indians was to protect the land."

At the end of this excursion with Ronald Cross, I am stupefied and incredulous when I hear him say that one must wish only for what is best for others.

"It's every morning when you get up that you have to think of thanking Him. Simply because the universe which He has created to astound us is still there.

During the meetings in the Longhouse, all the people can express their opinions. You just have to ask for permission to speak from the Chief who then lets people talk one after the other. The one who rises speaks his mind and then sits down again. Then it's the next one's turn. It's like in Parliament: The person says what's on his mind and sits back down. If it gets too noisy, the War Chief restores order and calms the assembly.

There are three meetings a week in the Longhouse. A first meeting for the men only. A second meeting for the women only. The last meeting is addressed to the whole community in order to discuss the problems brought up during the first two meetings. It's the way the Mohawks have been governing themselves ever since they became united. We were the first government here, before those of Canada and the United States. The American Constitution and the Canadian Constitution are based on the same system as ours. Except that we've always been doing it this way.

It is well known in history that this is how the government of the United States, the Constitution, was formed, because Benjamin Franklin used the Five Nations Confederacy as an example for the organization of the thirteen colonies. They'd seen how we ran our government among Nations and this is why they have states and they have their senators who sit down to take care of each place. The American eagle is actually the Iroquois eagle, only theirs holds thirteen arrows instead of the five arrows representing the five nations of our original confederacy. They'd seen how the Longhouse was run as a confederacy and this is where they took the example for their Constitution.

32

When the Europeans came here, there were no White governments, there were no White states, there was just one big continent and everybody was fighting to keep it. I mean the British were fighting the French and the Americans, they were all at war about who was going to control what because they had their countries overseas and they were fighting over our country and we were blind at the time not to see what was going on. Because we welcomed these people. We did not know at the time they were going to rebel against us and start taking our land the way they started taking it. They found riches here.

You read the books: They came here for gold, they came here for riches that were in this place to take back to their countries. It's a shame that our ancestors had to—at least according to the books—welcome them the way they did, because it's not nice to say it, but I wish things had been different and they just wouldn't have let them set foot on this land. They should have said, 'Hey this isn't your place.' But they were just as curious as anybody as to who these people were. They thought they were gods coming from the sea. That's how spiritual they were. They had a knowledge of things that happened in the past, of gods coming from the sun, from the sky, from the water, and that's what these people were to them, so they couldn't just destroy them, because they thought, 'These are our gods that are coming back to us. And if they're killing us, that's the way it's supposed to be.' They didn't understand that they weren't their gods, that these people came from overseas, like we do today.

It's also in the Longhouse that we have our political debates. There are three different sections in the house. Each clan has its section and there are three chiefs per clan, as well as three clan mothers. There's also a War Chief. He presides over the meeting, even though he plays many roles in our community. In times of crisis, he leads the men. *Rotiskenekete*, the carriers of the burden of peace, that's how the men are called. *Skennen* means peace; *kete* means carrying the burden. All the men are born as Warriors, but 'Warrior' is actually a White word.

Here in Kahnawake and Akwesasne, there's always been what the White people call a Warrior Society. It is a security force set up by what we call the men of the community. In English, the Indian word really means 'The Men's Society.' According to all our laws and all our traditions, the men are responsible for the safety of the Territory and the safety of the people in the Territory: That is their duty as men. So in times of a crisis or in times of national security, the men will come together and they will follow under the War Chief. There is a War Chief, and there are Assistant War Chiefs in each clan: the Bear Clan, the Wolf, and the Turtle. It's always been so, right throughout history there have been Warriors. We, as the men of the community, the village, or whatever you want to call it—it is our social role, our duty as men, to protect the land and to protect the people. And in a time of crisis the men come together and they are assigned their duties, what to do and how to do it. And, I mean, we're not talking without military experience. It's really not a military force but they work like one. They know communications, they know weapons, they know tactics. We teach each other. I mean, there was always, twenty-four hours a day, a security force working in the community besides the Peacekeepers. And there always has been here, because we only have two or three Peacekeeper's patrol cars for twenty-four hours a day, for a big community where there's people coming in here that you'd have to watch out for: people who abduct kids, people who come in drunk and start fights, and different types of things. And so we've always had our own security force. Really, it's tradition.

We kind of got stronger with it here in Kahnawake because we always knew that probably some day we would have these big troubles on our hands and people were going to come in here with guns and what not. So we had to update ourselves from bows and arrows and horseback to jeeps and automatic weapons. They are always under control. We've always had a working system where we had our own cars patrolling, communicating with the people or the Peacekeepers. It was a quiet society up to '90, a quiet thing that not many people knew about. And if there were Warriors who were on duty and seen in camouflage doing things, they weren't known to anybody, nobody knew who the Warriors were, not in this community or in any other community.

That was the thing with the mask, that's why they wore the mask. Because, if there was somebody from Kahnawake dealing drugs and the Peacekeepers never did anything about it, the Warriors took it upon themselves to gear up, maybe five or ten of them, and put on a mask so these people wouldn't recognize them, because it's one of our own people that we have to deal with, and go to his house and do what we have to do to stop him from selling drugs. And this way he couldn't turn around and take revenge on the people who did it because he didn't recognize them because they wore masks. And that's where the mask really came from. So our own people wouldn't recognize us and we wouldn't have this big confrontation in town with our own people. I mean people today are very vengeful.

If I go to a drug dealer's house like this and I smack him around and say, 'Quit selling drugs here or else I'm going to throw you off the Territory, or the men will deal with you'—and he sees it's me, sees it's my cousin or somebody, the next thing you know he's got his friends together and I've got to watch the safety of my family, because I'm trying to do something good. So that was the whole thing with the mask that nobody really understood. The mask is really like a uniform. It makes a distinction between what you are doing personally and what you are doing for the sake of the community.

It was more or less to be the unknown Warrior, in order not to escalate the situation where someone could take revenge on the person. That's why the mask was worn. Because there were times we had to take our own people and bring them back to the base and, let's put it straight out, knock some sense into them. I mean, that's the only way at certain times things work, you know. We've got drug deals all over, some people have them right next door, but the police never seem to do their job and get rid of them. If they do, there's another bunch there. So how do you deal with them? They go to jail for a week or two for selling drugs to kids and what not and then they're out on the street again. So they didn't get the message. You put them in jail for two, three years—they don't give a damn because they made two—three—four—hundred thousand dollars, or millions. They don't care, they'll go back and do it again. So sometimes you have to do it that way and let them know, 'Hey, we're not going to stand for it again, because if it happens again who knows where you're going to wind up.' And he doesn't know who's doing this.

If you are a traditional Indian, a traditional Mohawk, you know your responsibility as a man, what your responsibilities are to the community. But if you're brought up a church-going person or a Protestant, you don't know your cultural tradition or your constitution or your laws as a Mohawk. In 1990 before the Oka Crisis, I didn't know about it. I didn't know my obligations to the Mohawk people until later on, and neither did a lot of other people. That's why the Warrior Society was such a quiet society, without anybody really knowing about them. And all of a sudden it blew up in 1990, where Warriors had to come out in Oka and tell the rest of the men at the community level, family men and everything, that, 'Hey, this is what you're supposed to do. If you are a Mohawk man this is your obligation to your people. It is to stay here and fight no matter what it's going to take from you or whatever.' I had to learn that, and so did a couple thousand other men in this community. So the Warrior Society was no longer a secret as of '90.

Before '90, the members of the so called Warrior Society were really the *traditional* men of the community. And they always have been. The reason they were a minority is because the other people had forgotten what the role of the men in the community was. People had forgotten their tradition, their culture and their laws. They weren't taught it. Our people, like me, went to a White school. When my family moved back here from New York, I still wasn't taught my culture and my language. I went to school in Châteauguay. I always had to take French class, history, social studies and stuff like that. So I was brought up in the outside world—let's put it straight: in the White man's world. And so was everybody else in this community for the past 100, 150 years.

Today it's different because for the past ten or fifteen years we have had our own schools, right from kindergarten to high school. And in all these schools they teach the kids their language, they teach them their traditions, their culture. It's just like the French people: They go to French school—they teach you about your culture as a French person. They teach you French because they say, 'This is Quebec, that's our culture.' But here in Kahnawake, I didn't learn that. I didn't speak Mohawk. But my kids, my sons, they speak Mohawk. They know a lot more than I do. Now that we have our own schools we can teach it.

So our culture and our tradition have come back to us within the past fifteen years. The people are coming back to being traditional people. Before, we didn't know who we were because we weren't taught it. Maybe our grandparents told us stories and told us things about their lives and spoke Mohawk to us, but I never learned anything, because 75% of what I learned wasn't Mohawk.

Like I said, the Warrior Society was a tradition, that the men kept. And they trained themselves. The Warriors follow the orders of the War Chief. The people decide who will be Chief. When there's a clan meeting, all the debating positions are put on the table and each clan gives its point of view until all the clans agree on a solution to the problem.

There are many clans throughout the Nations and there's a lot more meaning to the clans too. People have to sit in clans to make decisions. I'm a Wolf, and when I walk into the Longhouse I go sit with the Wolves: They sit on one side of the house. The Turtles sit on another side of the house, and the Bears sit on another side. When a decision has to be made, the Council gets together and whatever you are making a decision on will be passed to whoever has the floor. If a Turtle has the floor, he will say: 'This came into the well, a decision has to be made on this, we pass it over to the Wolf.' So the Wolves will all discuss it amongst each other and make a decision on what they want to do and throw it back across to the Turtles and say, 'The Wolf Clan has decided that we agree with the Turtles on what they want to do, how they want to pass it.' It will then be passed to the Bears, and if the Bears all discuss it and say, 'No we do not agree with the Wolves and the Turtles,' it will go on and on like that until you come to a consensus where everybody agrees on each point and it will be passed back to the Chiefs and the Clan Mothers who will say: 'The Wolves agree that we should pass this, the Turtles agree, the Bears agree. So it is agreed by the whole assembly of the people.' Our government works that way. This system has been in existence since the very beginning of the Mohawk tribes. On any major decision, even with troubles in families or something, everything is decided among the people.

Years ago we didn't have police and if a Warrior went out and killed another person on the Territory, it would come to the Longhouse among the clans and they would discuss his punishment or what to do. If he was found guilty of murdering the person, then it would be decided what to do. Once it was decided, they would bring this person in and explain to him the decision of the people. So we never needed a police force or a court, because it was all in one, and the government is the people.

It's just like it's supposed to be in Canada: The government is supposed to be the people, because the government is supposed to be there for the people. But in Canada, it's not *all* the people making the decisions: It's the people you put in power, and you have to trust they're going to make the right decisions. That's not the Mohawk way.

A woman carries the clan. I myself was adopted into the Wolf Clan and brought into the Longhouse in 1990, because my mother is not Native, so my mother didn't carry a clan. My father carried the Bear Clan because his mother was a Bear.

Back then, we believed that we were all brothers and sisters and in one way or another we were all related to each other. That's how it started out. Even if you look at the Bible, Adam and Eve started Creation, so everybody is related to each other. Everybody has to be related one way or another. A woman would have children and if she was a Bear, her kids would be Bear.

The Mohawk People of Kahnawake

The Bear Clan	The Wolf Clan	The Turtle Clan
Three Clan Mothers	Three Clan Mothers	Three Clan Mothers
Three Chiefs	Three Chiefs	Three Chiefs

War Chief

There are other clans amongst other Nations. Some other Mohawks, like at Akwesasne, have different ones: the Snipe, the Beaver and the Snake. Here in Kahnawake we have the Wolf, the Turtle and the Bear.

Back in history if the Mohawks were at war with the Hurons and they took prisoners, maybe women and children, that weren't kin, they were adopted into the Mohawk Nation, so they were adopted by the clans. You read in certain books where there were Europeans that came to live with the Mohawk people and became brothers and sisters, so they were adopted into the tribe. They became one of them, they were no longer an outsider or a

White person, they were adopted in because there was love and trusting. There's a lot of good with this thing of 'taking in': They would never turn their backs on somebody they could trust and who they cared for. Let's go back in history and think of when North America was being settled, when they used to burn villages, and the Indians used to go and kill the men and take the women and children. And these women and children were raised like Indian people. They were accepted, they were adopted. Maybe twenty years later they would realize who they were, what they were, but that's not what they are now—they became Mohawk people, Indian people. If you were brought here as a child and raised by Mohawk people and you were accepted as a Mohawk—they adopted you—you would know nothing but the Mohawk ways. Even when, say forty years later, White people came in and said: 'He's a White child, we want him,' you wouldn't want to leave.

You can't marry someone from your clan. So if you belong to the Bear Clan, you can't marry a Bear Clan woman. This avoids all genetic problems of inter-marriage.

In times of crisis like the one we just went through, we have our own laws to obey and each person has their own role to play. We have our chiefs, our clan mothers, and the men who defend the land and the people.

During the 1990 crisis, there was a War Chief who was responsible for our strategy and word filtered down to the Warriors. The men would get their orders from the War Chief, who in turn got *his* orders from the Clan Chiefs and the Clan Mothers who would hold meetings with the community.

When a decision is made to go to war, we have to think in military terms. There's always a strategy to adopt when you're defending a territory. You think of the size of the grounds you have to protect, you measure the strength of your adversary, and then you try to guess where the attack will take place so that you can send groups of Warriors there to defend that sector, each in their turn. A leader is designated for each guard shift, and he takes his orders from the War Chief.

Different 'surprises' have to be cooked up in order to prevent any intrusion into the perimeter. We have to place certain devices around the perimeter that warn us of intruders. There are also patrols, made up of three or four people who try to get information from and about the enemy, count the number of combatants on the other side of the perimeter and find out what kinds of weapons they use. A real patrol should be invisible to the enemy but with the technology available, it's impossible to remain undetected. There are infrared goggles that allow you to see in the dark. When you're in a defensive position, you have a certain advantage because you're familiar with the area you're defending. Then the enemy often falls into your traps.

I always had the feeling that one day I'd find myself in a fight like this with my friends. I knew that one day we'd be in for it, that we'd have to rise up and fight for our lands. We all knew it. In spite of everything the Mohawks and the other Indians have done to try to protect their lands and their culture, the governments always come out on top.

We don't have the financial means or the legal know-how to win in court against the governments. We've been trying to resolve these territorial conflicts for a hundred years and nothing's been fixed yet.

North America was Indian country. The United States and Canada will never be able to make up for everything they've taken. If they admitted that they robbed us and they had to give us back everything they've taken from us, the price would be too much for them to pay. The territorial losses for both countries would be enormous.

Those people who are elected to government know that if they sit down to negotiate, they'll have to give us back our land. And that's why they don't listen to us.

We've been claiming our rights and our lands for too long. If we'd let them invade the Oka pine woods, what would they take from us tomorrow? The time has come for Indians to make a decision. If the White people want our lands, they'll have to kill us.

The Whites are ready to destroy everything for money. They're wiping out the planet for power and money. They don't give a damn if there's nothing left for our children. Our people could very easily get along with the White people, English or French. The conflicts come from the governments who won't be satisfied until they've taken everything possible away from us. They'll never admit that what they did was wrong.

If the White citizens think that the governments give us

money to just sit around and do nothing, they're gravely mistaken. You just have to think of all the resources that have been blindly yanked out of this land which was torn away from us. The priests and the monks have tried to convert us and erase our culture in order to turn us into Whites. We've lost everything except our pride in being Indians, and the Creator knows they've been trying to take even that away from us for a long time. But our spirit is strong and we'll never be broken.

I'd like the government to explain to us by what right it gave the Church enough power to sell our lands and rule on our Territories? How is it that, from one day to the next, our lands became the property of the priests, who themselves had always acknowledged it was ours, while they negotiated secretly with the British government to acquire it for themselves? These are historical facts.

The Mohawks don't ask to be given land. It's already ours. The Indians were sedentary people who lived in North America way before the Europeans ever got here. They were here first. The Indians were happy to greet Christopher Columbus, but the Whites kept on arriving in ever greater numbers and changing everything and pushing the Indians out of their way.

The Indians realized that the Whites wanted only to conquer and destroy and that their only ambition was wealth, money. I haven't studied history but I know this.

When Indians live on lands where there's oil, the governments move them off as if they were cattle, to take their oil and make money. They have no right to," Ronald Cross concludes angrily.

On this last point, lawyer James O'Reilly explains how the Alberta Natives found oil on their lands. They received quite a lot of money, he says, but the federal government refuses to allow them to control their own money. They have had to sue in court. (See Boisseau, n.p.)

In another case taking place in Alberta, it seems that "five agreements signed by the federal government were declared invalid, supposedly because they lacked some fine print, that the official seals were missing.... Understandably, all these cases have angered Natives," O'Reilly concludes (ibid.).

This is what I imply when I say that Mr. Justice Greenberg should have gone further in his decision concerning Native jurisprudence (see Appendix 1, below). Had he done so, he would have seen that each time a Native individual took his case before the courts, he simply got taken to the cleaners even more! And that, in such circumstances, telling the Natives that the courts are there to resolve their conflicts was like telling them politely to go to hell!

•

"No one has a right to own the land. Not the White man, not the Indian. The Indians care for it without it belonging to anyone in particular. We're all equal. It's not fair that one person be the owner of many acres of land while another person doesn't own any. All this is related to money. Money which becomes even more money, to the point where one person has so much money he can't even get rid of it. The poor get poorer and the rich, richer.

The Indians aren't interested in White lifestyles. They want to keep their own way of life. They have their laws, their religion. They're different. A lot of people say we should thank the governments for the money they give us, but we think they're not giving us anything they don't already owe us. They use our resources, our trees, our water. The money they give us comes from taxes they collect using our lands; they're profits made from products manufactured with our resources."

The biggest drawback to the many Indian claims, in the eyes of many White people, is that their opinions are all over the map. Some want to remain in the past, others complain that some reservations are still without electricity. And since I truly want to understand, I dare to ask another question that may offend: "You complain that money is the root of all evil, but when the governments give you welfare money, you take it. And in the end, we don't know *what* you really want. Woods in which to hunt? Or universities on the reservations? We've polluted your lakes and your rivers but you use cars. Draw us a clear picture of the kind of civilization you want. Do the Indians dream of living once more in the Longhouse?"

"You can't go back and live in the past," Ronald Cross replies, not at all embarrassed by the question.

"You have to live in the future. You have to grow with the future, but that doesn't mean you have to give up your traditions and your culture.

Indians today want to go to school, learn things, study. Fifty years ago, that wasn't the case. School was reserved for Whites. We got our schooling from nature—an education based on tradition and not an education based on money.

The Indians lived off the land and had no need for money. They had to learn to respect the land and their environment so that it remained a source of food and shelter forever. That was our education. Poverty didn't exist, neither did famine. Wealth didn't exist either. Indians needed nothing else to be happy than to discover how their ancestors had made it this far, and then to teach those traditions to their children.

The Mohawks aren't against anyone. We just don't want anyone to touch our lands. A lot of Indians work with the French-speaking people of this province, and with all the other nationalities. We have nothing against the Whites—the English or the French—but we do have a bone to pick with the governments that respect neither Indians nor Whites. Your society doesn't run the governments—it's the governments that run you. We Indians don't like it. That's where the problem is."

Well, what do you want? That we all go back to Europe? In a hundred years we'd still be moving people! And that's not all. I've been the victim of injustice too, because I paid for those lands! I did not get them as a gift. If you send me back to Europe and I have no more rights here, then I will have been robbed even more than you who got the land for free. I had to pay for it.

"We don't want anyone to leave. Just find some fair way to solve the issue.

You circulate on our lands and then you have the nerve to say you'll *give* us some of them? If someone robbed you and he told you afterwards 'I'm giving you back some of my loot, ain't I generous?'—what would your answer be?

The governments shouldn't exercise control over the Indian nations and what little we have left of our lands. We are a distinct people and we have our own governments and our own laws. We've never lost our status as a sovereign nation. To lose it, we would have had to accept to lose it, or to have surrendered it in battle.

The real issue is land claims and our own sovereignty. We never gave up sovereignty as a nation. We've been fighting for the past 500 years or however long. All the stuff that's coming over the media about our involvement in the cigarette trade and drugs and alcohol, their insisting that the public focus on that, is designed to tarnish our image as a people. They're trying to make us look bad because Canada's been hurt big time because of what happened in '90. In the eyes of the world it's no longer that peaceful country that it always said it was. That was proven. So governments have a lot to make up for, and what they think they have to do is turn the page, try to put it on *us* now, try to put the blame on *us* and try to make *us* look like criminals and terrorists and drug smugglers and shit like that. It's just to get public opinion back on their side.

One time I had an interviewer ask me about the cigarette trade and she says: 'What about the Mohawks and the illegal cigarettes?' I asked her, 'Do you smoke? Because if you do smoke, why are you saying cigarettes are illegal? Cigarettes are not illegal, drugs are illegal.' Sure, some of the Mohawks are involved in about 10% or less of the billion-dollar-a-year business that you call the illegal cigarette trade. Where's the other 90% of that trade? Who is involved in it and who's doing it? It's the people in Montreal, it's the people in Quebec, it's the people in Ottawa, it's the people in Ontario. So why just focus on the Mohawks? Why just tarnish the Mohawks' image? Every time you see a cigarette now, you think about 'illegal Indian tobacco,' right? It's always associated with pictures of Akwesasne or Kahnawake or Kanehsatake.

There's hundreds of borders that aren't manned where truckloads just drive right through at night. And the customs officers, they don't even want to come out. It's totally awesome, but the focus is always on us. That's the main thing. You talk cigarettes—illegal cigarettes, contraband, whatever—it's always focused on the Mohawks, and like I said, that's a billion-dollar-a-year business. And out of that billion dollars, maybe the Mohawk people are making 10, 20, 30, even 50 million. Who's making the other $950,000,000? Not us, and that's for damn sure. That trade is all over Canada, it's not only here in Kahnawake or Akwesasne. I mean, this is just two tiny spots.

It's never about the Koreans or the French people or whoever else is involved in the rest of the 90% of that business. But for them to justify taking control of these Territories, that's their reason.

Now if they came in tomorrow with a couple thousand troops and said: 'Hey, we went in there to stop the cigarette trade and all the illegal activities in that community,' that would be their justification. That's all it is. Because it's not a problem to them. The little money that we make isn't a problem to them. We have the right to sell tax free here. On gasoline, on anything brought into this community, we have the right to sell it tax free because we are tax exempt—*in* the community, *in* the Territory, we are tax exempt. I go to the store out there, I have to pay tax. And it's a hassle, filling out all those W4 papers. Either we're tax exempt or we're not. Half the White stores accept it, half of them don't. The government accepts it. I send my government gas receipts from Kahnawake here, I send my gas receipts every year, and they send me back $500-$600 dollars in tax money on gas. Now if I buy cigarettes for $46 a carton, I send in a receipt for the tax—am I going to get the tax money back? Probably will. Everything that we spend tax on comes back to us. I buy a vehicle, I pay the tax on that vehicle, I send the papers to the government. The government sends me the tax money back. So are we not tax exempt?

That's the thing—the 'illegal cigarette trade' is a big propaganda campaign to tarnish our image among the Canadian public, so that they can look at us in a different way: 'These people are criminals, they've got something to hide, this is why we're doing all this to them.' It's justification for what the governments have been doing to us and it's a strategy that they have worked out for a long time. They've always done that. They've always made us look like the bad people. For their own wrongdoings.

We never attacked them as a nation, we never tried to overthrow their government, but they're always trying to overthrow our government. And they don't understand: The simplest way to solve this problem is to just leave the Native people alone, let them go on about their business like the Two Row Wampum agrees it should be. The Two Row Wampum was created and given to them, and it states right in there the terms of the welcome extended by the Indians to the first White settlers: 'We can both sail on the same river, us in our canoe, you in your vessel, and we shall never set foot in each other's boat. We do not interfere with each other.' And that's been broken over and over thousands of times by the government, even by some of our own people and that's what makes it a hard situation for us to be in.

And by 'some of our own people' I mean the Band Council and those people in our communities who support them. Right now I don't know what kind of wheeling and dealing goes on within the Band Council here. The Band Council is supposed to be our government. But it's run by the Quebec government—it's not a *traditional* government of the Mohawk people. To be a Band Councillor and Chief, you're supposed to be voted in by the people, but the traditional Mohawks do not vote.

According to our laws and traditions, when things have to be done they are done by the people. The people make the decisions here, not a group of officials in an office that the government recognizes. See, before the Indian Act came into effect, there was no Band Council, we had a traditional Mohawk government. The traditional government, the Chiefs and the Clan Mothers of the Longhouse, are picked by the people. So it's the people who make the decisions. If we had to make a decision that we wanted new roads to come in or any other major decision in Kahnawake, the people would get together in the Longhouse and they would sit in their clans and it would be *all* the people who decided if it was good for them or not. And they would *all* pass that decision, not just a handful of people in a government office.

Traditional Mohawks don't have *representative* democracy. In other words, the way the Mohawk community works is that every major issue is decided by the people, all the people. There is no one person delegated to make the decisions on behalf of everyone else. It's the majority of all the people who decide. There's 8,000 Mohawks in Kahnawake now. If the Band Council was to make the decision, through their Band Council meetings, to build this casino they want to build, we would not recognize their decision because they work hand-in-hand with the government, and they're making decisions for the government—or the government's making decisions for us, whenever the Council passes anything. And these people on the Band Council are voted in there by only the 800 people who vote, out of the 8,000 who live in this community.

But an Indian does not vote a Chief into office. A Chief is

either hereditary or he's put in his position by the people, by the Clan Mothers. And the Clan Mothers have the right, if they feel that these Chiefs are not doing their job to the best of their ability for the people, to dethrone them, to take them out at any time if they are not working in the best interests of the people.

So only 800 people vote for this Band Council system, for the 'Chiefs'—they call themselves 'Chiefs'! He's a mayor and he's got his councillors! And in the Indian tradition there aren't any mayors and there aren't any councillors. There's chiefs and there's sub-chiefs and there's war chiefs and there's clan mothers. But when the majority of the people make the decision, the decision will stand, and nobody can overturn that decision.

When the Band Council turns around and makes a decision 'for the community,' there are only about 50 or 60 people at that meeting. So in their eyes that's the decision that's made with 'the majority of the people.' So if the majority of the 800 people who vote for the Band Council 'Chief' say, 'Yes let's build a casino,' he comes out and announces to the people that we're going to build this casino. So the people of Kahnawake get together, 4,000 people come up and sit under the one roof and say, 'Well, we do not want to have this casino in Kahnawake,' and *that's* the majority of the people in this community, and so he's not going to get it. Because he cannot override the majority of the people in his community. The reason most of the people here do not go out there and vote for the Band Council is because a lot of them are traditional Indians. They follow their Great Law, the Great Law that was passed down to us from generation to generation. It's been there for hundreds of years.

See, the Band Council does not respect the Two Row Wampum because they have one foot in the Indian boat and one foot in the White government's boat, which doesn't belong there because they're interfering. So they're going from our canoe into their boat, and they're bringing the laws of the foreign governments over into our boat, which is taboo, which is not supposed to be done.

The same thing is happening with the Peacekeepers. The Peacekeepers work under the Indian Act with the Band Councils. If somebody does a crime in Kahnawake, we have a court system here, right? But even the court system here is bringing Canadian law into our Territory, which is not right, which a lot of people do not accept and do not recognize. That's also why we do not recognize the SQ and the RCMP and the Army having jurisdiction over what goes on in Kahnawake.

Over the years here in Kahnawake we haven't had good relations with the Canadian police—the RCMP and the SQ. For years, a lot of them just did not work on a professional basis here. I mean, I had a cousin who was shot four times in front of his wife and kids by an SQ officer, supposedly in the officer's self-defence, because he came at them in the patrol car with a pool cue. So that justified the cop shooting him four times with a .357 Magnum? And this officer got away with it. He got a three-week suspension and he was acquitted of all charges. So justice is hard. If it was vice versa, if he went at my cousin with his night stick and my cousin shot him four times, claiming that he was in fear of his life, he would have been hung.

So since then—this was back in the late '70s—we evicted the SQ from the Territory, and that's when the Amerindian police force, the Peacekeepers, were organized here. After that shooting, when we evicted them, there was a riot here: Their cars were turned over, their men were beat up. And it's probably even got worse since the death of Corporal Lemay. I mean, he's got friends within the force and so do other cops that get hurt that come over here, you know. I'm not talking about Lemay himself here, but, like I said, a lot of the others don't work on a professional basis.

For a lot of years up till '90 the Peacekeepers were pretty well respected by the RCMP and the SQ. They kind of worked together hand in hand. I mean, they weren't allowed to come here, the SQ or the RCMP, so if a car was chased onto the Territory they would be in touch with the Peacekeepers here in Kahnawake and the Peacekeepers would take over from there because they knew if they did try to come into Kahnawake there would be people who would have stopped them and who knows what would have happened. So they would go up to the borderlines of Kahnawake, and there the Kahnawake Peacekeepers would take over. So they were working together, and they still are today. Not that the Peacekeepers are much respected by them any more after '90.

I mean, according to the RCMP and the SQ, they do not recognize a Kahnawake Peacekeeper as being an official police officer of Quebec. In 1990, during the crisis, the SQ pulled over the Peacekeepers and had them kneeling on the ground and took their guns and arrested them and charged them with weapons charges. These guys were Peacekeepers here in Kahnawake, and this is what the SQ did. It was on the front pages of the papers. But they recognized them from the time the SQ left here in the late '70s until the crisis in 1990. They were even recognized in their courts when they took our people out of their courts and brought them over here. They were recognized. And all of a sudden now the governments don't recognize them—because of all the stuff that went on in '90.

Because Kahnawake is a sovereign territory—it's Mohawk Territory—it does not operate under Canadian law. Even the criminal laws of Canada do not apply here in Kahnawake. It's we the people who have our own laws, our laws were laid down for us through the Great Law of Peace that we followed for hundreds of years. So as a traditional people we follow our own laws. If we go back to traditional government, it means the Band Council system and the Indian Act would have to be abolished. We are not answerable to Canada, but the Band Council is.

That's the whole thing with this Two Row Wampum—there's people in our boat who are stepping into Canada's boat, let's say more or less, and bringing over stuff from their boat to our boat without the consent of the Mohawk people. They're doing it on their own. The Mohawk people do not agree with it. It will come to a time—and it's not going to be long from now—when this Indian Act system and this Band Council system will not exist over here any longer. Because the majority of the people are traditional Mohawks and they will get control of their own government again and abolish the Indian Act, the Band Councils. The Band Councils have, I believe, ten years to start moving towards traditional government again. They have a mandate that they have to live up to from the Mohawk people. Back in '79 or so they had a mandate to start going back to traditional government. And they claim that they are still trying to go back to traditional government but that the people in Kahnawake are too split among themselves.

It's true: There are different factions, different groups here. We have a Catholic group, we have a Band Council group, and we have two Longhouses—the traditional groups—and all that creates a split in the community, so we can't sit under one roof, in order to have that traditional government again.

We have two Longhouses of traditional people in Kahnawake when there's supposed to be one. Neither of these two Longhouses support the Band Council system. Back during the French and Indian Wars, and during the American Revolution, they started arguing amongst each other in the Longhouse, and certain traditional people said we should fight as independent allies with the British, our trading partners who held the covenant chain of the Two Row Wampum, against the French and the American rebels. And certain other traditional people said 'We should remain neutral in these disputes.' And what they did was they made their own Longhouses: some of these people here, and some of those people there.

In the end, the British betrayed their allies from the Six Nations Confederacy, so the two Longhouses, they don't forgive each other, they don't agree with each other, so they won't sit under one roof—even until today. In order for traditional government to work here in Kahnawake, or in any other Territory, the whole of the people as one have to sit under that one Longhouse together again and think with one mind, and put that old division behind them.

But when the people do come together, like in 1990 with all the trouble we had, no matter what you were—a Catholic or a Protestant or from one of the two Longhouses or a Band Councillor—everybody came together as one to defend the Territory and the people. I mean, I was right next to a guy who was a Band Councillor, and the guy on the other side of me was a priest and we all worked together to defend the Territory, thinking as one. That's why we were so strong in 1990. The governments made a mistake by doing what they did because when all the people come together as one, that's the strongest you can make the Indian people.

So like I said, since the Indian Act came into effect, it split the communities in a big way. And the government knows that as long as a community is split it can never form a traditional government. And the government is very good at using the Band Council system to keep that split in the community going, because if it ever went away the Native people would be very strong.

I don't know why some of our people are asking for self-government: They're already self-governed. Nobody ever took that away from the Mohawk people. The Mohawk people never lost their sovereignty on this continent. They are a sovereign nation right up till today, and we still are and we always will be, no matter if Canada or the Queen or Quebec or America or whomever recognizes it or not. We never gave up our sovereignty and we never lost it in battle. We've never been defeated in a battle. I mean, in order to stop bloodshed and killing and the annihilation of our people, we had to give up some of the land that we occupied at that time and to come to where we are today, or we wouldn't be here today. The Mohawk people had to take measures to make sure that their people would survive. That's why we lost so much land. But the treaties are not lived up to. We made treaties with governments so that our people could live in peace without going to war with them. We had to compromise and the government would say: 'Well, you give up this part of the country and we'll give you this: We'll push you further north and we'll make sure that you have Medicare and you'll always have land to farm and stuff like that.' Treaties: Forget about it. There are hundreds of treaties with Native peoples. And we fell for it, and we took it in good faith and it was just more land given up instead of being paid for.

The people in the two Longhouses are all traditional people and they have their own groups of people who agree with them. And they each don't agree with the other Longhouse on the way they do things—but we all follow the same law, the Great Law of Peace. Neither of these two groups supports the Band Council system. They don't have anything to do with it. Even if a major decision is to be made by the Band Council system, these people from the two Longhouses will not go there and listen to them and say, 'Yes we agree with them,' because they'd be stepping from their boat into the government's boat.

Once we start dealing with the Band Council, we're dealing with the system of White governments, which have nothing to do with us. If I am a traditional Mohawk and I was to appeal to, or sit in on meetings with, the Band Council, and make decisions with them, I'd be stepping into the White governments' boat. I'd be interfering in their laws as they're interfering with ours. That was the whole concept of the Two Row Wampum—to live side by side together in peace and not interfere with each other, never to set foot in each other's boats. In other words, 'We will never interfere with your lifestyle; don't interfere with ours. We will never change your religion; don't change ours. We will never put our laws on you; so don't put your laws on us. Let's live together side by side and run each of our separate lives the way we see fit, but never interfere with each other.' But down the line they didn't respect that Two Row Wampum. They started interfering with our lives. They started putting us on reservations and trying to control our people. And that's exactly what they've done up to today.

These events in '90 created a situation where more of our people are trying to learn about our traditions, to become more spiritual, to work on ourselves, to become stronger human beings. I see it more and more as the days and months and years go on. I see more of the people going back to the Mohawk tradition, the way it was. There's a lack of knowledge because the young ones never bothered to learn from the elders, and the elders are passing on very fast. We're losing a lot of our elders, and a lot of the stuff that they know. You know they can teach it to many people, but the thing is they don't go out there and grab you and say 'I have to teach you this.' In the traditional Indian way of learning you have to go to them. In order to learn and to get the knowledge of these things of what we're supposed to do, we have to go to them, because if you don't know to ask, nothing they will teach you is going to mean anything to you anyway.

And like myself, and a lot of the young ones in my generation, that wasn't our way, man. We thought we didn't need anything from anybody, we didn't understand who we were. I think more people today understand who we are as a people and what we need to survive. We all have a feeling that something's going to happen in the future where we will need to know who we are and how to take care of our business as a people. I mean here in Kahnawake, this was a Catholic community. Our parents and their parents were brought up by Catholics. They were called the 'Praying Indians.' They worshipped the Church and the priest. I was brought up in the Church, right, so now I have to learn on my own all over again—when I'm in my thirties—who I am as a Mohawk, and that the Church is not my religion and that their God is not my god. But there's only one god for all of us. If you call him God or you call him Jesus or whatever, there's only one Creator in this world. And we're all created from the same Creator, but have different ways about it.

I think things are going to be in the young peoples' hands now because they're learning their language. I mean, kids two years old—my own son, he knows more than I, he understands more than I do, because he's being spoken to in Mohawk and in English. He can go to school here in Kahnawake and learn his culture and his tradition and his language. I missed that. The generation before me missed that. The generation before them missed that. Because they were brought up in White schools and with the Churches. And now the younger generations are moving away from the Churches, they're going back to traditional ways. We know, we have that feeling now, that that's what we are, who we are as a people. Because if I go back twenty years, on a Sunday the church would be totally packed with people. You go there today and it's getting emptier, emptier, emptier. It's just the old ones that have been going all the time that still go. The young ones have a choice today. Twenty or thirty years ago, the children didn't have a choice, they didn't have a say in who they were or what they were going to be. Because my parents were Catholic, I was brought up as a Catholic. I didn't have a choice. But my son—my wife baptized him in a church, but I also named him in the Longhouse. He has a clan in the Longhouse. I bring him to the Longhouse, to the socials and the dances and he goes about his business. And if my wife goes to church once in a while, she takes him there also. So he's going to get to an age where he's going to understand religion. I mean, I'm going to teach him the things I know, I learned, about my people and the way to do things in the traditional way. But he's got that choice which will be his own. We didn't have a choice, the generation before me didn't have a choice—we were brought up with the Church. Now a lot of people are going back to the tradition.

The men over the past couple of years have gotten—really, the young ones anyway—pretty militant. There were not enough young ones going to the Medicine People, the seers or the healers, for help. They said, 'I don't need help'; they felt that everything's good. I was pretty militant myself, I got pretty militant. And I started feeling that it wasn't right. It wasn't right for me to get that militant, to have me ride around the community with radios and weapons in my car, weapons in my house and every-thing—you know, just in case. It can make you feel safe in the beginning to have all this. But it wasn't for me because I was setting an example for the young ones. You know, they would stop me or we would talk and there were weapons in the car, there was gear in a military fashion, we had our communications, and always security—security, security, security. Like I said, the Warrior Society was a very secret society here in Kahnawake. Now it's out in the open, and everybody knows who's in the Warrior Society. Everybody knows who's on checkpoints and communications. It was always there before but it was never seen, it was a secret society. But now it's in the open and the young ones, they're involved in it too. Because the young people also go to the Longhouse and there's a lot of things that go on there. The men work hard.

So the thing for me is to set a different example. I speak to the children in schools, to the very young ones and the older ones. I speak to them about drugs and alcohol, and about healing and traditional things. And they kinda listen to a person like me, because they know how I am: They've known me all their lives; they've seen the way I was. And they see the change in me for the better. I can't set a bad example for them anymore by riding around town on a nice day and drinking beer and smoking joints. Because they've seen that in me before and it was wrong. And I did it because I'd seen that from the generation before me. I'd seen these young guys always cruising in nice cars with their girlfriends and drinking and thought: 'That's all right, I'm going to do that when I get older.' But it's wrong. And I have to explain that to them, and I have to tell them what it did to me. Just tell them my experiences. The kids are smart: They know the laws and they're really turning against all that, because drugs and alcohol killed our people big time—and they still are. Last night I just lost a twenty-two-year-old friend of mine, who was coming back from a bar up the road here. He was in the car, and some people got killed. Two weeks ago, same thing: My cousin had an accident coming back from that same bar here. It has a Quebec liquor licence to sell booze in Kahnawake, which the people don't want. But the people have to get together to remove that place because there's not supposed to be alcohol and drugs in this community.

Now the kids are taking a stand in this community to fight against it, and they're going to wake up the older people and we're going to have to support the young kids to close down these bars and these clubs. We've got Moose clubs, Knights of Columbus, the Legion, bootleggers, that all have to be closed up. Because it's easy access for booze and drugs to the kids. I'm not talking heavy drugs. There's cocaine in this community, there's hash and marijuana, like every other place. If they don't get it here, if they want it, they're going to go out of town to get it. But it's not going to be smoked here. We took a stance as a people.

In 1989 there was a problem: The kids were caught smoking up and selling hash in the school. So the people took it upon themselves, and the men backed the women of the community, and we made a list of all the people who we suspected were selling drugs or who we knew were selling drugs, and we went to each and every one of their houses, and we gave them a warning. Maybe fifty or a hundred people of the community: We walked, and the women told them, 'We give you our notice as of right now: If we hear you're selling drugs in this community, or if we see you selling drugs in this community, we're going to banish you from here. You're gone. You're out of here. You'll never be allowed here again.' And we had to enforce that. And we put a stop to it, because we enforced it, we said 'That's the truth. We catch you again, we hear you're selling again, you're never coming back here. So you'd better think hard about it.' And it worked.

We have to do this every so often because it's been a couple of years now, and they're slowly starting to do it again. So with the kids—I think there's a need for more healing. I'm in the healing process, bettering myself, so I can teach the kids the right things. Plus I could not say something to these kids, and then turn around and do the opposite. I could not go there and say, 'Hey, you kids shouldn't be drinking or smoking up. It's no good for you'—and turn around and I'm down the road having a beer and they're watching me. I wouldn't be walking my talk. So now I have to do that: I have to walk my talk, and that's the way I have to stay. So to me it's like a mission; it's my duty to solve something about being here.

I don't think anyone really knows until later on in life what their real purpose in life is. The real purpose in life is to work hard and bust your ass and die of an old age and accomplish something and help people. It's the Creator. He'll lead you on that path to what you have to do. Right now I have to make a difference because it makes me feel good and it helps me. And that's what this community needs. If we could all turn around and maybe start doing the things I'm doing, too, there would be more love in this community and more people helping each other. Because that was the thing with the Native peoples. Their way of life was to help one another. Nobody was ever hungry. If that family had no food, everybody supplied food for that family. They were never cold. Everybody helped everybody, that was the thing. Nobody was better than anybody; we were all equal as a people.

But today we are not equal as a people because we have millionaires here, we've got high class and middle class and poor ones here. They forgot about that thing of helping each other and caring for each other and showing love to the young ones and the old ones. It got really bad, we got really twisted, but we're trying to straighten it. And it's hard to straighten it when the governments keep saying things and putting things on us that split the community. And that's what split this community: the governments' doings. Their interfering in our lives is splitting this community more and more. Because people start pointing fingers at each other and blaming each other and start hating each other for things that are being said on TV. And it's crazy, the things the governments are doing to split our people. That's the way they work, you know. We work on each other, we do it to each other, but it's them that's creating it. And they know that. They know how to create that division.

But now there are more young people gradually coming to see the old people and the healers and learning the Mohawk ways. It's hard for them to start doing this because of all the problems we're still having, dealing with keeping out these outside forces and all the harassment that's going on. They don't feel safe when they walk the Territory. It's hard to get that hatred out of you, that anger, that they've seen since 1990. They've seen a lot of racism. They've seen their families, their fathers, their uncles, their brothers beat up by soldiers and beat up by SQ, and their mothers and their kids harassed. It's totally like martial law. When you leave this community you have to be on the alert, you have to be very alert. I mean, even me: I know what I'm looking forward to. Especially the SQ. I know what I'm going to deal with when they pull me over and I stop like a good Samaritan, and they pull over and I say 'What's the problem?' 'You're the fucking problem—that's the problem,' that's what they're going to say. 'You're the Indian—you're the fucking enemy,' let's put it that way. It still gets to me, but I learned how to deal with it. In the beginning every time I got close to them, I was tense, I was nervous, I was scared. I went through a lot of shit with those people. Now it's like they don't take any of my power away at all. I won't stop for them if I am close enough to my Territory where I can put a little chase on and get home. Because I've seen all the harassment and the stuff these people have been going through.

And it's not only Indians: It's a lot of White people who come through this community. They get harassed more than we do. It's been on the radio shows and talk shows and TV. It's the White people that took the pressure off us with the SQ and RCMP, because they were being harassed more than we were, or just as much as we were. So they put a little pressure on their government and said, 'Enough is enough, I don't think you need those police forces all over that community like that. You're creating the problem now.' And they finally got smart and backed off. It's been quiet for the past couple of months. Once in a while you get a little incident here and there, but it's been very quiet up to now."

RONALD CROSS—A HERO'S LIFE

The Myth of the Italian
Living in New York

Ronald Cross was born on November 9, 1957, in Brooklyn, New York. Indians have been living in this central urban neighbourhood for over a century. Most have been lured there by the enticing prospect of jobs working the high steel, a form of labour which has opened doors to Mohawks all over the world and especially in the United States.

The origins of the Cross family in Brooklyn reach back to the 1920s, when Ronald's grandfather, Joseph K. Cross The River, well-established in Kahnawake with his family, got the urge to try his luck in the US. His whole family followed him. That's how his son, Gerald Joseph Cross, found himself in Brooklyn at the start of his teen years, where he kept up with his schooling and later became an ironworker, like his father before him.

There Gerald met Ann-Marie Casalaspro, of Scottish-Italian descent. She immediately caught his eye; they were married on February 18, 1955.

"Right away my parents had their hands full," explains Ronald Cross. Glenn Gerald was born in April 1956; Ronald in November 1957;

Donna-Marie on May 31, 1959; Terry and Tracy—the twins—were born in 1962; and Joseph K. was born on January 5, 1968. All the siblings were born in Brooklyn, except for Darren Guy, born on September 6, 1976, in LaSalle, Quebec.

Of his Brooklyn childhood, Ronald has nothing but happy memories. He continues his story slowly, and I have no desire to interrupt him.

"As a child I was rather quiet. I had what you might call a peaceful disposition. I went to grade school at St. Theresa of Avila in Brooklyn. It was a private Catholic boys' school, run very strictly by the nuns. That's where we were baptized, where we had our First Communion and where we went each week for dominical mass. This school was located very close to our apartment.

Leonard Cross, my father's brother, lived nearby and sent his kids there too. My cousins, my brothers and I were the only Indians in that school. We had to wear suits and ties. I was a good student and my grades were among the best in my class. I didn't have much freedom but I didn't complain; at that point in my life I liked school a lot. In my free time I really enjoyed exploring my surroundings. My folks were always looking for me. I guess I was like every other kid my age raised in the big city. I was very curious.

My father, who belonged to Local 361 of the Brooklyn ironworkers' union, was a hard worker who was a good provider for his family. We lived quite comfortably. We were neither rich nor poor. You could say we were middle class and we could always get what every other kid could get. I'd say I had a happy childhood.

The last New York apartment we had that I can remember as a kid, was a two-storey house. We lived on the first floor. There were three bedrooms, so we couldn't each have our own room because there were eight of us. Only my sister had her own room, which didn't bother us at all. The boys' room was very big and we had double-decker beds.

My father was a sober man. He drank only rarely, and the few times he did were on special occasions. Some people drink once in a while but with him, it was less than once in a while. He'd go out with his friends sometimes but I never saw him drunk. He was a man who enjoyed life and who was uncommonly strong, very good at sports, a good baseball player. When he was a

60

young man, he got an offer to try out with the Brooklyn Dodgers. Instead, he married my mother. A lot of his friends still talk about that today and tell me stories about the time when he played baseball.

Later we played in the same league in Kahnawake: He played for the Knights of Columbus while my brother and I played for the Moose Lodge. He was still a great player, even though at that time he had only one eye. That happened in an accident in the early '70s in New York, after our family moved back to Kahnawake permanently in 1969, and he started commuting to his job in New York from Kahnawake every week. But he still remained the best at everything he did. He had a lot of friends and everyone respected him.

I've always liked Kahnawake. When we lived in Brooklyn, we spent almost every summer vacation there, living at my grandparents' place. That house was near the main road, on Malone road near the St. Lawrence river. I grew up with the Kanes, our neighbours. Mr. Donald Kane had six kids: five boys and a girl. All of us kids were pretty much the same age. We were pretty close, having spent all our lives together. I was always very happy in June when school ended. The idea of spending the summer in Kahnawake and seeing all my friends again filled me with joy. We lived a hundred yards from the river and everything was so peaceful. I'd spend the whole summer swimming with my friends. The days were never long enough to do everything we wanted to do.

Besides the river right next door, we had a lacrosse field right in front of our house. Lacrosse is an old sport, a very rough game played by Indians. It's played with sticks on a field that looks like a hockey rink, with a net and a goalie at either end. It's played with two teams. You pass the ball from player to player and you try to score goals against the opposing team. There's a lot of checking, a lot of physical contact. It's a way of forgetting your frustrations. I often played lacrosse when I was younger and I still play it from time to time with friends, just to work out.

My grandfather owned a place called Joe's Dance Hall. It was a snack-bar that served hot dogs and fries. There was a big room with tables, a juke-box and pinball machines. I liked that place. I worked there to help my grandfather. That's how I spent my summer vacation the year we got here, when we left New York for good in 1969.

Joseph Karentanoron Cross The River settles in New York with his family in the 1920s

Marie Kaweiennitakhe Montour

Gerald Joseph George Awennakenra Cross. Born in Kahnawake, 22 December, 1934; died 16 April, 1976.

Louis Anthony Casalaspro, of Italian descent. Born in New York in 1919. Served in World War II. Died in May, 1955.

Georgiana Walton, of Scottish descent. Born in New York, 9 November, 1918; died in New York, 1988.

Ann-Marie Casalaspro

(Married 18 February,1955)

Ronald Cross. Born in Brooklyn, 9 November, 1957.

This page: Ronald Cross' genealogy. At right, from top to bottom: Ann-Marie Casalaspro, Ronald Cross' mother, in front of the Brooklyn Museum, 1962; Ronald, Donna and Glenn Cross in Brooklyn, 1966; Ronald Cross (L) with his father Gerald (R) in Kahnawake.

Clockwise from top left: Ronald Cross in 1970; 1975; and in Kahnawake, 1975.

Top: Terry Cross playing lacrosse at Oka. Bottom: The Cross family home in Kahnawake.

This page, top: Joe McComber in Hamilton; bottom: Jimmy and Kevin McComber, in Hamilton—both c.1976-77. Facing page, top: construction site in Manhattan; bottom: Ronald Cross at work on construction site, Manhattan.

Life in Brooklyn was getting more and more dangerous in the late '60s, and my dad had decided to take his family back home to Kahnawake. He built us a house right next to his father's. Roads and cars had turned what used to be an impossible trip into something much easier, so he was now able to commute to New York during the week and come home for the weekends.

I hated school here as much as I liked it in Brooklyn. I came here from the United States, where the school system is one year behind the one we have here. Their First High is the same as being in the sixth grade in Canada. I should have done my sixth grade over, but I was sent to Howard Billings High School in Châteauguay instead. In the States I'd already skipped my fourth grade and gone right to fifth because I was ahead of the others. By making me skip another year here, it really became much too difficult. I didn't say anything to anyone, but I was being buried alive by my grades. I was two years behind everyone else and I lost all interest in school. I started thinking I'd find a job to get out of all that. Still, I got up to my third year of high school. Then in 1975 I quit; my idea was to become an ironworker, like my dad and my grandfather before him. My older brother Glenn had been working with my father in New York for a year already. Later, in 1976, after I had been trained, Glenn and I were involved in the construction of a new post office in Montreal, along with a lot of other people from Kahnawake.

In the spring of 1976, my brother bought himself a sixteen-foot boat. In early April some people were saying that there were trout to be had near the St. Constant locks. So on April 16, the three of us—my father, Glenn and I—sailed off on a river we weren't very familiar with. The weather was nippy that morning and the water was still icy. After a few hours of fruitless fishing, we decided to go a little higher up river. But the current was so strong that it dragged us irresistibly towards the Lachine rapids. The boat, now uncontrollable, tipped over and we were power-less to do anything about it and all three of us ended up in the water. We were too far from the shore to swim over and we couldn't reach the boat anymore. The water was freezing us and our wet clothes were pulling us under. In spite of the fact that we were all excellent swimmers, the turbulence of the rapids was dragging us to the bottom. We tried to stay together but it was impossible. The rapids were in control. Still, I succeeded in taking off my boots and my water-logged clothes. I managed to reach my brother, and helped him and my father peel off their clothes, as well. I couldn't tell you how long we stayed like that in the water, struggling and fighting the current.

I remember opening my eyes and realizing that I was in a boat with a stranger who kept asking me if there had been only three of us in our craft. He could see my brother and my father. I told him yes and while we were pulling in my brother, my father sank right before our eyes, in a second. My brother and I were in a state of shock. I didn't understand what had happened. I was completely lost, as if I couldn't grasp the horror of the situation.

The man brought us back to shore, where an ambulance was waiting to drive us to the hospital. The doctor told us it was a miracle that we were still alive. Logically, a man couldn't survive more than five or ten minutes in water so cold. He'd die of hypothermia.

Later we found out that the man who had pulled us out of the river was an officer of the Sûreté du Québec. He was watching us from the shore while he was putting his own boat in the water. I also learned that we'd been in the water for at least twenty minutes.

A month went by before my father's body was found. As for me, nothing of what happened had sunk in. I guess I never really wanted to face up to the reality of it. In my mind, my dad had gone on a trip. Not a day goes by that I don't think of him. He's always in my heart and in my mind.

I never saw his body after they found him and that's probably why, to me, he's still alive somewhere. Sometimes I see him in my dreams and when I meet him, I always ask him the same questions: Where was he in the water and why did he have to leave us? I often wonder how my life would have turned out if he'd remained with us. He was a big influence on me. I admired him. I admired his wisdom. I liked the way he talked to me.

My father's death was tragic for all of us. He loved us deeply and we know that he would have given his life for his children. My mother was deeply affected. Suddenly she found herself having to raise seven kids alone. In spite of this, she took responsibility for all of us and did the impossible to make us happy.

If God was to take someone else from my family, I'd rather it had been me. I would have preferred sacrificing myself for those I love."

After Gerald Joseph Cross' funeral, the family pulled itself together as well as it could. His sister, Donna-Marie, married Louis P. Stacey, an American sailor, in Scotland in 1977. Ronald Cross went to work in Hamilton, Ontario, with a family friend named Jimmy McComber and his two sons. Jimmy took them under his wing and taught them the dangerous job of the ironworker. The slightest error at such heights on the construction sites could prove fatal. As an apprentice, it's essential that you learn from the best workers: You have to be able to get your work done well and swiftly while never neglecting any of the basic safety rules. Jimmy McComber taught them the job until he was confident enough in their abilities to let them work by themselves.

"We worked in Hamilton for almost a year, commuting every week as my father had done and his father before him. I was the third generation of ironworkers in the family.
Working with Jimmy helped me get over my father's death. Not only did he teach me my job, he also taught me how to handle my own responsibilities. I was able to fly by myself now and I had Jimmy to thank for it, as well as his wife Juney whom I consider to be like my second mother, and the rest of his family. They helped me get through a very hard time in my life and they always treated me like a son."

After his apprenticeship in Hamilton, Ronald Cross decided to work in the US. At the time, Ronald Cross had been going out with Darleen Stacey, a Mohawk from the Kahnawake reservation. They broke up and he went to work in Detroit, Michigan. When he returned, she was pregnant; she had been for a month previous to his departure for Detroit. His first son, Ryan Cross, was born on February 22, 1980.

"I spent some time with Ryan when he was a baby. After that, I was often gone and I almost never saw him for many years. We got together again after the 1990 Crisis when I was released from prison. I regret not having seen him grow up, but I was young and I didn't know what I was doing. Luckily I still have the chance to make up for it because he's still young and he's a very good kid. Darleen is an excellent mother and Ryan is lucky to have a stepfather who loves him. We all get along quite well with each other."

Top: Darleen Stacey, Ronald Cross and their son Ryan, born 22 February, 1980. Bottom: Ryan Cross at his High School graduation ceremonies.

In 1980, he settled in New York but returned to Kahnawake every weekend.

During this time, his mother, Ann-Marie Casalaspro, met Rolland Simon, a Mohawk man from the area around Oka. She decided to live there with him and they bought a house.

"I was on my own at a very young age, and when my father died it seemed like I became more mature than the others in certain ways, in the sense of making my own decisions and taking care of business. My brothers, even Glenn who is a year and a half older than I, were still kind of young in their ways. So in a way, my family started to look to me as the 'oldest,' and I started taking on a kind of fatherly role. I was working on my own, I had my own place. I guess I could always take care of myself.

As a young guy I was, I have to say, a tough guy, too. If I had to straighten somebody out physically, I would do it. I mean, not with my family, I never got physical with my family. And if there was a problem that my mother couldn't handle, like with my brothers or something, she would come to me. I could control a difficult situation, I wouldn't just fly off the handle, I would always resort to solving it in the best, most mature way. I didn't even realize this myself when I was young. I was a little wild, I liked to have my good times, but there were times when I had to be serious and take care of problems in the family, and my mother always looked to me for help. And so did my brothers. If they were in trouble, they could trust me, they could say anything to me, and they could count on me to deal with it. I would get down and say 'Well, you did what you did—it's done and let's fix it, let's fix the problem.' That's why they looked up to me, because my brothers, they used to get into a lot of trouble, and they had a rough time in Oka too.

My mother and my brothers were the only family from Kahnawake ever to move to Oka, so that was another thing. There was a lot of jealousy—the people at Oka didn't accept them at first. There were a lot of fights, a lot of brawls, and any time they got into trouble I was always there to back them up. I didn't live there but I used to go up to Oka on visits and my brothers would say, 'Well this guy beat me up and he's going to do this and that,' and I'd say, 'Yeah, well let's go take care of it.' So I would take care of it, and I kind of gained their respect. We had family feuds over there with other families that didn't like us, and one time some of the toughest guys in this family—we had to go head-to-head with them. There was no reasoning, so there was this fight, because these guys were drinkers and they were brawlers and that's all they knew. So it had to be settled that way, and I took care of business with these tough guys from Kanehsatake, and I really let them have it good, and after that we were pretty well respected.

I hate to say this because it might sound like I'm bragging but I'm not, and I'm not proud of what I had to do at a young age. I used to get in a lot of fights. And, knock on wood, I fought guys six or seven feet tall, 300 pounds, two or three of them at a time, and I was a little guy and I always came out on top. I always thought it was because I never went to them looking for trouble, they always came to me, and I thought that as long as they came to me, and if I couldn't get out of it, well I was going to come out on top because I hadn't asked for it. That's the way I looked at it. I mean I'd take a good beating now and then, but I'd always wind up coming out on top, showing them: 'Hey it's going to take a little more than what you thought it would for you to do what you want to do'."

In 1988, he transferred his union work card from local 711 in Montreal to local 361 in Brooklyn. His family had now been members of local 361 for three generations. Many of his uncles and cousins were also members there during his ten-year membership in the union.

Ronald Cross first went out with Nadine Montour in 1979, and broke up with her in 1987. While in New York, he lived with someone else for a while.

"She had an apartment in New York and a house in Miami, Florida. You might say she was the best woman in the world and yet...I missed Nadine; I realized that breaking up with her had been a mistake. The American woman and I split up in March 1990, just before the crisis, and she knew that, once I returned to Kahnawake, I'd try to see Nadine again. We were friends more than anything else, and we still are."

•

He continued to work in New York with his friends until March, 1990.

"We all lived in the same neighbourhood. We worked to-gether, commuted together, lived and celebrated together. Between 1987 and 1990, I seldom visited Kahnawake. I'd broken up with Nadine, whom I'd been seeing for eight years. I had no reasons to go back there, especially since I knew I'd made a mistake leaving her."

It was during this period that he began drinking, taking cocaine and making trouble.

"It got to the point where I couldn't drink with my friends without it turning into a fight. I was even fighting with my friends. I thought constantly about suicide. I was very depressed and it got worse when I drank. I called my family all the time and they were starting to suspect that I might do something desperate or stupid. That's when they asked me to come back home.

One day I was talking with Louis, my brother-in-law, and he said he'd come get me. I told him not to waste his time, that no one could do anything without my consent. We talked for a long time and he knew I was in trouble. He made me promise to come back and finally I told him that I would, in a couple of days. And then no one heard from me again. So one day my brother-in-law and my brother Terry paid me a surprise visit in New York. I asked them what they were doing there and they said: 'Since you've forgotten the way back home, we've come to get you.' I knew then that it was time for me to go. New York City was destroying me and if I didn't leave then they'd surely find me dead somewhere soon. So I decided to go back home with them and to take charge of my life again.

That was in March 1990. I went to live at my sister's place in Kahnawake. Unfortunately, things didn't get any better since all my friends came there frequently too, and most of them had the same problems I did. So once again I found myself drinking and taking cocaine every night.

On May 13, 1990, I was involved in a brawl in a disco on Upper Lachine Road. I was pretty drunk and I overturned some tables. The doorman threw me out. As I was getting to my car, the police stopped me to ask me some questions. I don't really remember what happened after that but the next thing I knew they'd handcuffed me and thrown me to the ground. I woke up the next morning in jail. I was accused of assaulting an officer. I appeared in court the same day and was released after paying a $250 fine.

After that incident, I went to Oka to be by myself. I was serious about quitting drugs and booze. I told myself this would be easier to do there because it was so peaceful. I didn't have as many friends there; in fact, I was alone with my family.

One day in May while I was walking through the Pines, I saw a bunch of guys in a parked truck. I knew them and I stopped to talk to them. They told me they were on twenty-four hour surveillance duty to make sure no one cut down any trees and damaged the forest. I thought the people in Oka wanted to cut some trees for lumber or firewood, because no one had told me they wanted to build a golf course or put up condominiums there—we didn't get into that. So I let it go. The conversation ended and I went on my way. I knew there were people there from March on, just keeping watch on the place, keeping out trucks and people from coming in with their chainsaws and cutting down trees. But it was never a big thing to me really. To begin with, I wasn't involved in the goings-on in Oka because I didn't live there; my mother lives there. I live here in Kahnawake. So I wasn't involved in anything politically there; it made no difference to me. I'm sure they had their town meetings and their community meetings about it and so on, but it was nothing that I ever wanted to find out about or hear about. I was just staying there to get my life straightened out, and I wasn't politically conscious. I had never seen anything on the news about people wanting to go in there, so really it was something that I didn't pay attention to because to me at the time it was nothing.

You've got to understand the people in Kanehsatake are very laid-back people. They've lived there in peace for, I don't know, a hundred years or more, with the French and the English people. They're trilingual people. They speak English, they speak French and they speak Mohawk. So they always got along. It's only a population of 800 people, and there were never major things going on. It was a mixed—a checkerboard community is what they call it. You had French neighbours, Chinese neighbours, whatever, and Indians.

The Kanehsatake Territory itself, the Mohawk Territory is what they call a checkerboard community over there. Because it's not like a reserve; it's like a municipality. There's no economic development there for Indians. Sure, you've got a little corner store here and there but it's not like here in Kahnawake. Here we take care of all our own business: We have our own schools, our own hospitals, our own buses, our own road crews, whatever we need we have for ourselves and it's all Indians that do it. That's what we consider to be our own economic development right here in this community. But over there they don't have any of that. Their roads are cleared by the municipality of Oka, there's no Indian hospitals, there's no Indian clinics, there's nothing for them. So they were living like a municipality, integrated with the town of Oka. And that's the way it's been for a long time. There aren't many traditional Mohawks there. And the ones that did have all this concern about what was going on with the Pines were only a handful. They're the ones who put the guys there to watch and said, 'We're not going to give in to that.' The rest just laid back and didn't take an interest in their community, they didn't want to get involved—just like me at the time.

Every year there's a festival on the lacrosse field in the Pines at Oka, to celebrate the first of July. That day, I was bicycling on Route 344 when I saw a group of people with tents. I told myself there would probably be a big celebration this year. I didn't go because I didn't want to start drinking again. Anyway, I suspected there might be some fights caused by drinking. So I stayed away. A couple of days later, on July 3, I bicycled by the same spot and saw that there were still about 300 people there. I wondered what might be happening for the celebration to last this long. I spotted a few of my friends from Kahnawake and I went into the forest to talk to them. They told me what it was about and I decided to stay with them.

I mean if it fooled me, how many people in Kanehsatake didn't know what was going on. A lot of them didn't know why those people were there until July 11, until they blocked the road and said 'Nobody's coming in here.' When they saw the SQ coming in and trying to kill all the people, that's when the people came out of their shells and said, 'Hey we've got to stand up for this.' And there wasn't like 200 or 300 Natives from Kanehsatake that stood up to fight for this thing. We're talking maybe 20 or 30 people out of 800. And that group was formed through their Longhouse, and then they came to the other communities for help. Now why did they have to go through other Mohawk communities for help? Because they didn't have the help in their own community. People there didn't want to get involved. Most of them wanted to leave things how they were. People didn't know the exact extent of what was going to happen. Maybe in their minds they said, 'You know, they're never going to tear down that pine forest. It's too old, it's burial grounds—it's just too beautiful to cut or to lose to anybody really, to use a forest like that for a golf course.' I guess to them the golf course was this fantasy that would never come true and they believed that right to the last minute, when the Longhouse in Kanehsatake came to ask the people in the Longhouse in Kahnawake and Akwesasne to go there to meet with them, so they could get some help with their problem. And that's what happened. The traditional Chiefs and the Clan Mothers, in both Kahnawake and Akwesasne, went to Kanehsatake and they sat down and they talked with the people from Kanehsatake about what they wanted to do. And it was made clear to everybody that they would stand and fight and not let them take this piece of land away. I don't think anybody really believed until July 11 that that would have happened in Oka.

They never had their own police force, see. They're not independent like we are. They have their Band Council system and that's all they have. The situation over there in Kanehsatake is even worse than here because it's also a split community, with their traditional people and their Band Council people.

Like I said, it fooled me, how it escalated so fast. It really escalated from July 1 to July 11—those ten days were the biggest escalation of that whole thing. And if they hadn't come in and attacked the way they did, things would have never gotten to where they went. It would never have lasted that long. It would never have got to that. The people were negotiating. They negotiated until they had no more means to continue. In our laws we have to talk through every aspect that we can think of to settle a problem or a situation peacefully. We have to look at every aspect we can until we have no more, and there's nothing else we can do to resolve this situation. Violence is the last resort in any situation. If negotiations haven't worked, you have to keep trying and trying and trying. We've been trying for 500 years now. Getting nowhere. All we've been getting is lied to. So now we were backed into a corner, we had nowhere to go. No matter what we said and no matter what the environmental people said about cutting this pine forest down, it didn't make a difference to the mayor of Oka. And he's got the government behind him. So it doesn't make a difference what we say any more, they're still coming in and they're making that golf course, they're going to do it. So what do we do? There's nothing else we can do. So now we've got to put our lives on the line. We have to fight, we have to go to war. And if we have to die for the land, then we have to die for the land. Because there's no other means of settling this without them taking this land away.

Right now, I don't believe they'll ever get that land to make a golf course. They're lucky they still have the nine holes that they have. Even there, from my understanding, that land was leased to them for a period of ninety-nine years or something.

By bringing outside forces into our Territory—whether it be the Army or the SQ—war was declared on us, because they had no jurisdiction over Mohawk Territory as we consider it. Although none of our people were killed at the time, if anyone had been killed the message was made clear here at Kahnawake, through the media and television. Chief Joe Norton assembled 200 Chiefs from across Canada and the USA. And they sat in council here in Kahnawake. And they said to the government in the press conference they gave, 'If the Canadian Army goes in and attacks the Mohawk people you shall be declaring war not only on the Mohawk people but on all the indigenous peoples. We will consider it an act of war and you will be at war not only with the Mohawks but with all the other tribes in North America.' If the Army would have come in forcibly—you know, shooting any people—there would have been a civil war throughout this country between Native people and the governments. That's a fact that we know. But the government coming on us so hard with all those forces, like I said—they were at war, even though they didn't declare it.

What that confrontation did was to give something back to us that they took away from us a long time ago, and that was the ability to come together as one nation. The Six Nations have been separated by this Indian Act/Band Council thing, like I explained, which created different factions among the people, so the people cannot get together as a traditional government because they have different ideas and they follow different ways. But when the people come together, when all the people of the Territory come together as one, they are strong. It's what we call 'of one mind.' It's like when the Six Nations Confederacy was created a long time ago. The thing was that one nation by itself is one arrow and can be broken very easily, but six nations together is six arrows and they will have a very hard time breaking all the arrows at once. So that's what the Confederacy is, and that's what happened in 1990. By the governments doing what they did, they brought all the Indian nations back together as one, thinking as one mind.

The ceremonies that our people did at that time to help us get out of that situation were very powerful. We were protected very well because everybody was together as one mind: There was no bickering amongst each other, there was no hatred, there was no anger—it was all together as one, as brother and sister. So it made us very strong in 1990. Spiritually, the odds were totally against Canada and any forces that came against us. It's like getting a religion you believe in a hundred percent: You have faith in it; it's there for you when you need it, as long as you don't abuse it. That was the spiritual situation in 1990.

But once 1990 was over and things started to get back to normal, the factions came back into place, and people started pointing fingers at each other and blaming each other, so it pulled our people apart again. It's a shame people only do come together when there's a crisis. It's like a family that hasn't been together in a long time and somebody important in the family, maybe a grandmother, passes away and all of a sudden the whole family is there again and maybe you dislike your cousin or something, but there's none of that. You forget it, you pay your respects—there's just understanding. You go in there with a clear mind. You don't go in there carrying that hatred, because you survive together again as one. And that's what it takes to bring people together: a big crisis—something that is going to ruin everybody. There is such a division in so many aspects of the community.

Being 'of one mind' is something we lost a long time ago. But if we ever gain it back, and sit together in one Longhouse, it is very strong, very powerful, because in '90 we got back to the way we were, to where our culture and our traditions were."

•

Memories of Oka or, Bitter Memories

Which of these two situations would you say is the most dangerous: working on construction sites in Hamilton and New York, or being a Warrior during the Oka Crisis? In terms of danger to one's person, it would seem that defying the White people's laws holds the greater hazard.

At Oka, the violence made itself up as it went along. Starting with the simple construction of a barricade, the rest was improvised from day to day.

Everything began on a nice day in March 1990, when the Municipal Council of the village of Oka adopted the proposal to expand the area's golf course. In one stroke, Oka's Pines and the Mohawk cemetery at Kanehsatake were threatened. In order to protect their land and the graves of their ancestors, the Mohawks erected a barricade to make the Whites understand that they intended to protect this land against all invaders.

Knowing the power of the law, the Whites struck back by pleading in Terrebonne's Superior Court. Mr. Justice J. Bergeron decided in their favour and ordered the barricade taken down. From that moment on, the fight took on historic proportions. What could the Mohawks do, legally, to prevent the Whites from building the golf course they cherished? Nothing, except to negotiate and to hope naïvely that someone somewhere in government would understand their claims and their feelings.

Thirty years previously, the Mohawks had lived through a similar nightmare. They had been opposed to the building of the first golf course, and had hired a lawyer, Mr. Emile Colas. They then sent him with a delegation to Ottawa to try to prevent the development. There, in the name of the Mohawks of Kanehsatake, Mr. Colas addressed a joint committee of the Senate and the House of Commons, proposing the establishment of a Commission made up of an equal number of Whites and Mohawks to settle the issue. These attempts at settling the dispute in good faith failed, and the Commission was never established. Result: The golf course was built anyway, in spite of the protests and discontent of the Native population in Kanehsatake.

Not satisfied with their earlier victory, the Whites came back for more thirty years later. This time they wanted not only to expand that same golf course, but also to add a condominium development to it. And once again, it was just too bad for those pines and that cemetery. The Indians are against it? So what? The Whites will simply get an injunction and the Indians will just have to retreat deeper into the forest.

Considering the events of 1961, what Mohawk of average intelligence would not understand that Indians do not matter and that the White People will get their golf course anyway, simply because they decided they would? What are those pines and why do they mean so much to the Mohawks?

"As to the Pines, Grand Chief Peltier described it as, 'Very precious, spiritual, a sacred place, the heart and soul of my people. The elders use it to gather medicines.' Also, he explained that the trees in the Pines have to hold down the soil, which is sandy and fine and had, before the planting of those pine trees, a tendency to erode and blow away" (see Appendix 1, below). To demonstrate the latter, a report entitled "Historical Study of the Forest Around the Village of Oka" was submitted in court during the proceedings concerning the Indian barricade (ibid.). Considering its contents, it is astonishing that this document did not weigh more heavily in favour of the Natives. It states clearly that "fundamentally, the Oka forest protects its inhabitants from being sanded in."

Part of Oka was once buried under an avalanche of sand. Michel Girard concluded his report: "The tree cutting that would be necessary for the expansion of the Oka golf course could once again trigger erosion and soil instability. In the near future, the village of Oka and the lands of the Grande Commune would once again be threatened by soil collapse" (Lamarche 89).

So the Mohawks had more than one reason to worry about the future of their Pines. But how could they get themselves heard? If only peaceful protest went anywhere...who knows whether Ronald Cross and all the others would have taken up arms on that fateful day in July, 1990.

"Our only preoccupation was to put a stop to the destruction of the Oka Pines by protecting the woods with barricades. The mayor of Oka had provoked this crisis, first by successfully obtaining a court injunction and then by the way he tried to have it enforced by the Sûreté du Québec. We saw no reason why the Sûreté's SWAT team had to be brought into this, court order or not. We were in the middle of negotiations and everyone knew we weren't about to give up our Pines and the cemetery of our ancestors. Without taking stock of the enormity of what they'd done and the possible consequences, they wanted to demonstrate their superiority with a show of force when it was perfectly obvious that the Mohawk people were going to defend their territory. They didn't know exactly how far we'd go and neither did we. We really didn't expect an armed assault, but we were ready for the worst because we'd decided never to bow to their demands concerning the expansion of the golf course.

We didn't necessarily want to take the risk of triggering a war; we just wanted to defend our rights. The idea wasn't to start a fight but rather to reclaim the ownership of our lands. We never thought we'd win a military victory against the government forces, but at least we made the leaders aware of our state of mind, our weariness of always seeing our territorial negotiations pushed further down on their agenda of priorities.

We knew we had to reach an agreement quickly if we wanted to avoid an attack that would leave many victims on either side. At first, we wanted to concentrate exclusively on negotiating land claims. But as soon as more people got involved, there were suddenly more and more points of contention and the situation deteriorated.

At Oka, the Army was facing around fifty people and in Kahnawake, where we had blockaded the Mercier Bridge in support of the people at Kanehsatake, around two thousand. They could have wiped us out. But if they'd killed us all, they'd have triggered a civil war. There are more than a million Native Indians in Canada who would have rebelled against the Canadian government. What would the government have done then? Kill all the other Indians? Would they have declared martial law throughout Canada, like they do in totalitarian states? Not that they didn't act like fascists during the crisis!

There had been a meeting in Kahnawake where the 200 chiefs

present made their decision public. If the Army attacked the Mohawk people, it would be considered a declaration of war on all indigenous peoples. If the governments found the situation difficult at Oka and in Kahnawake, what would they have done if they'd had to face thousands of us?

We may have lost a battle but we won the war. We did our jobs and we couldn't have accomplished any more without sacrificing some lives. Now the whole world knows of our problems. And the governments have to deal with them. Native land claims and Native wishes for autonomy are now high on the agenda. I think it's a victory for our people.

Unfortunately, the only time governments listen or take action is when someone dies or when lives are in danger. If they'd respected us and if they'd taken our claims seriously from the start, this whole mess would have been avoided. During the crisis, we'd listen to the news on TV to see how our negotiations were moving along. And we kept hoping that it would all be over soon. The journalists we had allowed into our compound were very honest—they didn't distort the truth. Their reports and articles reflected exactly the statements we made during the press conferences, but after the conflict escalated, their reports never got outside the barricades.

The Sûreté du Québec falsely accused the journalists of being on our side. The force was frustrated at not being able to keep the press out. The press witnessed all their abuses at Oka.

The media that was inside the Treatment Centre, a lot of their stories did not get out until it was over, because the Army prevented the media from using their cellular phones and faxes, from sending film out, from sending tapes out, from sending any footage or anything out at all. So they were stuck in the Treatment Centre for the last thirty-something days without sending out reports, without sending out pictures, without sending out film or tapes. And the coverage the media *did* use came from the reporters who were only *around* the situation, who weren't allowed into our compound, and they weren't dealing with facts. It wasn't until later on—after the crisis—that the truth of the situation came out in the films, because that's the footage that was shot *inside* the Treatment Centre.

And I'll tell you, I've got to say, a lot of French-speaking Quebec journalists, a lot of Quebec French papers, did not work on a professional basis. They took matters from their own feelings and opinions. A reporter who does not work professionally is not going to have a true story. Like even folk today, you pick up French papers in Quebec and all they do is dump on the Mohawks. You pick up a *Gazette*, or *Times* or something, and it's got the true story in it, what the facts are. But if you pick up a French paper, they do not deal with facts, these people. I don't know if their editors or whoever put these stories out, but they do not deal with the facts. They deal with hearsay. The professionals to me were the ones who stayed inside. These people on the inside were getting it right from the horse's mouth, and outside they were not getting it from the horse's mouth, they were getting it from the horse's cousin. To me, the ones on the inside, no matter if it was bad for us or good for us, they got the facts.

The ones that stayed on the outside got everything that was floating along the lines, all the hearsay. And then they went to people in the community, asking them questions about what we're doing inside and what's going on. How do those people know? They're not in there. They were getting hearsay from the Army, hearsay from the village of Oka, hearsay from government officials. They take a little situation and blow it so far out of proportion that the public, they just eat it up. Like creating the myth that the Warriors were criminals and terrorists and Mafia-involved. That came from Brian Mulroney's mouth, not from the community.

There were reporters from all over the world, French as well as English. We refused access to some of them at the barricades because of the inaccuracies in their reports or articles. Others had no influence whatsoever and were asked to leave. Except for those isolated cases, all the reporters were welcome, but we had to watch them twenty-four hours a day so that they wouldn't blunder into a danger zone."

•

"During the crisis, I told my brothers I didn't want to see them involved in this conflict. I was thinking of my mother and I told myself it was bad enough for her to risk losing one of her sons. Besides, I had enough problems as it was without having to worry about my younger kin on top of it.

In spite of this, two of my brothers were arrested during the crisis. My brother Terry was arrested by the Sûreté du Québec for illegal possession of a firearm and he spent a weekend in jail. He was one of the first to be harassed and arrested at Oka.

After the crisis, my youngest brother, Guy, was also arrested, during a party. The scrap was predictable. Cory Jacobs, a Native Crown witness—hence a witness against the Indians during the crisis—was also at that party. They'd both had a few drinks and got into an argument. My brother was arrested by the Sûreté du Québec for having made threats to a Crown witness. The judge sentenced him to six months in the Saint-Jérôme jail. My brother was eighteen years old and had no previous criminal record. He'd never been arrested before. Even though both of them were drunk at the time, only my brother was arrested.

During the crisis, I think my brothers were afraid for me and wanted to help. But at the same time they knew I could get out of it and I could take care of myself. For many years after my father's death, I was always gone and my brothers grew up without me. They always respected me as being the 'eldest,' like I said. When I was there they asked for my advice. They know how I am. Each time there's a problem, they know they can count on me. I've never let them down.

When I was in the TC in 1990 I got a call from Germany from my brother Tracy, who's a career man with the Army. His buddies who were on leave for the weekend, they were doing a party thing. And they were really upset with what was going on with the Army, with the Vingt-deux. It's an English Army in Ontario so they've got a different perspective on what goes on with the Vingt-deux, which is the Quebec Army. I mean they're not even well-liked among their own people. The reasons, I don't know. I guess my brother and his buddies, they are an elite unit, to them the Vingt-deux are just a bunch of sissies. But they were feeling no pain and saying things on the phone that was being bugged at the time. I mean calling down their own Canadian Army which is supposed to be as one, and they're telling us to kick their asses, and I tell them, 'Just take it easy, watch what you're saying'—but they were feeling no pain.

Some of the things he said on there could have really hurt him, his career. But he feels it's been hurt already: They're not going let him get any higher than a Sergeant. They're not going to commission him to be an officer because he's a Native, a Mohawk Native from Kahnawake. They're not going to give him the power; they don't have to do that and he knows it. In 1990 he was harassed: He was under surveillance twenty-four hours a day by CSIS, or whoever the Special Services for the Army are, to watch him, tap his phones, follow him all the time, because they knew who he was and they knew who I was. But he just does his job as a soldier and that's all he does. Just like a lot of young guys who were in Oka.

Tracy Cross (third from left, standing), Terry's twin, a sergeant in the Canadian Armed Forces.

They had a job to do like we did. We were there voluntarily because we also had a job to do, but they had no choice but to be there. I spoke to many of these young guys outside, right on the lines. They didn't want to be there. They wanted to be home, they wanted to be elsewhere, they didn't want to be in Canada bringing up arms against their own people, that's the way they felt. They felt like, 'Why should we be here? Because the SQ started something and now they're too unskilled, like a bunch of sissies, to finish what they started. They have to involve us. But we don't want to do their job, and that's what we think we're doing, and we don't want to be here.'

I used to walk the lines and talk to these guys—they're guys you meet on a street or in some bar, young guys who meet each other with some respect. The problem was the older guys—the officers, the Sergeants—they were the real instigators. They tried to set an example of how to be tough in combat to the men. They were under orders and their orders were to be hard. A soldier is supposed to be hard, he's supposed to fear no evil, he's not supposed to be afraid to die. That's a crock, everybody's afraid to die.

Ronald Cross and his mother, Ann-Marie Casalaspro. Photo by Francine Dufresne.

The members of my family in New York took it upon themselves to publicize the Native Indian crisis in the United States. I think there was a news blackout about the subject, in the papers and on television, until I took the initiative and called a New York newspaper. I was behind the barricades and I arranged for the reporter to get in touch with my aunts in Brooklyn. Then they published my story.

My aunts then went to the steelworkers' union, who got its members together to go protest in front of the Canadian Embassy in Manhattan. Several demonstrations took place and several articles were published in the papers. The New York members of my family met with black organizations to ask the Reverend Jesse Jackson if he'd serve as a mediator for the Native people.

The people in my family did all they could. They got in touch with embassies, Senators, members of Congress, New York leaders. My mother also got heavily involved. She handled the publicity in Canada so that the public would know exactly what was going on from our point of view.

They did everything possible to get funds for our defence. They contacted everyone who supports our cause and tries to help us."

•

"At Oka, we were short of men, of leadership, and the territory we had to cover was much too large. We had a lot of trouble forming shifts. Most of the men couldn't be relieved so they had to sleep in 'bunkers' to ensure a twenty-four hour presence.

At first, we had a lot of fighters. Natives came from everywhere to help us. Then it was easy for us to be relieved, which allowed us to relax a bit. After a few weeks the situation degenerated. It became harder and harder to go in and out of the barricades, so that in the end we could count only on those who were already there. We had a lot of inexperienced kids with us. We had to make sure constantly that one of them wasn't doing something dumb, because the fire-power around us was very strong.

Tensions between both sides were very high and we didn't want some green kid to forget a bullet in his magazine and fire a shot by accident.

A simple mistake like that could have cost many lives. The older ones had to keep a sharp eye on the younger ones. We made up our teams in such a way that there was always someone responsible in each group whose job it was to make sure that the men understood that we were in a *defensive* situation, not an offensive one.

There's a lot of men in our communities that served in all the wars: There's guys here that served in Vietnam and Korea and World War II, World War I. There's a lot of veterans. I could say probably in this whole community out of maybe 3,000 men, maybe 1,000 of them are veterans who have seen action. They've been in the Marines, they've been in the Army, they've been in the Airforce—you name it they've been there. And a lot of them came to the aid of preparing the men too. But we also had a security force—the Warrior Society—that ran the security in Kahnawake for the past twenty years or thirty years. These are the *Rotiskenekete*—'the men of the community,' 'the carriers of the burden of peace'—and we had our own base, we still have our own base, we have our own communications system, we have our own—not a military force really, but we work like one. The men know communications, they know weapons, they know tactics. We teach each other. I mean twenty-four hours a day there's a security force working in the community besides the Peacekeepers. If you are a traditional Indian, a traditional Mohawk, you would know your responsibility as a man, what your responsibilities are to the community. But if you're brought up a church-going person or a Protestant, you don't know your cultural tradition or your constitution or your laws as a Mohawk.

Before 1990 I didn't know about that. I didn't know my obligations to the Mohawk people until later on, and that was the same for a lot of other people.

Like I said, the Warrior Society was a tradition made up of men who kept that traditional obligation alive. And they trained themselves, you know, how to run a security system for the people. And when everything happened in '90, there were a lot of green people. Even myself, I didn't know about an automatic. I'd never shot an automatic weapon or even had one in my hands. I mean I was taught, and in those few months a lot of military tactics just came to me by common sense. But we had to know what their plans were in the outside forces, how they were going to react to us. This was where a lot of older guys, the veterans, were really helpful. They knew the military tactics, the psychological game of it. And that's what it was, there was a lot of psychological warfare. We didn't want to pull the trigger but we wanted to make a point of scaring them and letting them know: 'Hey, it's not going to be that easy to come in here.' We could feel, psychologically then, that they thought we were trained, and we had them more scared than we were. And you'd have to be crazy to say you weren't scared. But we had them more unsure about what we had and what we were doing than we thought we did.

In Oka, they always thought there were 400, 500—600 Warriors inside the Pines, for all those three months. They could never get a head count on us because we had so much coverage there. And we did so many different things to make them think: 'Hey, there's a lot of men out there,' when really we had about 40 men throughout the whole thing. This is why we never contradicted the whole Vietnam thing in public, and we let them believe we really did have 400 guys in there with us. If they believed we had just as much heavy artillery as they did, they were thinking twice about moving and coming in. If they thought we had the whole place surrounded with booby traps, they weren't coming in there at night to start fooling around—they didn't want to get blown up.

We made do with what we had. We went out on the golf course, we dug a little trench about a hundred yards out, then we dug a hole, making sure they were watching us. We knew they were watching us twenty-four hours a day. We dug a hole and we got a couple of flares, let's say they were flares, taped them up. We put the bundle in the hole, put a silver can on top, then we ran a wire from there all the way into the bush. They'd come to places like that, and what did these people think? They'd think it was dynamite.

Same thing on the Bridge. They took pictures of dynamite on the Bridge, big rolls of dynamite. Flares, that's all it was, with wires coming out of them. We just had to make them think that. No matter what they said about heavy artillery and that, it didn't go that far. I mean, we had some stuff. If you want to get truthful, we had some stuff, but not what they think we had. For them, they saw to it that a lot of it came on TV to justify their own enormous firepower. But we fooled them. We'd get pipes, six-inch pipes, right? We dug a trench. We put up sandbags. We put a tarp over it. We put this six-inch pipe sticking out with arms and with a scope on it, you know. That's all it was, a pipe.

The team I worked with had no fixed position. We had to patrol the entire Territory day and night, trying to eavesdrop on our enemies' conversations in order to get as much information as possible. We also had to make sure that everything was going well in all the sectors, that all the men were in good condition, and to get reports about the activities of the groups of Warriors. And we also had to act as a police force among our own people so that no one drank alcohol or made any trouble. The men were on duty twenty-four hours a day and, many times, the women relieved the men so that they might get a little rest.

Usually, when we had questions to ask, the War Chief answered them. There was a War Chief there, an official War Chief, from Akwesasne, guiding all the men from Kahnawake, from Akwesasne and Kanehsatake. It should have been a representative from each of these communities that made the decisions. Dennis Nicholas was the one giving orders to tell the men from Kanehsatake their responsibilities, so he was more or less like Assistant War Chief. But in the long run, after July 11, when the War Chief from Akwesasne had left—it was never official for meetings or anything—Dennis Nicholas was calling the shots because it was his Territory. He lived in Kanehsatake, so he should have been calling the shots for the men, telling them what to do, and working on a system to make sure everything was working out.

But instead we were out one day in the four-wheelers doing surveillance, going through the back of the Pines and he flipped over on the terrain and busted up his knee a little, so we ran him back to the camp. One of the girls there, she was a nurse and she started taking care of him. And he was single, and she was single, and one thing led to another and the next thing you know they were bandaging up each other at his house. He was under a lot of pressure and I guess he just needed to be out of the picture for a while. So after that, myself and Noriega [Gordon Lazore] and a couple of others were pretty active around the clock, twenty-four hours a day.

We never took a fixed position in Kanehsatake. We were what you would call a recon team. Our duties were to make sure that everything was going well at all the checkpoints, that the men were alright and they were doing the right things, and during both day and night to cover the whole perimeter, our whole perimeter that we had secured on foot to make sure that the Army wasn't setting up booby traps, and they weren't sending their own recon teams to come in and do things. Also, if there were any problems at any of the checkpoints or any of the perimeters, our recon team would be called in and we would tell the men what to do and how to handle the situation, or we would do it ourselves. If any outsiders or media were seen, we were the ones called to take care of it, instead of having guys leaving their positions. So for two or three months we were active and visible twenty-four hours around the clock.

There were five of us in this team that was constantly called to deal with any situation, any problem. In other words, the men, if there was anything wrong, would call myself or Noriega. And we would go over there and take care of it, then continue our job.

Ronald Cross in the Pines.

It was a big load. I mean, we walked thirty square miles every day. We'd rest a couple of hours, sleep and do what we had to do, then go on. And with the shortage of men, we always had to be there. So that's why, I guess, being called so much on the radio and being at all these different places at all times of the day and night, we were seen a lot. I mean, anywhere we went, whether we went by car or by bike or by four-wheeler or on foot, there was always the media there. And we were always on the radio, our names were always on the radio, more than anybody else's. That's why they got to think of me as one of their scapegoats, because we were always in the picture, showing up somewhere or doing something or taking care of something. And that's where the SQ, I guess, thought they had the leaders of the Warrior Society, because they figured the names they heard the most and the individuals taking all these responsibilities, 'had to be the leaders.' Really all it was, was that we were an elite group that made sure everything was maintained, and nobody did anything stupid. Because the War Chief was out of the picture now.

Even if Dennis was there, they would still come for us because that's the position we took. We'd take care of the problems, we'd take some of the load off the acting War Chief because not everything could be put on his shoulders. So we'd have to take some of that away from him, to not burn him out, so that he could make the right decisions too. So it was a big role. We were always in the picture and in the limelight. I mean, it couldn't be helped. We could be 400-500 yards away in the bush, and there'd be a guy we can't even see with a huge lens on the camera and he's taking pictures of us. So we couldn't stay out of it no matter what.

In the beginning, for the first month and a half, we tried to keep all the media in one spot. We didn't want them along any of the perimeters taking pictures of the bunkers, or what we had laid out in the bush or anything. I had a couple of problems with a couple of reporters, we almost scrapped it out, because they said, 'We can go anywhere we want.' 'Oh no you can't buddy— you can't just ride around Kanehsatake. 'No way,' I said, 'no way.' 'We're not going to take pictures,' they said. 'Okay, I'll take your word for it, sure.' We had to keep them out because the next thing you know there it would be in the papers and on TV: our bunkers, a headcount, they would have known all our fixed positions. So that's why we had to herd them like cattle. And they were getting restless, we always had to go and catch them sneaking through the bushes.

We did it for their own safety too, but they didn't understand that. We had rigged up things in the bushes that could really seriously hurt a person, take them out of commission. We didn't rig up things that would kill a person but we rigged up booby traps where, if a person got caught, he was going to be out of commission. I mean, he might lose a leg or an arm or something, get hooked in the eye, but nothing to kill a person. Just to let the Army know if they want to fool around in the bush, they're going to get hurt. It wouldn't kill them, just let them know, 'Hey, I'm going to take you out of commission.'

With the Clan Mothers there, when a big decision had to be made, it wasn't just made amongst the members of our team. If I had a problem that I felt was going to jeopardize our stuff, our safety, I would go to the people, and say 'Look there's a problem over here—what are we going to do about it?' We would discuss it among the men and the women and make a decision, then go and do it. Like digging up the roads, taking the tractor and making mounds of dirt across the roads and trenches for tanks to go in. We didn't just do that, we had to discuss it, how it would effect everybody in the community.

I found myself having to make decisions that the War Chief should have made. Very often those decisions had to be made on the spot. After a while, it was almost always the same ones who were defending the area. Most of the guys from Kanehsatake would come to patrol for a few hours and then go home to eat and sleep while the Warriors from the other communities were there twenty-four hours a day. Only a handful of men from Oka stayed with us. A lot of us got fed up with the people from Kanehsatake because they weren't there to help us. They had asked us to help them, and as soon as the shit hit the fan they hid or they ran away.

A lot of people wanted to negotiate. We all wanted to negotiate. But when the pressure was turned up, they left us holding the bag. Of course, they were worried about what would happen to their lands, but they didn't worry about history and the pride of the Mohawk people. In other words, sure we didn't want anybody to die and we didn't want war either. But did that mean we had to shame ourselves in the eyes of our ancestors by giving up the fight?

Throughout the history of the Mohawk Nation, our people have never surrendered to anyone. To give up would mean that all the battles waged by our ancestors had been futile. So the decision was made that we wouldn't surrender, that there had to be another way for us to get out of this, or else we'd fight to the death."

Lasagna

"I'd been seen a few times on television and in the papers. At first, the police didn't know who I was, because in all the pictures that had been shown of 'Lasagna' up to September, I'd been wearing a mask. They eavesdropped on our radio transmissions from the first day of the conflict and the same names kept coming back constantly on the airwaves. From this they deduced that 'Noriega,' 'Nicholas' and 'Lasagna' were the leaders.

The police kept hearing 'Lasagna, Lasagna' without knowing who I was. August 31, one day before the Army moved forward, Ronnie Bonspille got away from the Oka territory. It was he who gave my real name to the Sûreté du Québec. The LaSalle police had a picture of me and quite probably a file too, ever since the incident in the bar on Upper Lachine Road that happened four months before the Oka Crisis. But all they knew of me was my first name, Ronaldo, my mother's maiden name, Casalaspro, and a New York address they found in my wallet. Because I hadn't answered any of their questions during my arrest, I guess that's why they said I was from New York.

I decided to take off my mask the very day that they showed my unmasked picture on television. That was in early September. My identity had been supplied by Ronnie Bonspille and Francis Jacobs, the two Indians that had fled from Oka in August, 1990.

There are people out there who would sell out even their own mothers. There are traitors, even among Indians. Some people are weaker than others. But that doesn't mean that the police and the governments are angels. For them, anything goes when it comes to getting information, and when they want to make you talk, they're worse than the criminals: They become criminals with badges."

The Francis Jacobs Affair

Francis Jacobs is the Mohawk who was beaten by other Mohawks during the crisis. The White people looking at this on their television sets could not make heads or tails of it except to think that "Lasagna" was probably behind the whole thing, trying to take over leadership of the reserve on behalf of his "Mafia masters." When the cameras showed Jacobs' swollen face, people started saying that those Indians were "savages." Who is Francis Jacobs and what was his role during the crisis?

To Lasagna, Jacobs is one of the two traitors who gave his name and picture to the Sûreté du Québec after having left the Oka area to collaborate with the police.

During the crisis, Jacobs' duties, like those of many others, was to patrol his sector in order to prevent robberies, break-ins, and vandalism. In spite of all these patrols, many homes were robbed and vandalized, which contributed to blackening the reputation of the Warriors. According to Lasagna, Jacobs himself, before leaving the reserve to become a police collaborator, was responsible for some of the break-ins and the vandalism that occurred, which he then blamed on the other Warriors. So even before Jacobs informed on Lasagna, Ronald Cross had more than a personal reason to discipline him. Adding to this animosity, that very night the television news reports featured the Mongeon family farm, allegedly ransacked by Warriors. Francis Jacobs' name appeared in the report, as well as footage of Ronald Cross' motorcycle which someone had set on fire.

On the night of September 1, 1990, while Ronald Cross was at his brother Glenn's house, two friends came to visit him. Their idea was to get even with those who were sullying the Warriors' reputation.

The description of the ensuing violence, as told by Ronald Cross, terrified me. I was discovering a Lasagna whom nothing would stop and whom I did not recognize. But at the time of the original news report, I was unaware of what had gone on between Jacobs and Cross. Jacobs appeared to have been beaten just for disagreeing with the Warriors' philosophy.

Out of context, the sight of Francis Jacobs savagely beaten for no apparent reason simply reinforced the idea that the Warriors were beating up anyone who was not on their side. The Warriors started losing public support because the media were portraying them as not only ransacking houses, but, worse still, as brutalizing their own brothers. Terror seemed to be reigning on the Territory, and it bore the names "Warriors" and "Lasagna."

For their part, the Sûreté du Québec claimed to have no reason to suspect Jacobs of having committed such misdeeds. It is necessary, at this point, to remind the reader that Jacobs is still a Crown witness. It is also necessary to remind the reader that many of the items looted from these ransacked houses were later found to be in the possession of none other than Francis Jacobs and his associate Ronnie Bonspille, who claimed, during Ronald Cross' trial, that they were "storing the goods and kept an inventory" (Horn 45).

The Famous Face-to-Face Encounter

"I don't think we were the aggressors. The Army was the aggressor. The military was supposed to keep the peace but what they really wanted was to show us how superior they were. They did everything possible to trigger a gun battle with us. They tried at least a dozen times to provoke us so that we'd fire at their positions—at their tanks for example, which would have justified an assault by the Army.

If the government thinks its Armed Forces showed a lot of cool and discipline, they're wrong. Most of the young soldiers *were* very disciplined. But their officers and the men in charge of the soldiers on the battlefield were instigators and troublemakers. They were itching to find some way to end this thing with a blazing display of what their young soldiers could do. Invariably, it was always the older ones who made trouble—not their men. Whenever the soldiers themselves got near us, it's because they'd received orders to. You just have to recall the day the Army went into the forest and we had to retreat to the Treatment Centre.

That night, they were bivouacked near the lacrosse playing field. We had all previously agreed that none of us would move. Everything was quiet and it started getting dark. Some of the men had gotten together near the entrance of the Treatment Centre around a campfire they had going. There were some media reporters, women and children sitting around the fire. Suddenly there was a machine-gun burst from the lacrosse field. The bullets sprayed everywhere around us. Dust was flying and bits of rock ricocheted all over the place. Everybody hit the dirt. It was a three-shot burst. The guns used by the Army have a button that allows you to shoot in semi-automatic mode or else in automatic three-shot bursts. When the soldier pulls on the trigger, the gun fires three bullets at a time.

Then everything was quiet. 'Mad Jap,' 'The Big Red One' and I went to their lines, face-to-face with their sergeant to ask him was he was trying to do and why he was shooting at us. The sergeant just laughed at us. He looked at his men, then he looked at us and he said: 'Gunfire? I didn't hear any gunfire.' Then he turned to his men again and, with a big smile on his face, asked them: 'Did you guys hear any gunfire?' With that big ear-to-ear grin of his.

That man was supposed to be a squad leader, the officer in charge! We told him he'd almost shot one of the reporters, that there were women and children, that he'd almost shot them and that if this happened again, there would probably be a civil war throughout Canada. Why had they done that, if not to provoke us?

Even though the Army had often said on television that the soldiers wouldn't be the first ones to open fire, we had to face several incidents of that type. They opened fire many times and, because of television, the whole world saw them shoot at us. They opened fire on a group of unarmed Mohawk men, women and children, who had only their fists to defend themselves. I even have a friend in Kahnawake who was shot in the knee by a soldier with his M-16.

I believe the Army wanted to goad us into taking regrettable or insane action, so that they could then tell people that even though they didn't want to do us any harm, they had to retaliate. The Army wanted to be able to say it was merely in a defensive position. To do this, they had only one tactic: to provoke us into firing the 'first shot.'

If the Army didn't want to start any trouble, all it had to do was not set foot on our land, because no outside force has any jurisdiction on Indian land without the consent of the Indian people. Invading Indian lands or entering them without the consent of the Indian people is an act of war.

The face-to-face encounter with the soldier was to show them they had no business on our lands and that they wouldn't intimidate us with their guns. We had a cause to defend and we weren't leaving. It was also a psychological ploy to make them understand that it was going to be far from easy for them."

The Mercier Bridge

"We had to come up with something even better than the barricades at Oka to make them respect us. We had to find a pressure tactic that would keep them quiet. That's why we blocked the Mercier Bridge. After a few days the population went nuts and started taking it out on Indians all over. We'd blocked the bridge that they needed to go to work! But who started that war...the Whites or the Indians?

We didn't take over the Mercier Bridge because we had something against the Whites, but because it was our only means of applying pressure. We didn't want things to get to that point but, unfortunately, violence is the only thing some people understand. From that moment, as long as we retained control of the bridge, their troops were paralyzed. They had to listen to our demands. We knew we were outnumbered and that the next assault would be a major one. But they knew we weren't novices, that we were very familiar with our Territory, that they would be forced to come and get us and that they'd lose a lot of men in a fight like that. I knew they wouldn't take that sort of risk. No one wants to be responsible for launching an attack where people get killed."

The White people, deprived of their bridge, did not understand that the Mohawks were victims as much as they were in this affair. And yet it is not the Mohawks who triggered the Oka Crisis. First they were provoked and they retaliated. They never wanted any war or battle or slaughter and yet, during the crisis, they had to bear the brunt of all the spiteful criticism. On a television program shown on Radio-Canada [the French CBC], Jean Cournoyer summed up the Oka Crisis with these words: "The Mohawks are nothing but eighteen armed bandits who are holding an entire population hostage."

With the bulldozers poised to destroy the Pines and the Mohawks' ancestral cemetery, what were they to do? Send a telegram to the Environment Minister just to find out, after the cemetery was ransacked and the woods destroyed, that the government concurred with their position? Could the government regrow century-old trees and return the dead to their graves?

At best, the government would have apologized. Then, as is customary, it would have blamed some minister or other who, in turn, would have blamed another. The Indians had to act fast and, unfortunately, violence is often the only way to shake ministers into action.

Everyone recognized and admitted that this problem had been dragging on for months. It required an explosion such as this one for governments to get involved. And what involvement! They played bureaucratic ping-pong: One said it was a federal matter while the other claimed it was a provincial one. As we know from the constitutional debates, it is easy to imagine what would have happened to the Oka lands had the Mohawks sent telegrams instead of taking up arms.

Indians who fight back, who put up barricades, who block the Mercier Bridge, do not do this in order to provoke the Whites or to have fun. They do not do it because they enjoy holding the public hostage. They do it because they know it is the only way to bring a vacationing minister back home.

A lot of people were upset over damages caused to White people's homes, and rightly so. But why is it more scandalous to vandalize White people's property than that of the Indians?

"When something of ours gets ransacked," says Ronald Cross, "it never matters. It's unfortunate that it's always violence that gets the upper hand. But without that violence, without this fear of the bloodbath, what would have become of Oka? What could we have done once the trees were chopped down?"

The Retreat With No Surrender

"When the Army decided to move forward, we decided to fall back. There was no other choice. We didn't want to get involved in a fight that would end badly for both sides. But we'd decided to fall back only to a certain point and that if the Army tried to push us back any further, we'd fight our final battle. We didn't want to surrender to the Sûreté du Québec.

During the entire crisis, the Sûreté tortured and beat up Indians and arrested innocent people for no reason. They wanted to hit back for the humiliation they felt at having made so many mistakes. There was no way we'd surrender to them. The Army agreed: If we were to surrender, they wouldn't hand us over to the Sûreté du Québec.

The day before we left the Treatment Centre, September 25,

the Chief of the Confederation told us we'd done our duty, that we couldn't do any more. They asked us to think of a way by which we could get out of this and go home.

The Treatment Centre at Oka. Photo by Francine Dufresne.

Since throughout history the Mohawk people have never surrendered, and we didn't want to be the first to do so, we had to find a way out of this without surrendering. We held a meeting and we decided on the following strategy: We would leave the Treatment Centre and go back home in our battle dress, but without our weapons. The weapons were to be destroyed.

The Army knew we were going to leave the Centre on the 26th of September. We lit a huge bonfire, dismantled the weapons, threw all the combat ordinance into the fire and destroyed any other object that could be used as a weapon. The weapons were burned along with all the documents and the faxes. All the ammunition was also destroyed. Some of the Warriors, including me, had decided at first not to leave the Treatment Centre before the agreement was put on paper. Once the ceremony had begun, however, I changed my mind. There was no reason why I should remain alone in the Centre. I took my gun and my munitions, I went behind the Treatment Centre, I threw my gun in the fire and I got rid of my bullets. Everybody was glad I'd changed my mind, even though they knew I was terribly hurt inside. It was difficult for me to give up the fight.

Everybody knew that, once they got their hands on us, I was one of those who would get it worst. We were afraid that some of us might be killed by the Sûreté du Québec. I was number one on that list. That's why some of us weren't entirely ready to give up. But we had to think of the women and children and we couldn't risk their lives along with ours. So we decided to finish it.

The Army had agreed to pick us up in a bus right in front of the Treatment Centre and to take us to the military base in Farnham [90 kms east of Montreal]. After giving it some thought, we came up with another plan. If they wanted us, they had to capture us. Why should we surrender to them? That's why we decided to leave by the east side and to disperse. And good luck to the ones that got away. Being unarmed, we knew they wouldn't gun us down—so they had to catch us. This wasn't considered a surrender.

We put boards on top of their barbed wire so we could leave by the east side. The Army was taken unawares by our break-out on that side. They'd put their big guys near the exit where they were expecting us and their smaller soldiers on the side where we weren't supposed to go. So we threw ourselves over their barbed wire, right onto the smaller soldiers. The Army being unprepared, it was much easier for us to get out. We took advantage of the confusion created by our tactic. They took a long time to react and to send reinforcements.

Already many of us had reached the bottom of the hill. A reporter asked Noriega where he was going. Noriega said: 'We're going home.'

The Army succeeded in rounding us up and handed over three prisoners to the Sûreté du Québec. We were sorted out by the SQ and the military. The SQ wanted to get the guys that they figured were in charge of all this, who had run the operations. They thought they could get more information out of us by interrogating the head haunchos. In their minds we were the head haunchos because we were the ones who were most talked to on the radio and on our communications lines. We were the most visible. They had been listening in on our lines, on our communications from day one, so they could figure out who was calling the shots and who was doing what. So they figured that they had the leaders or the chiefs that were in charge of organizing this thing. Once they found out who we were and what we were, they found out they had nothing, they had a bunch of ordinary guys that just stood up and did what we had to do to protect our lives.

I think they knew the public was more sympathetic to the Mohawks, that they would never be able to actually put the forty people from the TC in jail. I mean, there were women and children in there with us, so they could never really get enough of a case to put them all in jail, so what they were trying to do was to find scapegoats to pay the price for what had happened. I think they knew they would never find out who actually shot Lemay as well, so somebody had to pay the price for all that had gone on.

They really had acted like the Gestapo in the Nazi days. They weren't only unprofessional and racist towards the Mohawk people, they put their foot down on everybody. There were White people—there wasn't anybody who wasn't harassed by the SQ at the time they had their barricades in Oka. They made themselves look really bad because they harassed a lot of people besides the Mohawks. I mean, they took reporters at gunpoint, their phones were taken away, their tapes; they put guns to innocent peoples' heads; they interrogated ordinary citizens because they thought they knew something about the people on the inside. They were so hard on everyone, trying to find information on who these people were, who the Warriors were, who the people inside were. So they knew their image as a police force was totally shot to hell because of what they had done during the standoff.

The thing that I believe is the SQ had made arrangements with the Army to take certain people on their behalf, like Dennis

Nicholas, Noriega [Gordon Lazore], 20/20 [Roger Lazore] and me. Because the arrangement with the Army was that when we were captured or whatever, we would all be taken to Farnham, we wouldn't be put in the hands of the SQ. Everyone knew the SQ would do the most damage, that's why the Army was moved in in the first place.

The four of us were separated from the whole group of people, because the SQ wanted to deal with us themselves."

What happened in the hours that followed?

The Hidden Facts of the Oka Crisis

The day following his arrest, Ronald Cross appeared in the Saint-Jérôme courthouse in a sorry state. His face puffed up and swollen, he looked like a man who had taken a serious beating.

"When we were captured," said Ronald Cross, "I was sure I wouldn't be released with the others. The Sûreté du Québec was working hand-in-hand with the Army. They wanted to get the 'Oka bigshots.' That's why they picked out Dennis Nicholas, Gordon Lazore and me."

What had happened to him that he looked so terrible in that short interval between his arrest the previous evening and his court appearance the next morning?

"The Sûreté du Québec had put up a tent in the Pines. That's where they brought us when we were arrested. They made us kneel and then they handcuffed us with our hands behind our backs. A man in a green suit came into the tent and the soldiers guarding us left. The man in green came towards me and said: 'Hey, boy! You're not dealing with the Army anymore, you're dealing with the Sûreté du Québec.' He showed me his badge, kicked me in the face and pummelled my ribs.

A few minutes later, two officers of the Sûreté du Québec put me in a car. One of them drove and the other one sat in the back with me. The trip lasted forty-five minutes during which the guy in back kept hitting me. He told me I was a dead man. I thought they were taking me somewhere to kill me. I didn't realize then that I had become some sort of celebrity and that this would make it difficult for them to explain my death to the rest of the world."

Ronald Cross then found himself at Parthenais detention centre where, he says, he received several beatings at the hands of a number of police officers.

"We had gotten out of the Treatment Centre at 5:30 p.m. and I got to Parthenais at 7:30. They beat me till around 4:30 in the morning. Almost eight or nine hours straight. They questioned me and wanted me to sign some papers but I kept refusing, so they beat me. They told me it didn't matter—that I'd end up in jail anyway. That they were going to charge me with so many things that I'd stay in for life. They showed me a pile of papers and said I would be seeing a lot more! The SQ interrogator showed me a list of papers in the SQ station and said, 'These are all the charges we are going to lay on you.' I mean, fifty-nine charges was kind of ridiculous. They had about nineteen or twenty separate weapons charges.

Now let's put that into perspective: Either I was carrying a weapon or I wasn't, so why does it have to be twenty individual weapons charges, you know. Either I was carrying a weapon or I wasn't carrying a weapon. And they couldn't prove I carried a working weapon anyway, because they never have found any weapons that were workable—you know, that could fire shots—so they could not charge us on a weapons charge. That's the way the law is. Then there was the matter where I had made death threats to one soldier. Okay, I made death threats to soldiers because they had made death threats to me. I was defending myself. In the courtroom, soldiers admitted to making death threats, as did the police. Soldiers had been assaulted, so had the Indians. I mean, they had guns, we had guns, but there's no justice for us.

There were witnesses, they came into our trial from Oka, who owned homes in Oka and actually said, 'Well if I had a gun I would have killed the sonofabitch.' So he was making a death threat right there in the courtroom to the judge. He said, 'I was going into the house and I was going to kill them.' And he got away with it. The balance of the justice system was totally on their side. No matter what my lawyers did to justify my actions it didn't make a difference to the judge.

Around two in the morning I started having trouble breathing and they had to call the paramedics, who told the Sûreté du Québec I had to be rushed to the hospital. Someone called my lawyer, Pierre Poupart, to ask him to get to the hospital. He sent his assistant, Guy Cournoyer.

After a brief medical examination, they brought me back to Parthenais. My lawyer was there and we talked for a few minutes. I told him they'd keep on beating me. He said: 'Now that I've seen you and how you are, they'll stop.' I had no more marks on my face; they'd cleaned me up before calling the paramedics.

The Sûreté guys who beat me knew all the tricks of how to hit someone without leaving a trace. Instead of hitting right in the face, they hit you on top of the head and box your ears. They put a phone book on your chest or on your face and hit it with a truncheon, which hurts a lot but doesn't create any lacerations. Several times, while they were trying to hit me on the head or on the ears, I turned my face right into their fists so that I'd have some marks. It worked pretty well except that it upset them and they hit me even more.

The next morning, a woman from the American Embassy came to see me; she took note of my injuries and of the beatings they'd given me. The police then drove me to the Saint-Jérôme courthouse. My lawyer didn't believe his eyes. He told me he'd never thought they'd continue their beatings, but he had to admit it was obvious that they had."

So ends Lasagna's recounting of the hours that immediately followed his capture. The police claimed that his injuries had been caused by a fall in some bushes while running away from the Treatment Centre in Oka (Maclaine & Baxendale 93).

In March of 1992, Amnesty International published two photos of Ronald Cross, taken at twelve-hour intervals. The first was allegedly taken on September 27 at 4:40 a.m. and the other at 5:00 p.m. One of the pictures clearly shows the swelling under Lasagna's left eye (*Amnesty International* 3).

On April 17, 1991, I accompanied Ronald Cross to the office of the Director of Ethics, in Montreal's Palais de Justice, where we were promised that an investigation would be conducted, after Ronald Cross formally identified the officers who had beaten him. In the intervening three years, no such investigation has ever taken place.

"I pointed out certain individuals from pictures, and they know what kind of witnesses I have to the beatings. They said they were going to bring them up on charges, that there was going to be an inquiry into it. I haven't heard anything since that day. It's the same kind of justice that Indians get all the time. Injustice."

Lasagna: Hero or Victim?

When you examine the life of Ronald Cross, you wonder who is writing his fate. Each time he decides to straighten up and fly right, he finds himself on a path that is both unpredictable and catastrophic.

Back from New York with serious intentions of getting a grip on his life and kicking his drinking habit, he is instead catapulted to the very heart of an Indian crisis and becomes a hero of the revolution! And instead of the life of peace which he dreamed of, he finds himself in jail smack in the middle of Montreal's criminal life, when his only previous brush with the law resulted from having overturned some tables while drunk. It is as if fate did not want him to have his life of peace.

Granted bail on March 9, 1991, released on March 15, 1991, and determined this time to stay away from drinking and his drinking buddies, he decided to marry Nadine Montour. When he returned to Kahnawake in April of 1990, he had started seeing Nadine Montour again, as he always knew he would. He took advantage of his release from prison to marry her and go on a honeymoon to Niagara Falls. The tattoo on his left arm shows the date of his marriage: May 25, 1991. He now lives on the Kahnawake reservation with Nadine and their son, Jerry, born on December 5, 1991.

Once again, his intentions were noble: to be a good husband and a good father. His friends, wanting to celebrate this event with the traditional bachelor party, arranged for Ronald Cross to become, though quite grudgingly, the butt of the party. And since such a celebration includes getting drunk and getting its main victim drunk, Ronald Cross is pulled down into this whirlpool at the hands of his good friends.

Ronald Cross' bachelor party. The Mercier Bridge is in the background.

Many beers later, they are all drunk, and they get this great idea: to free Ronald Cross' brother-in-law who is under arrest for having driven while under the influence. Together they decide to go plead for his release with the Peacekeepers.

But once there, our merry bunch of would-be lawyers, all even more under the influence than their "client," are unsuccessful at convincing the Peacekeepers to release their friend. The next thing you know, every Indian on the reservation with a walkie-talkie has heard about the get-together at the Peacekeepers' station and soon there are more than a hundred people jostling there.

Marriage of Ronald Cross and Nadine Montour, 25 May, 1991. From left to right: Louis-P. Stacey, Ronald Cross, Nadine Montour and Ronald's sister, Donna.

Faced with this, the Peacekeepers grab their nightsticks and try to scatter the crowd. The situation deteriorates and once again Ronald Cross is accused of assault, this time for having allegedly thrown a radio at a Peacekeeper's head.

"All these events," Cross explains, "happened because a lot of us had had too much to drink and we lost our heads." The incident, for which he was not the only person responsible, would not have taken on such pro-portions if the bunch had not consumed so much alcohol, says Cross. But he does not think the Peacekeepers' brutality was justified. They showed up in force, and then the pushing and shoving started. They tried to use force against Lasagna and he defended himself. One of the police-men came at him with his nightstick to hit him. What was he to do? Let himself get beaten to avoid further trouble?

The end result: Far from freeing his brother-in-law, Cross is himself again arrested.

•

That evening, in an interview on Radio-Canada, a Native who was a boatman during the 1990 crisis said that he had taken Cross on the river many times, from Oka to the Kahnawake reservation. "He'd take these little vacations from time to time," he added.

Imagine! Lasagna ducking out of the revolution for a brief moment to meet his betrothed in the woods! Shades of the *Great Gatsby*! So many different men under that mask. Not once did I think of him as ferrying weapons, supplies or information. Lasagna found this story, appealing as it might be, very amusing. He never confirmed or denied having gone on these boating trysts, content merely to smile.

•

Never a dull moment with Ronald Cross! Released on bail on March 15, 1991, he gets mixed up two months later—Saturday May 11, 1991—in the assault imbroglio against the Kahnawake Peacekeepers, which brought him right to the Palais de Justice in Longueuil. He found himself incarcerated once again in the Saint-Jérôme jail for about a month during the summer, after which he was released.

During that month in Saint-Jérôme, I pay him a visit. He is tanned. Outside, the weather is superb, except for the wind which blows too strongly. The prison is located in the very heart of a green field. All around are kilometres upon kilometres of flat terrain. He cannot wait to leave this place. He has all sorts of plans. When he leaves here, he will spend six weeks in a detox centre. Prison is not, as some might think, the best place to dry out. At Parthenais he once told me: "Here you can get anything…except beautiful women!"

He seems happy today. Why does he feel this way? His confidence in being granted bail soon, the recent visit by his wife and son—in fact, they both left just before I arrived—or maybe simply because it is springtime. He talks about this detox centre with such enthusiasm, I do not dare remind him that such an experience can sometimes be crueller than prison.

Speaking of which, he hands me a series of articles published in *Reader's Digest* that deal frankly with the problem of alcoholism on the reservations (see Richardson). His decision is made. He'll go to the

Akwesasne Detoxification Centre. He then resumes his previous train of thought: "The Canadian government refuses to admit that the Indian crisis is a political matter. It obstinately persists in saying it's a *criminal* matter. I consider it a political matter. No one can deny that there was a war. In that case, I'm a prisoner of war, not a criminal."

And, faced with my silence, he insists: "They sent the Army! It was a war!"

●

Of the four men most wanted by the SQ, Dennis Nicholas took a plea bargain with the Crown.

"The Crown knew him: He'd been in trouble with them before for working with the Warrior Society as a communications man. He was found guilty on weapons charges in the past, for which he took a plea bargain also. So every time they arrested him for doing something he figured the fastest way out for him would be just to take the plea bargain that they offered him. He did consult with the rest of us. We thought it was a big mistake for him to plea bargain this time: But in his mind he was doing no good for his people behind bars—so the faster he got out, the sooner he could help on the outside. So that was his attitude towards it.

The Crown also offered bargains for all of us: He offered me five years; he offered Gordon four years; and Roger, two. We told him what he could do with it. We said: 'No criminal charges here. We'll go to court and we'll fight till our last penny is spent. We are never going to take a plea bargain because we're guilty of no criminal charges.' And that was our stand. And he should have taken it too, but he had his own mind made up. We figured he set a precedent for the rest of us to be charged as criminals, because up to that point they had laid criminal charges on all of us. But we could have fought it politically.

I don't know if he knew this at the time. See, we didn't realize it at the time either. We were considered by the people to be prisoners of war, because although war was not declared on us legally—through papers and what not, and the governments' declaring, 'We are at war with the Indians'—by bringing outside forces into our Territory, war *was* declared on us, whether it be by the Army or the SQ, because they had no jurisdiction over Mohawk Territory as we consider it."

In prison, Ronald Cross talked to a lot of people—social workers, psychologists—and all of them see him as a prisoner of war. But that does not change how the prison treats him.

•

His trial concerning the criminal charges laid against him during his involvement in the Oka resistance movement began in September, 1991 in the Saint-Jérôme courthouse. An empty chamber. Hopelessly empty. In the accused's box: Roger Lazore, Gordon Lazore and Ronald Cross. I had expected a full house, a crush of journalists. Nothing of the sort. There is almost no one here. There are more Sûreté du Québec officers here than spectators. Forgotten heroes? In the third row, a *Gazette* reporter; in the fourth, the Justice's private chauffeur; in the back, two officers of the Sûreté du Québec; spread out here and there, two or three Natives; and at the bar, five lawyers.

And while these five gentlemen behave as if their very lives depended on a particular interpretation of an article of the Criminal Code, I try to understand how a story like this can unfold in such indifference. It is true that the Saint-Jérôme courthouse, in the middle of winter (the trial lasted months), is likely to attract fewer people and, consequently, much less publicity than the Palais de Justice in Montreal. Doubtless that is what the authorities want. As for the Indians, why should they make such a trip every day at their expense, risking snowstorms, just to hear some lawyers squabbling for hours on end about points of law? I understand all this, but I am disappointed for him.

Ronald Cross does not belong in this Saint-Jérôme courthouse. The Crown has tried to obscure something that should have been carried out in the full glare of day.

On my way back home, a phrase from history haunts me: "Napoleon was too great for France and too small for Europe."

•

There have been countless petitions to the Court in the Lazore and Cross case. It is a way, like many others, to let the affair drag on while reducing the accused to unemployment and emptying their purses. This is in fact the best-known and most frequently used tactic of many legal offices: Multiply the petitions until the other side runs out of money and thus is forced to give up. Is the lawyer who plays this game really serving justice? It is by taking advantage of the Indians and their wallets that the Crown awarded itself the glory of this new jurisprudence.

Court proceedings in Canada have always been undertaken in the language of the accused. In fact, this fundamental legal principle is a basic right of every Canadian citizen. I don't know of a single francophone who would tolerate that his or her trial take place in English just because the prosecutor and the Crown were anglophones. In this case, the proceedings were conducted in French: All three of the accused in the Cross-Lazore case, however, are anglophones. It was decided, after weeks of debate—and at the expense of the accused—to give them headphone sets and force them to put up with a translator buzzing in their ears. Once again, the media should have had a field day, but they remained silent.

The idiocy did not stop there. In the hallways of the court building, the reporters were in a tizzy over Lasagna's attitude: "He doesn't give a damn about the Court," they said. Cross tolerated the headphones for a while, then he put them down and shut his eyes, as if it were not his own trial. Contrary to what the reporters were saying, I thought this was a smart move, since it was not in fact his trial, but rather that of the lawyers.

And I thought to myself: What do they expect of him? When he rebels, that proves he is a violent man. And since no one has any pity for the violent, he will be given a harsher sentence. When he sleeps, he lacks respect for the Court. And he can be given an extra fifteen years, just to wake him up.

Thankfully, the Court of Appeals reversed the Superior Court's decision, and the trial was allowed to continue in English. Did the Crown prosecutor not know this right from the start?

The Criminal Code requires that the accused be tried in his own language. As Julio Peris noted, it was the Mohawks—who wanted nothing to do with our laws—who had to demand that the Criminal Code be respected. The Crown prosecutor, whose job is to make sure the Criminal Code *is* respected, was attacking the Code's validity.

A lawyer thinks like a lawyer. For my part, it was the first time I became aware of the fact that the accused pays for all the hours spent debating, the endless discussions, the hesitations, postponements, restaurant meals, parking fees. My God, you have to be rich to go to Court! If the opposing lawyer resorts to wearing down the accused with delaying tactics, inevitably there will come a time when the accused, innocent or guilty, will have to give up, being no longer able to afford the luxury of wanting to be acquitted.

"During this legal case, we were approached by some very skilled Indian lawyers.

A writer-lawyer named Bruce Clark wanted to represent us on the question of the Indian people's sovereignty. He's been studying Indian cases—the question of sovereignty and the political implications of sovereignty—for twenty years now. Unfortunately these lawyers couldn't do much for us, because these are criminal accusations we are facing and not a constitutional debate on Native sovereignty. They also depend on our defence strategy. But with our case in St. Jérôme, there were a lot of things that could have been done differently. Like to have a change of venue to Montreal with the rest of the people. They were to be tried in St. Jérôme, but they wanted their trial in Montreal, and the same thing could have been done for us.

And the thing is—the lawyers had a choice, because our lawyers were the lawyers for the others also. Not all of them, but most of them. Who was going to trial first, the four of us or the thirty-nine? How would it have worked out to our advantage? That itself was a mistake. Who was to be charged first was a decision made by the people here in Kahnawake, by the Longhouse. The decision was made by figuring that we three were hit the hardest by criminal charges, and there was nothing we could do but turn it around to politicize it. After the first Mohawk, Dennis Nicholas, accepted to plead guilty—in exchange for two years less one day—the Crown had the right to bring criminal charges against all the others. The precedent had been created, allowing the Court to try us as criminals. The lawyers we had at the beginning should have acted immediately, should have taken all the appropriate actions at the very start to protect us from this injustice. Dennis Nicholas' guilty plea didn't have to be turned against us.

We had no court experience. On the reservation the lawyers and the defence strategy were in the hands of the people. It's the Nation's bureau which finally brought one of our present lawyers, Mr. Owen Young, into court. Our other new lawyer, Mr. Julio Peris, was chosen by a committee made up of one representative from each of the three communities: Joe David from Kanehsatake, Joe Deom from Kahnawake, and Lorren Oakes from Akwesasne. These two lawyers finally did a good job. But when they got the case, it was too late to fix the blunders of those who'd been there before them. Owen Young and Julio Peris took our cause to heart. They didn't do it to fatten their bank accounts like the other lawyers we had before.

I can't tell you how many times the judge had to cover up his own mistakes. He was passing judgment on his own errors. During his opening comments to the jury he was giving them instructions which favoured the Crown. He prejudiced the defence's case and our lawyer moved for a mistrial. This same judge had to decide whether or not his instructions had influenced the jury in favour of the Crown to the point where a mistrial was necessary. Of course, the motion was denied!

How can a judge be his own judge and render a decision on his own mistakes? It's as if you asked me if I thought I was guilty or not.

Before the trial gets started, the Crown has to reveal to the defence all the evidence which it has so that the defence can prepare itself adequately. In this trial, this procedure was not followed. So, right in the middle of the trial, the Crown would show up with new recordings, new photos which it claimed it had just gotten from the Sûreté du Québec or the Army. Witnesses' statements were used in court without those same witnesses, who'd *made* these statements to the Sûreté du Québec, having to show up in court. In this way, we were deprived of our right to cross-examine these people about their statements. This irregularity occurred several times and the judge always overruled our lawyer's objections and always favoured the Crown's. The points of law that were in our favour were always overruled.

During this trial, our lawyer would regularly request that the Crown submit its evidence beforehand. The Crown would retaliate by showing up in court with new evidence about which our lawyer had no prior knowledge.

With a jury made up of Whites judging three Indians, we didn't have much of a chance. The Court said we were to be judged by our peers. My peers are Indians, not Whites. Every member of the jury had watched the crisis on TV or had read the papers. They all knew 'Lasagna' and 'Noriega.' None of them could possibly be innocent of any knowledge of the crisis, or never have heard of us. I don't think anyone there could put all that publicity out of their minds and give us a fair trial.

There was not one minority person on that jury. I was not judged by my peers. I was judged by *their* peers, by the governments' peers, by the White people's peers. So to me it was like going back to the plantation days when the coloured people had no rights in America. And they brought a coloured person to court for whatever reason, and he was judged by his peers: all White hillbillies. He didn't have a chance. He was hung from the minute they brought him in there. If they want to bring me back to trial and judge me by my peers, then they've got to put twelve Mohawk people on that jury, and erase all their thoughts about 1990 from their minds! Because this is what the jury was asked when they picked the jury. Every single one of those jurors—I don't know if we went through 300-400-500 of them—every single one of them knew who Lasagna was, who Noriega was. Every single one of them knew about the Oka Crisis. That's all they'd seen on TV in 1990 and in the papers. So how could they put all that happened in 1990 out of their minds to judge me fairly on what I was being charged with? There's no way in hell."

•

A few days before the case was scheduled to end—January 8, 1992— Ronald Cross failed to show up in court. And I happened to make the full Montreal-Saint-Jérôme trip on that very day!

"It was pure pressure: pressure of my everyday court appearances, of not working, of having money problems—things weren't going my way at all. I was down, I was depressed. I was still drinking at the time. I was using drugs, cocaine, and I just had enough of it all. I started drinking and partying, and one thing led to another. The partying went on and on and on, right into the next day and, although I knew I had to be in court, I didn't care anymore. I said, 'I don't care, to hell with it! They're running my life, maybe I should just,' the thought came through my mind many times, 'get up and leave, to hell with the court and what they think and the system and screw the fifty grand I put down on bail.' If I got away, I could go to another country. I wanted to run—I just wanted to end it and get it out of my life. So it was just a party, to forget about all I was going through. That's the reason why, I think, a lot of people drink and do drugs: to forget about their pain and their feelings. It makes it go away. I forgot all about the courts and the police and the harassment. I thought about it and I didn't want to deal with it, so that was my escape. But the next day I went in voluntarily, and I was thrown in jail. They had a warrant out for my arrest.

We went to a mini-trial for breaking bail conditions. I won because I was being charged with breaking the bail condition that I failed to appear in court. But when the judge let us out on bail, he never put it in the original bail conditions that I was to show up for court appearances. So I won that. Although I won it, they still kept $10,000, figuring that I couldn't come up with another $10,000. And if I could, it would take me some time, so they had me behind bars.

They went through every avenue they could to keep me behind bars—in other words to show me that, 'Hey, you don't have control of your life—we do. And we can grab you any time we want to and put you behind bars.' I had to watch myself when I was in jail also for things like that, but I was given good advice: 'Just mind your own business—hang on to that. Just do what you've got to do; don't get involved with a lot of people. There's people in there for all kinds of things.' And that's what I did: I just took care of me. I minded my own business; I did what I had to do."

The Sûreté du Québec started a search for him and brought back into court the next morning. As a result of this latest escapade, he was once again incarcerated at Parthenais detention centre, where I visited him almost every day until he was transferred to Ste-Anne-des-Plaines.

•

"I've been locked up for a while now, around eleven months in all. In what you might call maximum security. The most important thing to me is my freedom. I've always been a free spirit. I go anywhere I want to go and hardly ever have a problem with anyone. So being locked up was pretty difficult but I knew I had to accept it no matter what the consequences were. I never thought it would go as far as it did. I still don't believe it today. It's an experience that I'll share with my kids. There are movies and tapes and books on these events, and they're going to have to understand not to make the mistakes that we made. We all learn by our mistakes. But I'm not saying that what happened in '90 was a mistake."

And to think that, had he pleaded guilty, it would all have been over by now. That is what following principles will get you.

●

After eleven long months of detention and imprisonment, interrupted by brief periods of freedom which he quickly lost, Ronald Cross gives his impressions and comments about the prison system, the world of lawyers, of judges, of prisoners. Justice seen in less than lofty terms...

"It's a lot harder doing time in a detention centre like Parthenais than in a penitentiary like this place. I've known both kinds. I've been in this federal institution for six weeks and I'm tired of being here, but I have to admit that the federal prisons are much better. The provincial prisons are disgusting!

There is more freedom in a federal prison. You can go outside when you want, from one in the afternoon till eight at night. You can play volleyball, tennis and lift weights. We have three television rooms: one for the French, one for the English, and one that shows nothing but movies. Even Alcoholics Anonymous comes to visit us.

During a trial, you're kept in the jail which is closest to the courthouse. For example, if you go to court in Montreal, you're held at Parthenais. And if your request for release on bail is turned down and your trial is pushed back further in the calendar, sometimes months later, you can be sent to any prison in Quebec.

Parthenais could be called the 'Guilty House' because, after having been held there for some time, the accused has a tendency to plead guilty or to plea bargain, just to get it over with as soon as possible. That prison's been designed to make you feel like pleading guilty. Trust me, it's a nuthouse. There's no room to breathe, no room to move, to have some peace, to be by yourself. Really—no freedom. You can't even go outside to get some air. One hour a day you're allowed to go to the gym and that's it. During one twenty-four hour period, you're out of your six-by-eight cell for around seven hours. Two hours in the cell, two hours out of it. It gets pretty depressing. You're locked up for seventeen hours a day in a tiny room. I did six months under those conditions.

The system has good ways of getting to you. Those guys know how to play with the prisoners' heads to make their stay here painful. The law, the courts, that whole system knows how to make you languish, stretch things out so that you get weary, so that you become broke. And then you can't defend yourself anymore.

Of course, there's always Legal Aid. Call those guys and you'll stay inside for sure. I think one lawyer in fifty in Legal Aid is capable of taking your trial to heart. For the others, it's a money thing and a power trip. Everybody knows everybody else in the system. You can be facing the same accusations as some other guy. For the same trial, you get away with it if you hire such and such a lawyer. With another lawyer, you rot inside. It's not only a question of money: It also depends on the judge which your lawyer wants for the trial. Lawyers know how to end up in front of the judge of their choice. And that makes all the difference.

The law: That's a bunch of lawyers having lunch, saying 'Lawyer X went in front of Judge Y, and that this judge can't stand that lawyer for something that happened in the past; that this judge really slapped this lawyer in the face and gave his client twice the sentence he expected, just so he could show the lawyer who was holding the big end of the stick.'

How many people have paid a big price only because the judge and the lawyer couldn't keep their private lives out of the courtroom? I guess people would know more about our system of justice if those lawyers wrote books on how to outwit the judicial system and win in court. But they won't do it because it would ruin their reputations and prevent them from winning cases in the future.

If you have two lawyers who always argue and don't get

along, one day one of those lawyers could become a judge and find himself face-to-face in court with the guy he didn't get along with. He'll make him understand real easily, like 'Now *I'm* the judge and *I'm* calling the shots.'

The judicial system is like every other system: It's filled with corruption. It's a system controlled by money and power. I recognize that we need the judicial system and the police. Violence, murder, rape, robbery—all crimes need to be punished and I think the guilty should pay for their crimes.

A lot of people would be surprised to learn that it costs almost $50,000 a year to keep a single person in a penitentiary. When you lock up 200 or 300 people in a jail, then multiply that by the number of all such institutions in Quebec—and in Canada as a whole—you can see that it represents a lot of money!

When someone is locked up after having done something bad, he can try to learn what to correct in order not to do it again, but it's also possible he can become worse and hold society responsible for what happened to him. When he gets out, he can become an even greater risk to the public. It's not true to say that the system is focused on rehabilitation: Eight prisoners out of ten are repeat offenders. They're two-time losers, they've been in here before. Still, there must be a way to come up with a program that wouldn't make them bitter towards society.

I've spoken up and I've made a lot of friends here, because a lot of guys here are all right. It's been a long time since I've met people like that. I often wonder what they're doing here. So much money is invested in detaining people who wouldn't hurt a fly. I've been with them for months now. Not once have I seen them get violent, or act frustrated, or angry. I've never asked them what they are in here for, but I think it's probably drug-related or else it has something to do with…some illegal way to make money.

They're not a threat to society. They just need to be helped."

●

Lasagna understands that he has been picked as the scapegoat for the entire 1990 crisis. He is the one designated by the authorities to bear the full weight of what happened that summer.

I talk to him about all the other Mohawks who will come to trial later. "They'll all be acquitted!" he says.

I look at him and I wonder if he is starting to play the victim or to wallow in self-pity. Does he want me to feel sorry for him?

"When he read his decision on our case the judge said: 'The governments of Quebec and of Canada have been ridiculed by these events.' Their image has been tarnished and they looked like incompetents in the eyes of the world. Somebody has to pay for that.

The governments have spent a lot of money because of the Oka Crisis and now somebody needs to be punished for it. I've been chosen to serve as an example. The judge also said: 'Years ago the court hanged horse thieves to make an example of them: Other people wouldn't steal any more horses afterwards.' They've done the same thing with me. They're punishing me so that the other Indians won't rebel anymore.

The Sûreté du Québec absolutely wanted to get me, even though I strongly suspect they know I've never actually been a member of the Warrior Society. But some big names had to be the scapegoats to keep the rest of the people in line.

When those in power see that someone has a lot of influence with the Indians or the Mohawks, they try to shut him up. They make him disappear, they lock him up. They know that these influential people are a threat to the government because they won't give up the fight and because they have the power to draw the people into whatever they decide."

But in the summer of 1994, while he still awaits the day his case will come to appeal, the image of that empty courtroom still lingers. If the courts hadn't asked the people whom Ronald Cross considered to be his peers to sit on the jury, why had the Mohawks not come to his trial in greater numbers? Where was the solidarity of those with whom he had spent all that time on the front lines? And why does he not attempt to communicate with Ellen Gabriel, with Dennis Nicholas, with any of the other key figures so intimately involved in that long battle for the Pines? What's happened? Has he made a conscious decision to work on his own spirituality and to stay away from those people? Does he not want to discuss those events? Do they bring back bitter memories? Is there a division in the community? Is this a conscious decision on his part, or have they just drifted apart? How could he have risked so much for his people only to be left to pay the price alone?

"Well to tell you the truth, it's a little bit of everything you said. I haven't talked to any of them, especially the group as a whole from the Treatment Centre. I feel that the three of us who took the fall and were sentenced, were let down by these people and we weren't supported enough by them. I feel that the thirty-nine who were tried separately and acquitted had more support and more help than we did. We needed it the most and they weren't there for us at the time.

You see, the two separate trials caused a split between lawyers. They took on a lawyer that half of us didn't agree with. We were in jail for six months before we got bail; the thirty-nine were out in the same week. I mean, in the beginning they supported us, they came to the court. But during the trial and everything else, there was no support from these people. They weren't there for us. We lost communications with them. Different lawyers were being brought in all the time, different strategies were being worked on by them.

Also, in order to save face in the courtrooms, certain people who were involved disagreed that they asked the Warriors to be there. They went against the Warriors. Certain people said 'We never asked the Warriors to go there.' Which was not true because they did. The Longhouse in Kanehsatake had asked the Warriors to come in and help them. So they contradicted themselves. With Dennis Nicholas, taking the plea bargain that he did, that was it. For the three of us, he had given in to the police who were putting a little pressure on him. Even though we don't deserve what we're getting, we should take it—because we're never going to give in to them. We're never going to give in and say we're criminals. He made the wrong decision: In order to get himself out of the system as fast as he could by taking that plea bargain, he went against *our ways* by giving in. And the way he gave in was to agree that we were criminals. So Dennis Nicholas was now out of the picture. It was brought up in meetings when we got out on bail and came home, and I see him now and then and we talk. But he knows the men in the community have lost a lot of respect for him, or he is not to be trusted.

You see, he never really was the War Chief. He was just acting as the War Chief because there was no other War Chief in Kanehsatake. He was never officially made a War Chief by the Longhouse. And Kanehsatake never officially had a security system like the Warrior Society here in Kahnawake. They had, like I explained, *Rotiskenekete*, the men of the community. And that's what the people call the Warriors, the men. They had their roles to play. But over here we had a different security force. Nicholas was involved in it big time: He was a communications man, and he knew everything that was going on. But he didn't live up to his responsibility to fight our opponents to the end. He went along with them.

We all made mistakes during '90 and that was one of his. But I'm not going to condemn him for it. He still has a lot of friends within both communities. I'm not saying he's a bad person: He just made a bad decision that I didn't like personally, and a lot of other people didn't either. Just like I made mistakes during Oka too. I made mistakes by sometimes drinking and doing drugs while on duty, creating situations that put a lot of lives in danger. I'm not proud of them—but they were mistakes, and mistakes that we learn from. So he's not the only one. I wasn't condemned for the mistakes that I made. I got a lot of flack for them, I got a lot of hell for them because I jeopardized a lot of things.

If I knew then what I know today, I would have done things a lot differently. I might not have been as aggressive as I was then, because I was pretty aggressive. It was very easy to piss me off. It was hard for me to hold back my anger and, instead, to show my emotions, my Indian emotions. I was more gung-ho into the battle itself than I was into resolving it. I wasn't thinking of a way of resolving the situation; I was thinking of a way of defending ourselves. I was more militant than I was spiritual. What was on my mind was that we were coming down to a war and there was going to be a shootout, and 'If we're going to die we're not going to die alone, so let's do the best we can to take as many as we can with us.' That was my attitude at the time. But it started to change towards the end. Towards the end it was like it didn't really make a difference. What happened, happened. I wasn't getting as angry, as aggressive, as I was at the beginning. But it's something that happened and something that has to be put in the past, and we've got to work on the future now."

And what does that future look like to Ronald Cross in the spring of 1994, while Lucien Bouchard and other members of the Bloc Québécois seem to be advocating that the Army be sent in again to deal with the so called "criminal activities on Mohawk lands"? Has Oka not made a difference to the question of Native rights in North America? What is it with these rumours? Is it likely that the Army is going to come in? Why does the Bloc seem to support such an action?

"Since 1990, the government is still trying to justify its reasons for attacking our people the way it did. Like I explained earlier, they were defaced in the eyes of the world. Canada got a very bad image. Canada was always seen as this peaceful nation that had its peacekeepers all over the world, and they were the ones that had never created a war. And that's exactly what the Canadian governments did in 1990: They created a war among their own people in their own country. People who they were supposed to be protecting and taking care of—they went against them.

I think they are very much afraid of Native people having power in this country. To have the power to run their own lives. The government wants control of everything. They want to have their forces in here to push their lies on us. And they're going to go to any lengths and justify any means that they can to their public to show that they're doing the right thing. Like I explained, they're afraid of rich Indians, they're afraid of educated Indians. They're afraid of us having the power to make our own decisions. They're afraid of dealing with land claims for all they will lose, and all we will gain, because land claims issues are just gain for us and loss for them. They're not happy unless they have full control of this whole nation they call Canada, which is Indian Territory. And they're going to justify doing it by any means—true, fabricated, or whatever.

We haven't been at peace here since 1990. We still have our checkpoints up in Kahnawake. I mean, we're still keeping these outside forces out. Our people are still being harassed every day. Men are being arrested. Men are being beaten up by the SQ, taken to jail for fabricated charges just because they're Mohawk. They're not going to rest until they have control of these Territories. The head of the RCMP came on TV the other day and said, 'The SQ and the RCMP—there's nowhere in Canada

124

that they cannot go, so nobody has the right to tell us we cannot go there.'

Well we have that right, and we fought for that right, and we're still holding that right because we haven't let them in here yet. And they're going to do whatever they can to get in here, to have their powers and heal their loss, to try to make us the Canadian citizens that we're not. And that goes back to, like I said, the Two Row Wampum. We do not force our laws on you— on them—why do they want to force their laws on us, on this Territory? When I leave Kahnawake, I have to abide by the laws outside because that's their laws. I am no different from anybody else. If I go speeding down the highway in Kahnawake, that's fine, if I don't get caught. If I go outside Kahnawake and start speeding and a cop pulls me over, I've got to pay that speeding ticket, because that's their laws. And when they come into our Territory, they have to respect *our* laws also. We have laws too. But we do not accept them pushing their laws on our Territory when we already have our own laws enforced.

We take care of our own. We have to take care of ourselves, because as a people, as a Mohawk people, we have nobody to defend us. We have to defend ourselves. We don't have a Canadian Army or an American Army or a Canadian police force or anything to defend us, because they're all against us. They're all fighting against us. So we have to form our own society to defend our people, just like Switzerland does. If I'm right, that's one of the only countries that doesn't have a standing army but in times of a crisis they will form an army to defend the people and the land. The same thing in the States. Who protects the Natives against the State Troopers and the FBI and the government and the National Guard? They have to form their own society to protect themselves, because throughout history they've been making war on our people.

I think any Indian nation that gets in a situation like this— where outside forces come into their Territory and attack them— will have the support of all Native communities. That's how Custer lost his battle. He got fooled. He thought he was up against one nation, but what happened was the nations came together as one and destroyed him, you see. He didn't know that would happen. He never thought they would do that—that they would stick together as a people. But really all Native peoples are one people: The continent of North America is Indian country. And if they have to fight and die together, they will die together because things have gone far enough now. Our people have lost so much, and we can't afford to lose anything else in our lives. The only thing they never took away from us was our pride, and that's all we have left. And now we have to get back all that we have lost. We have to get back our culture, our tradition, our languages—as a people. We have to get back to Mother Earth, to make sure that she is protected too, because we are the caretakers of the land. And that is our duty: to take care of the land. Not to abuse it. She takes care of us, we have to take care of her. So in the future, if anything comes up, we have a lot of support.

As long as we are living, as long as the blood flows through our veins, we'll be ready to do whatever duties we have to. And if it has to happen again, it will. Our men are prepared for it. We are not going to let them take from us anymore. It's time we are dealt with fairly, rightfully. Instead of hurting us, help us. Try to help understand our ways instead of always contradicting us and putting us down. Try to understand what we're going through, too.

We are all human beings, but societies are different. Each has its own ways. We do not change White people into Indians, why are they trying to change us into White people? They've been doing that since they landed here. And it's a very difficult thing to accept. Our forefathers accepted it. But today, like I said, we are educated people, we know the difference. And you look back fifty or a hundred years ago. There was no Native-run education for Indian peoples. Fifty years ago, they didn't go to school; they had to work to survive. They didn't have time or money or the necessities to go to school and educate themselves. But after so many years, our people are getting educated. You can't pull the wool over our eyes as easily as before. We know how to fight back now. We lost so much over the years and years and years of being raised and going to school on the outside, we lost all that we needed to know about Mother Earth and how to take care of ourselves.

Medicines and ceremonies, everything has a meaning for it— in our culture it's all about respect and love. This is what I am learning. I was in a sweatlodge last night. I was in there for five, six hours—and you have to experience this. It's like you can have visions in there, you can go back in the past, you can go to your ancestors. You get back to Mother Earth: Going into a sweatlodge, it's like going back into a woman's womb because it's warm in there, and you go in there naked and it's just the rocks and the fire. You put medicine over the rocks, and cedar. There are different sweats for different things: for cleansing, to heal you, to take the negativity out of you and make you positive. You could ask the Creator for what you need in life, to walk a good walk. These are things I've learned just over four years, and I'll be going on with it my whole life. I'll be an old man and still be learning. Everything I've learned I have to remember and I have to try to *know*.

They say the Creator will leave tools for you which you can use to better yourself, to find the necessities to live a good life. You have to be conscious of his message to you, to better your life so you can pass it on to your children, and they to their children. It's the good life is what it is—it's getting back to nature, back to Mother Earth. Because she's hurting big time right now, as we can see by all the destruction that is going on in the world, and they say Mother Nature is acting up. That's exactly what it is: Mother Earth is hurting from all the destruction they're causing to her, everything they have taken away from her. You've got to pay a price for that. She'll cleanse herself some day, like a woman cleanses herself, a woman when she's mooning, she's cleansing all that negativity in her body, she's getting rid of it. That's how a woman cleanses herself. She doesn't need as many sweatlodges as a man does. A man has ways of smothering himself with sweetgrass and sage, with which you tell the negativity to leave the body, it's not welcome. And if it doesn't leave, you are going to turn it over to the Creator, the Spirit, whoever he is. That's how a woman cleanses her body. So now once a month when she's mooning I have to take my feathers and my medicine and hide them somewhere so the negativity doesn't go over to them.

In sweatlodges we burn tobacco and sage, and clean our medicines and our feathers. It's all been passed down for thousands and thousands of years, and we survive—we survive all the hard times. And that to me is my new purpose here in life: to know what my Native ancestors knew. I'm having a hard time right now because a lot of ceremonies and different kinds of praying are in Mohawk, and I don't speak much Mohawk. The words I do know I have to say, but it's a tone in the Mohawk words that carries the message to the Creator, through the waves in the air to the Creator; it's like burning tobacco. When we do our prayers and that, we burn tobacco and the smoke will take the message to Him.

To me, the more I learn the better I feel, the better I make myself. I've got lightness in my life now. I may not have an easy life—as I said before, I was a wild and crazy guy when I was young. I used to do things and I didn't care what happened. I used to abuse everything I did: I abused drinking, I abused drugs, I abused the earth, I abused the animals—just like a typical mischievous kid, you know. I wasn't that bad—I didn't go robbing or hurting people. I was a kid, like a lot of other kids, checking things out...experimenting, whatever, abusing everything. Later on in life, they say, you'll pay for the things you do in your life. That's a truth I know. I believe that. The medicine people, they tell me, 'Well you've got a price to pay to get yourself clean and walk your talk.'

You know, it is a price I've paid, and this is all part of that price—the suffering I did in jail. I still haven't got control of my life because of this case. It's been four years now, that my life has been on hold because of the courts and signing in every week on bail. They've still got a hold on me. I'm not a free person: I do a wrong thing, they've got my life. I don't think anybody has the right to do that. I don't believe in criminals getting away with what they do, and they deserve what they get, you know. 'If you can't do the time, don't do the crime.' I believe in that.

That's the thing: to face your fears. It's a scary thing, you know. There are only two things we have to do, and that's to live and to die. We all do it. Every single person in this world, we do that. But it's the question of how and when and why. We live for today, not tomorrow. Today's the day, this is today. You can't have a foot in the past and a foot in the future because then you're not going anywhere.

That was one of my major problems: to take the weight of my people on my shoulders, to try to carry all our problems. I took the burden that was put on our people since hundreds and hundreds of years ago, unsolved things that happened hundreds of years ago with our people that are still not solved—I've been taking that burden, which is wrong for me to do. I did not create it, and I cannot solve it alone. So I should just leave it and just live for today and work on myself for today, instead of going back into the past. Because I'm trying to solve things that happened 100 years ago—500 years ago—that still haven't been solved. But somebody's always trying to solve them: the problem with the poverty in the Territories, the racism in the world. There are so many problems in the world that not just one person can solve them. But he could contribute to helping solve them.

If I could change myself, maybe I can make a difference with one of the kids in the community, or one of my cousins, that might start to think the same way I do. And that's where the change comes into effect. I have to change so that I can set an example for them, for the children, for the young ones, so they can see: 'Hey, it's not right to hate; it's not right to carry grudges; it's not right to be angry. Use it in a positive way, not a negative way.'

I went to see a Medicine Woman the other day and she says, 'A lot of people, they come to me and they say, oh Christ things ain't going right in my life. Who's hexing me? Somebody's got a hex on me: Things are always going bad and I'm always in pain and somebody's working on me.' And the answer is, 'Nobody's working on you. You're working on yourself. You're doing it all to yourself. You're creating this. It's a monster of negativity around you that works on you and that will come back to you. You think negatively about a person that you have a grudge against for a long time. If every time you see him he makes you angry, the sonofabitch makes you angry, it's not him that makes you angry—it's you that makes yourself angry. So you're taking the power that you have in you, a positive power, and you're turning it negative and it's no good. It's hurting you. So you're hurting yourself.' That's it. If people could understand that, then all this negativity, when it comes toward you, it looks at you and says: 'Oh, this guy—he doesn't go for that. He's saying I don't want no part of that negative shit, get away from me.'

It's like when we clean our homes, we burn sage or cedar. What we do is we have a fire, then we take the cones and put them in a bucket, and we take a lot of sage, and we come into the house with a Medicine Man who takes his eagle feathers and he cleans your house. He goes around and never backtracks, he's always going forward, throughout the whole house. He smokes the house out, everywhere, opens the doors and everything. Because when you're in a home, sometimes there's arguing that goes on in the home, sometimes there's bad feelings in the home, there's yelling—all the negative stuff. Maybe you drink in the home, get drunk in the home, there's fights in the home—all that stuff stays in there. It's hiding all in your house. And while it stays in there, it's always coming on you, always coming on you. So that's what they do: They smoke it out with the sage and the cedar until the house is smoked right out. And he tells it, 'You're not welcome in this house anymore. When the owner of this house tells you to leave, you better leave or the Creator will deal with you.' And it's afraid of the Creator, the Creator knows that. The negativity just has to leave. We smoke out the house.

I just learned this myself, how to clean the house. All that negative stuff, all that arguing, all the bad thoughts that I have in this house, the drinking. I say, 'I want you out of this house because you're no longer welcome here. I want you out now or else. If you don't leave on your own, the Creator will deal with you.' I open all the windows, all that smoke goes out. I light a couple of candles and let the house air out and—phew. And the Medicine Man comes back in and he feels how the house is.

Sometimes you feel uncomfortable in the house. There are certain spots in the house where you just know something's wrong. You get a feeling. And that's the way it is. If you learn how to do that, it's good. Like I said, I'm just learning all this myself. I feel good about it because it makes me feel good. I can come into my home and know that it's clean and that there's nothing but good in here. It's like the creation story. To me, even when I wasn't into this Mohawk traditional culture, I knew there was always good and evil in the world. Everybody knows that. Even when a newborn baby comes out of his mother—how can you think this baby could have any evil in him, but he does. They're born with it now. They say in the Adam and Eve story, since she ate that apple, she brought evil into the world. That was the mistake, because before that there was nothing but good and love and harmony; they didn't know about hatred, they didn't know what hatred was, or bad things. That's what brought it in, they said. To me, I know there's good and evil in every person, but the battle within yourself is: What are you going to let take control of you? Are you going to let 60% of the bad take control of you or 60% of the good take control of you, so it overpowers the bad in you? So you fight within yourself, always to remind yourself, 'I'm going to let the good have control of my body and my mind.' Because there are times in our lives, I guess, when we do things that we regret later on."

●

It is not widely known that one of Ronald Cross' bail conditions is that he not comment on the events at Oka in 1990. Quite apart from the fact that the imposition of such a condition is a violation of his Charter rights by the Crown, Lasagna, as usual, interprets this condition in his uncompromising Mohawk way.

"These are my feelings. If it jeopardizes my bail or not, it doesn't make a difference to me. I think the public has a right to know these things. I think the public has a right to hear the facts. I do not talk about things I'm not supposed to talk about. I have bail conditions not to talk about the Oka Crisis. I'm not talking about the Oka Crisis: I'm talking about the Mohawk Nation, the situations that we are facing. Whether it be in Oka, whether it be in Kahnawake, whether it be in Akwesasne, or whether it be in Ganienkeh—these are the situations we are facing today. And the public has a right to know that. They have a right to be aware of exactly what's going on in these Territories. They have a right to know that our people are trying to bring peace to all these communities around us, and peace with the governments—peace with them. I set out to do this book to educate the people about the situation in '90 and to justify myself to them, to show them that I am not a criminal.

This is like taking a history lesson, which even I'm still learning today. I was never politically involved until the events at Oka in 1990. I was a steelworker—a young guy living a young life, a young man's life. I was living high on the hog: I had a good job, nice cars and parties, and I was not too politically involved. I didn't know anything about my own culture, my own tradition, or anything that went on with Native people throughout this continent. I didn't care about it and I didn't want to know about it.

But after what happened in 1990, I guess I had a lot of time on my hands in jail. Also, I got this thing within me, something just saying, 'Hey, it's time you learned. It's time you make a difference with these people. Maybe you can teach somebody something to make a difference. Maybe I can teach myself.' And that's what I'm doing. I'm teaching myself all the time. To me it's a knowledge that could go on forever, to learn about these things. But I also remember a lot of the bad things.

I guess that's what drives me, that drives me to want to know more and to learn more. But I like to learn facts, exact facts. I don't like to read things in the paper. You pick up a newspaper—you can't believe a lot of things in there. Even the other day, they said on TV: 'Kahnawake is a big safe house for the cocaine Mafia.' Hey, I live here! I know what goes on here, you know. It's just something that was made up, something to create animosity, or whatever the word is, to turn public opinion. They've been trying since 1990 to turn public opinion against us, because we have a lot of sympathy from a lot of people across the line. Throughout Europe, throughout Canada and the United States.

In the beginning, you know, their own people were against their governments for doing what they did. And they had to turn that around; they had to get public opinion on their side in order to justify themselves. They always have to justify themselves. They will never admit to doing wrong. That's one thing: It's such a big, free country here in Canada, and the government is supposed to be honest; it's supposed to work for the people. Why can't they ever admit when they make a mistake? Why can't they just come out and say, 'Look it was a mistake. We're going to learn by our mistakes. It's never going to happen again.'

When I do something wrong—if you're an honest person and you do something wrong and you know it was wrong and it was a mistake, you have to apologize for it. I never see that. I never see that with any government official. They'll never apologize for their mistakes, they'll never admit to a mistake. You don't justify sending 200-300 armed police, riot squads, SWAT teams with M16s and concussion grenades, on a group of women and children at six in the morning and come in there blasting.

Really, what were they looking for? So maybe they did know there were weapons in the Pines. Even so, if they would have come in and just removed the people, the people would have been removed. But it's the *way* they came in that forced our people to retaliate in the same way. We just weren't going to stand there and get knocked down. If they would have come in with their shields and their nightsticks—and we could see that they had no weapons, no firearms, no tear-gas, whatever—I think the people would have gone. They would have had to drag them off, but they would have gone. I know that for a fact. But when all the shooting started breaking loose and there's bullets flying all over the place, and they're not coming from us—what are you going to do?

I did what I had to do as my duty, as one of the males in this community, as a Mohawk male. I have a role to play and I have to follow that role. So that's why I set out to do this book. And also to let the people know on the outside, mainly in Quebec and Canada, and in the United States, that the Mohawk people did *not* pick up arms, or did *not* have to defend themselves, against the *people* of Canada, but that we had to defend ourselves against the *governments* of Canada and the United States. That's what I wanted to point out. Because there was so much racism that went on during 1990. Racism against us. It seemed like it was like the *people* we were fighting because we had that bridge blocked. They took the fight into their own hands, like we were fighting against them, committing acts of war against the Canadian *people*. That's the way they acted. They wanted to come in here and kill us. When little did they know it was a political situation. It wasn't a thing meant to hurt them when we blocked a bridge and we blocked the roads. It wasn't to hurt them: It was to protect us. And they should have stuck with us. They should have put pressure on their governments because they put those people in office. They should have put pressure on them to sit down and negotiate and settle this thing with the Mohawk people, instead of going about it the way they did, to prolong it for three months, for the governments to get their way once again. Because they said they were willing to have the standoff as long as possible. Why didn't they just sit down and deal with it. And make decisions to settle this once and for all, so it doesn't happen again. Yet it's four years later now, and we still have these problems, and there's still a lot of tension. The people here in Kahnawake right now are on red alert for fear of an invasion. The men are on red alert in this community."

A Man Free and Fearless

The interview with Julio Peris in this section was conducted in August 1992, by Francine Dufresne on behalf of Les Éditions Sedes.

Who is Ronald Cross, a.k.a. Lasagna? For Julio R. Peris, one of the lawyers delegated by the Kahnawake Longhouse, Ronald J. Cross— whom he sometimes refers to as "Ron"—is "friendly, funny, intelligent and not very demanding. He hasn't been criminalized. His way of thinking is pretty logical. And he's not a man who's afraid." Moreover, "Ronald Cross has a drug and alcohol problem, but he's the first to admit it. I like him," he says, smiling.

Mr. Peris' sense of Ronald Cross is far removed from the worn-out image of Lasagna, loony braggart. Besides, statements made by several soldiers confirm the fact that Ronald Cross is not an arrogant man.

As for the famous photograph which has been seen around the world, it was proven beyond the shadow of a doubt, during the trial in Saint-Jérôme, that it does not show Ronald Cross, but rather "some unidentified Warrior."

The near tenderness with which Mr. Peris speaks of his notorious client is somehow touching. This is understandable considering not only Ronald Cross' apparently likable personality, but also the young lawyer's awareness of the political, historical and judicial facets of what the world has called the "Oka Crisis." Beyond the mangled, distorted and fabricated media image, Ronald Cross, "the real man, is a free spirit. In English they say 'an affront to authority'. He's not a 'good little Indian', well assimilated. He's not afraid and this absence of fear is perceived as a slap in the face of authority. Which would explain all the energy that was devoted to locking him up."

"So he's a media creation?"

"Yes."

"A scapegoat?"

"Oh, yes!"

During one of our previous meetings at Ste-Anne-des-Plaines, Ronald Cross, while insisting on his and the Lazores' roles as scapegoats, had predicted that all the other thirty-nine Indians who had been charged in a separate trial with criminal offences would be acquitted, which in fact they were, on Friday, July 3, 1992. Because—in an important and fundamental decision—the jury had favoured the concept of "nation-to-nation."

In other words, by acquitting the vast majority of the Mohawks, their jury indicated clearly that this affair had nothing to do with criminal law, but was essentially a political matter to be dealt with through nation-to-nation negotiations. And this conclusion, in spite of the authorities' wish to criminalize the events.

There went $10,000,000 in public funds that could have been spent more wisely. Especially since, according to a Mohawk statement released on the day of the acquittal, "the issues of the golf course and other developments are still not resolved."

These words give even more weight to the observations, reasoning and conclusions of Superior Court Mr. Justice Benjamin J. Greenberg (Criminal Division), as published in his decision on the Cross-Lazore case five months earlier, dated February 19, 1992: "In regard to their actions of opposition to the wider non-native community, which, in the case of Ronald Cross resulted in the convictions enumerated above in the second group of counts, I am satisfied that he was not motivated by greed or reasons of personal gain. He acted out of deep anger, rage, desperation and a sense of hopelessness, all the result of the systematic discrimination and racism against his people over several centuries."

"Also, if the media featured him prominently as 'Lasagna' during the Oka Crisis, his public image as such is purely a creation of the media.

"For years, decades, even centuries, the aboriginal people of this country have endured, at best, indifference, neglect and unfairness and, at worst, open hostility, contempt, discrimination and racism." (See Appendix 1, below, for entire document.)

Contempt, discrimination and racism. They are finally out in the open, those big bad words that are at the very heart of the crisis. And does racism not grow from the manure of intolerance? The Native people occupy an important place in Canadian society. They were the first inhabitants of this country, of this continent.

Does it not make you smile, then, when you hear some individuals, snug in their living rooms, brag about being "Québecois de vieille souche"—"Quebecers from old stock"? How can you be of old stock when you have only been here 300 years at most?

And all the while, the present is right here, right now, open and generous. And as Mr. Justice Greenberg pointed out so well: "We live in an open society, free and democratic; probably one of the freest countries in the world." But then again, perhaps the Oka Crisis served as an outlet for the concealed racism of a society that has lived for too long folded in on itself and which misjudges, under the mask of contempt and indifference, its closest neighbours.

Mr. Peris has, from his very first dealings with the Native community, thought hard about people and the facts of the world—how, for example, ignorance or misjudgment of the other can be the root of many a misunderstanding. It is in these terms that Mr. Peris likes to describe his six-year-old son's, Matthew's, first visit to the Kahnawake Longhouse, one festival night. When, accompanied by his son, he entered a room where there were already at least 200 people present, the child exclaimed: "Daddy, where are all the Indians?"

The boy knew Indians only through the stereotypes propagated by American movies. No feathered headdresses, ergo no Indians. That is how prejudice and contempt are born: as son and daughter to ignorance and, ultimately, parents to racism.

Of course, the Mohawks, who adore children, found this very amusing. But for Matthew Peris, that night was one on which he learned one of his first great lessons of life: "He discovered that Indians are people like you and I." People like you and I, who wanted to protect the cemetery of their ancestors. A cemetery which some people wanted to turn into a golf course. People just like you and I, who wanted to cry out their refusal to be assimilated, to protect their culture, their way of life, their lands And on the other side, the soldiers of the Second Battalion of Company C of the Twenty-Second Royal Regiment, the largest peacetime mobilization of the Canadian Army in the history of this country. An armed siege of seventy-eight days, twenty-six of them—September 1-26, 1990—spent around a 300-metre area enclosed in barbed wire, imprisoning people like you and I.

And within all of this, Ronald Cross—a man like any other, but a man who was not afraid. "He wasn't afraid," Mr. Peris insists.

"That made him an affront to authority. Actually, the Crown was ticked off that he was released on bail. Ever since then they have been trying everything possible to put him back behind bars. If it hadn't been for that business with Francis Jacobs, Ronald Cross would have been acquitted a long time ago.

"They never pleaded; they stood mute to the indictment. And they stood mute all the way to the end and never testified in their defence.

"And after the Crown's case, meaning the evidence presented by the Crown against them during their trial, we felt that there was no case to answer, so why put our cards on the table?

"When you're dealing with anything to do with criminal offences, if you stand up before a court in Canada and say, 'You have no jurisdiction over me and the Criminal Code has no jurisdiction over me,' you're going to lose. You can close your eyes to it, but you're going to lose.

"The nation-to-nation defence definitely will have to be put on the table at some point. But as a criminal lawyer, and I was retained as a criminal lawyer, I have to have evidence against my client before I risk his conviction, or risk a defence of nation-to-nation, which hinges on the question of whether in fact the criminal courts in Canada have any jurisdiction over the Mohawk people or over the Mohawk Territory. You would have to argue that there's a parallel legal system that is enforceable by the Mohawk Nation. But we have no jurisdiction in a White court to enforce that law. So he would have to be given over to the Mohawk Nation to be dealt with accordingly. We didn't think that would succeed, and we didn't have the resources, either, to present that kind of defence. That would have taken us into another year in the courts, at least. We, with these three men, took a tactical approach that we felt was more successful than running the risk of losing under that kind of defence.

"They did not testify in their defence, they did not take the stand, because they felt they had nothing to answer to in the criminal case presented by the Crown."

When Ronald Cross says that his peers are the Natives and not the Whites, he is not entirely wrong. The cultural imperatives of Natives and non-Natives are so different that what helps the defence of one can sink the other. I will use as an example the testimony of Angus Nelson in the Francis Jacobs case.

Angus Nelson is a Mohawk sympathetic to the Warriors' cause. He is the one who, on the night of September 1, 1990, drove Cross and Lazore to Jacobs' place so they could talk. Once there, Nelson did not get involved in anything. He saw the fight but did not get involved. It was not his business. So he testified in court about that settling of accounts between Cross, Lazore and Jacobs. During his testimony, he described Jacobs as crying like a baby and pleading with his tormentors to stop beating him.

Angus Nelson is supposed to be Cross and Lazore's friend and, what's more, he supports the Mohawk cause. What got into him to describe the two of them in such a way?! And especially to insist on the fact that Jacobs was crying and whining like a baby without even trying to defend himself?

At that moment nobody would have wanted to be the lawyer of the accused. That testimony had just sunk them, especially since they had decided they would not take the stand in their own defence. It would never enter a White person's mind that Nelson was well-disposed towards the accused, and yet that was the case. Nelson had no intention of harming Cross or Lazore with his testimony. Quite the contrary.

To a Mohawk, a man is not a man if he cries and pleads for help instead of defending himself. To a Mohawk, whoever cries like a baby in such a situation does not deserve to have his beating stop, but rather deserves for it to go on until he learns to become a man. This different concept of manliness was used against the accused because the Crown was facing a White jury. Personally, as a White woman, I have a lot of trouble accepting this version of virility and the jury surely felt the same unease. For us, one of the lowest things you can do is continue hitting someone when he is down.

Julio Peris tried in vain to explain this cultural difference to the jury. But the White jury had formed its own opinion of the violence of the accused and there was nothing the defence could do to bring it back to the Natives' differing view.

Julio R. Peris. Photo by Francine Dufresne.

•

It is now June, 1994, and the legal team is preparing the Cross-Lazore appeal, which will probably not be heard by the courts until 1995. Meanwhile, Ronald Cross has spent over eleven months in jail, must sign in every week, and abide by a long list of bail conditions which restrict his freedom of movement, freedom of speech, and his ability to find work and support his family. It has often been said that "justice delayed is justice denied." How much longer will the Government of Canada continue to deny justice to Ronald Cross and the people he protected in the Pines?

•

The Lemay Inquest

The following is an excerpt from Kristin Andrews' article, "The Oka Inquest: In the Shadow of the Pines."

In 1781, eleven chiefs of the First Nations gathered to assert their right to land which the Sulpician mission claimed as its seigneurie. The Mohawks called the land Oka. According to a 1974 history thesis by Claude Pariseau, these chiefs presented a Wampum, a long belt covered with symbolic design.

They explained the design this way: "The two dogs at either end guard the limits of our land. And if someone wants to trouble our ownership, the dogs must warn us by barking; and this is what they have been doing for three years." By this (conservative) calculation, the dogs have now been barking for 215 years.

OKA: TWO CENTURIES LATER

On January 18, 1993, Coroner Guy Gilbert opened an inquest into the death of Corporal Marcel Lemay. Lemay was shot and killed during the Sûreté du Québec (SQ) raid on the Oka barricade in July of 1990.

But for many people, the important question to be determined at the inquest is not "Who shot Lemay?" The inquest will bring to light a history of SQ harassment of Native people, and a government which was complicit in allowing an armed invasion of Oka that was both illegal and unnecessary.

Tensions between Native people and the SQ have been mounting steadily since the early '80s, Pierre Lepage told the inquest on March 9, 1993. Lepage prepared a document called "A Collective Shock" for the Québec Human Rights Commission, in which he details a number of complaints of physical and verbal abuse of Native people on the part of the SQ, both before and after what Kanehsatake residents call the SQ crisis.

While four complaints of police brutality were submitted after the 1990 Oka conflict, the Police Ethics Commissioner refused to address any of them because they were received after a new Police Act came into effect, Lepage wrote.

Thirty-nine officers were set to appear before the Police Ethics Board to address concerns about improper conduct during the Oka raid. Their cases were thrown out in January, 1993, on a technicality.

But the SQ did not act alone when they went into Oka on July 11. "The decision for the raid was taken at the very highest level of government, in conjunction with Robert Bourassa," said Jim Duff, a reporter for CJAD radio. Duff has covered First Nations issues for twenty years.

"It was a preemptive strike. They were trying to break the back of the Mohawk buildup," he said.

"This was a civil dispute, over land," said Richard Corriveau, the lawyer representing the Mohawks at the inquest. "The use of force was so disproportionate to the protests. This shows what happens when you abandon a political process and go for the police option."

SO WHO *DID* SHOOT LEMAY?

"I don't think that a Mohawk bullet shot Lemay," said Duff, who was behind the barricades at Oka on July 11. "I know two things. The SQ opened fire, and they were using live ammunition."

Deborah Etienne, a Kanehsatake resident who was also at the barricades, agrees. Etienne's testimony at the inquest forced the SQ to admit, for the first time, that they did indeed shoot their guns during the confrontation on July 11, 1990.

In January, 1993, three SQ officers testified that they shot into the air, using only blanks. Etienne produced photographs of trees and of the boards on a nearby lacrosse court which were both riddled with bullets at

140

chest level. The trees were in the SQ's direct line of fire.

"They were shooting straight at the people. If the media hadn't been there, I think a lot of us would be dead now," Etienne said.

Etienne accused the SQ of perjury. "They lied about the guns. They lied about the bullets. They lied about how many officers there were." While the SQ claims three teams of five men approached the barricade, Etienne and others say there were at least 100.

She also said the SQ tampered with evidence, removing bullets from the pines soon after the conflict. The bullet-covered boards on the lacrosse court were mysteriously replaced immediately after the stand-off.

Luc Adoury, a public relations official for the SQ, said he could not comment on any aspect of the inquest or any related incident. "We never comment on investigations in progress," he said.

The crux of the argument that the Mohawks shot Lemay has rested on the claim that the SQ was not carrying the kind of ammunition used to shoot their officer. But Richard Corriveau, the lawyer representing the Mohawk people at the inquest said the SQ and the Mohawks both carried the same kind of weapons, and the same ammunition, a .223 calibre metal jacket bullet. Corriveau said witnesses he will call as the inquest proceeds will prove this.

The warriors would not have shot at Lemay, Etienne said. From their position, in order to shoot at Lemay, they would have risked hitting the Mohawk women and children who were standing behind the officers. "Why would they risk killing their families?" she asked.

Etienne turned the focus of the inquest around, accusing the SQ of breaking its own laws. "This was a civil injunction," she said. "They had no right to come in here with teargas and concussion grenades. They had my 13 year old daughter in a ditch with a gun pointed at her forehead, locked and loaded."

John Cree, who testified at the inquest...also accused SQ officers of unnecessary violence during the summer of 1990. He cried when he described an officer pointing a gun at his three-year-old son....

SUBTERFUGE AND HARASSMENT

...Corporal Lemay was shot during 28 seconds of rapid gunfire coming from both Mohawks and police. "They will never be able to determine whose gun shot Lemay. That's just not the point," said CJAD's Jim Duff.

The inquest can bring to light, however, the circumstances leading up to the SQ's July 11 invasion of Oka. A history of subterfuge and harassment is already beginning to emerge.

One SQ officer testified that he had posed undercover as a reporter in Kanehsatake in order to gain access to information about the Warriors.

Jacques Imbault, a member of the anti-Mohawk Regroupement des Citoyens d'Oka, testified that he assisted the SQ in recording the license plates of out-of-town vehicles which visited Oka, also in an attempt to track Warrior activities.

Jim Duff has said he's sure FBI or CIA agents were present at Oka during the crisis. Denise David Tolley of Kanehsatake radio station CKRK said that she too noticed the presence of American federal agents.

Many anonymous sources suggest that SQ officers are heavily involved in the cigarette trade they are presumably trying to stop. Some say the SQ supplies arms to an anti-Warrior group in Akwesasne.

This bundle of "conspiracy theories" cannot be more fully substantiated precisely because many Native people are afraid of the consequences of testifying against the SQ.

"After I testified, there was an SQ car parked outside my home," said Deborah Etienne.

Richard Corriveau said people's fears of going on record about harassment has made finding witnesses for the inquest difficult.

THE PINES CAST LONG SHADOWS

...The stand-off at the Pines in July of 1990 was not an isolated event. It continued a centuries-old fight on the part of the Native people, who want to retain their land and their autonomy.

"This is part of history," said Etienne, "and our truth will have to be a part of it."

(Excerpted from *The McGill Daily*, 8 Apr. 1993: 8-9.)

•

It would seem that the hopes of those who would like the larger issues behind the events at Oka in the summer of 1990, addressed in their appropriate historical context may well find an opportunity in the proceedings of the inquest into the death of Corporal Lemay. The lawyer representing the Coroner at this inquest, Mr. Richard Masson, stated in a telephone interview in February, 1994, that the prime purpose of the inquest was not to discover who had fired the shot that killed officer Lemay, but to bring to light the facts and circumstances leading up to his death, so that in future, these kinds of civil encounters, leading to the injury and death of *any* person involved, can be avoided. In a case so fraught with profound historical significance, it is astonishing to find, in this inquest, a forum where these issues can finally be addressed with an eye to the future, informed by a knowledge of our shared history.

On March 15, 1994, Ronald Cross was called before the Lemay inquest, where, despite the condition of his bail that he not comment on the events at Oka, he took the stand to testify on the facts pertaining to his involvement in the events of July 11, 1990.

Amid the endless details of his movements on July 10 and 11, two items in his testimony stand out: He was armed, on the morning of July 11, with an AK47 (a rifle not manufactured anywhere in the world in .223 calibre); and he did not fire his weapon during the confrontation.

Prior to his appearance before the inquest, in the course of completing this book for publication, Cross had spoken about the circumstances surrounding the death of Corporal Lemay on that fateful day.

"We believe there was a conspiracy, between the governments of the United States and Canada in 1990, to overthrow the Mohawk Nation. The United States and Canada were working together in a joint operation to overthrow the Mohawk Nation in '89 and '90, to bring their forces into Mohawk Territory and to enforce their laws and control our activities in the Territories.

This golf course issue, to me, was just to justify their actions, just to rile up the people. Because they knew damn well that if they were to go in at Oka, the people in Kahnawake would retaliate. They knew we would because we had done so before. We had trouble here before, with the SQ and RCMP, and what we did was shut the bridge down. So they knew that if anything went on in the Mohawk Territory over in Oka, Kahnawake would retaliate, and that would justify their doing whatever they did.

At the inquiry going on into Lemay's death, the SQ have contradicted themselves and made themselves out to be such liars. They started out by saying, in '90 and '91 and '92, 'We don't know who gave the orders,' and everybody's blaming everybody else. But now things are coming out in this inquiry where the higher-ups knew there were weapons there, and they never told the guys what was going on in there. The guys that went in and did the raid—they didn't know that there were guys there fully armed and everything. Why didn't they tell their men that these people were heavily armed, that 'If we go in there, there's going to be a shootout'? Why didn't they tell them that? And so their men went in thinking that, 'Hey, these guys are in there with a bunch of baseball bats and sticks.' I heard afterwards that even his widow made an announcement that she did not blame the Mohawk people for his death, because she did not believe that the SQ should have gone in there the way they did. She blamed the SQ. And that's who I blame. I blame them."

Several days after Ronald Cross' testimony before the Lemay inquest, another Native, Allen Gabriel, was reported to have testified that he distanced himself from the Warriors early on in the events at Oka because of what he described as the "racist attitudes" of the men defending the community.

Is "Lasagna" a racist? In answering that question, we have come full circle in our search for "the man behind the mask." Ronald Cross was born in New York of an American woman of Scottish-Italian descent, who had married a Mohawk man from Kahnawake. In his teen years, Ronald Cross' life and that of his brother Glenn had been saved by a man who was an officer in the SQ. His brother Tracy is a "career man" with the Canadian Army, a career choice that Cross has supported throughout his life. Is it reasonable to assume, given his personal history, that Ronald Cross could ever develop racist attitudes? Does military service in the defence of one's nation against hostile forces automatically and necessarily turn a man into a "racist"? Here again, Ronald Cross speaks most eloquently and simply for himself.

"I'm not a racist person. I treat an individual as an individual, based on how he treats me and other people. It doesn't matter the colour, race or creed of that person, it doesn't make a difference to me. I judge a person by his actions, by the way he treats people, how he treats me. I was brought up that way, to respect people, that you never get respect if you don't give respect. That's the way I was brought up.

I wasn't brought up to hate any individual or any group of individuals. Even the SQ. This is three years later and after all the hell I've been through with them I still don't condemn them

144

as a group. But certain individuals who work within that group, I can blame them for a lot of the bad actions that came down on their behalf. I mean, even the Mohawk people themselves were not perfect. But like they say, just because there's a couple of bad apples in the bunch doesn't mean the whole bunch is bad. So with every group of people, every race, it's like that."

Nadine Montour and Ronald Cross.

THE ROLE OF THE MEDIA
IN THE GOVERNMENTS'
"PUBLIC INFORMATION STRATEGY"

"The Mafia"

At the beginning of the crisis, his mask barely removed, the media portrayed Cross and his band as "criminals" well known to American police. "Warriors" and "Mafia" quickly became synonymous, and this portrayal quickly discredited them in the eyes of the White population that had supported them. At that point, even I shut off my television set: Those crooks did not deserve my sympathy. Then I had second thoughts. What if the reporters were lying?

So, when I met Lasagna, I was expecting to encounter a gangster with a thick criminal record, a long list of serious crimes. Instead I discovered a Mohawk who was very well-informed on the history of his own people, whose rap sheet consisted of a single item: a drinking spree in a disco.

I never understood why those reporters, who had gone to such lengths to paint him as a tough guy, never retracted their stories. If they had only double-checked their sources instead of using them stupidly, they would have found out that Lasagna had only a minor criminal record, that he was not an Italian from New York—or worse, a stranger on the reservation with no blood ties with the Natives, and that he had not accepted this job just for the thrill of holding a gun in his hands. They would have found out that he was a Mohawk, the proud heir of a long line of Native people on his father's side, and that he had lived most of his childhood on the Kahnawake reservation.

They would have also discovered that his mother lives in Oka, and that one of his sons, Ryan, lives in Kahnawake. They would then have understood that Ronald Cross was entitled to become involved in the Oka Crisis, on any number of grounds.

Bad publicity never helps the accused. Even if a reporter retracts, there are always people who remain unaware of the corrective action. Once launched, an accusation, truthful or not, follows its own inevitable course. This tactic is one many lawyers use court. They ask questions they know they are not allowed to ask, and make claims they know they have no right to make, all the while fully aware that the impression thus made on the jury is now irreversible. They know that even if the judge orders their comments stricken from the record, the harm is done, the seeds of doubt and suspicion have been planted.

Could any jury really be objective with all the hearsay that was circulating about the Warriors? How could anyone sympathize with the Warriors when the papers said that even the "good Indians" did not like them, and were in fact afraid of them?

"Internal Conflict"

Word quickly got around, in both the White and the Native communities, that the Warriors were dangerous criminals, and that some Natives had told the media they feared them. Some are supposed to have said: "We're anxious for the Warriors to leave; they're from the Mafia. After the crisis, they'll stay on the reservation and run the place." The Minister of Indian Affairs, Harry Swain, called the Warriors a "criminal organization." Jacques Parizeau, leader of the Parti Québécois, had branded them "terrorists." And Mike Mitchell, Council Leader of the Akwesasne Band Council, is supposed to have stated: "Warriors are walking around with guns, declaring war on whoever gets in their way" (*Maclean's* 6 Aug. 1990: 22-23).

How can a Mohawk want to protect people who speak of him so negatively? And, in particular, how can Ronald Cross accept spending part of his life in prison for people who, far from thanking him, actually insult him?

"No one involved in the Mohawk crisis had a criminal record," says Ronald Cross. "We are not criminals."

"There were only a handful of individuals who didn't want the Warriors to defend the land. Those who are against the Warriors are those who support the Band Council. If you remember that the Band Council is run by the government, it's all very easy to understand. Like I said earlier, in order to choose a Chief and form a Band Council you need a community vote. In Mohawk tradition, Indians don't vote.

When you go along with the government, it's only one part of the reservation that makes the decisions: the elected part. Now, in Mohawk tradition, *everybody* has to be heard one after the other and the majority opinion wins. If the majority agrees with a proposition, the law decided upon by the majority is accepted. At all times it's the community that decides, and not the Band Council.

The great majority of Indians in the territory are traditionalists. Those who slandered the Warriors were thinking of their own skins, and there aren't many of those. They didn't offend me personally; they offended themselves by refusing to respect the traditions and laws of the Mohawks. They also offended their ancestors who gave their lives so that future generations might survive. They covered themselves in shame. The Warriors, who are also traditionalists, have always worked for the community according to Mohawk law, in the manner of our ancestors."

If the Warriors were not wanted by the FBI, had they at least gone to war in Vietnam?

"Vietnam"

It was often said in the media that most of the Warriors had learned their trade in Vietnam. Far from being a killer with experience in Vietnam,

Ronald Cross has never gone to war. This crisis at Oka was his first experience using guns, just as it was his first real brush with the law.

"I never went to Vietnam but I know a lot of fighters who did. They told about how things had gone over there, what kind of war they'd fought. I've also read several books on the subject. It was a racist war, useless as all the others, whose aim was to invade someone else's land. Even though the American government was the much greater force in the conflict, the politicians and the bureaucrats tied the military's hands. If not for that the soldiers could have repaved the entire country and stuck the American flag right in the middle of it.

I have a lot of respect for those who served in Vietnam. And it's easy for me today to imagine what they must have felt. When all you see around you is death and destruction and you go back home while fifty or sixty thousand of your buddies will never return, you have just one question in mind: 'If I survive, is it because I didn't fight as I should have? Because I didn't fight to the death, didn't fight until I'd accomplished the mission I was sent to do?'

Often I regret having come out alive of the Oka Crisis. I'm glad that it didn't turn into a bloodbath and that it ended peacefully. But in my head and in my heart, it's not over yet. And it might take quite a while before we see the end of it.

The media's associating us with Vietnam, making people believe that some of us had fought in Vietnam, was one of the tactics we actually exploited to make the Army think it was facing fighters who had a lot more experience than the Canadian soldiers did. And it worked very well because, thinking that we had surely set booby-traps, they never sent out reconnaissance teams or patrols. They figured that men who had gone to Vietnam were better than anyone else at setting traps and protecting a perimeter."

Is it possible that this fact—that the Mohawks, during the stand-off, strategically never contradicted the false media stories linking them to Vietnam—was used against the Warriors? Part of the White population who were at first sympathetic to the Mohawks, started to regret their compassion. Everything they saw, heard or read in the media seemed to prove that they were supporting "crooks," maybe even gun-toting wackos. Men wanted by the FBI and who had fought in Vietnam, could not be fighting for a just cause—rather, they certainly must just be out to cause trouble!

The "Lasagna" of the Famous "Face-To-Face Encounter"

The well-publicized photo of Private Patrick Cloutier's face-to-face confrontation with the Mohawk Warrior. CANAPRESS photo by Shaney Komulainen, taken on 1 September 1990.

Had there been two, three Lasagnas? Maybe more, but certainly not fewer. During our first meeting at Parthenais, Ronald Cross had told me he had often been confused with other Warriors, so that he sometimes had to take the rap for what somebody else had done. Any Warrior of similar height, wearing the same disguise, automatically became "Lasagna" to the media. And many of the accusations of violence weighing him down could very well have been the actions of other people.

151

This revelation, added to all the others, stunned me. How could the reporters covering this crisis not have known or ignored such troubling facts?

It is so banal to find out that the famous photograph of the nose-to-nose encounter between Private Cloutier and Lasagna, this picture that popped up everywhere around the globe and often landed on the front pages of the largest magazines, was actually the photo of Private Cloutier and another, unidentified Warrior.

If it were possible, on that one day, to confuse another Warrior with Lasagna and push this case of mistaken identity so far that it was eventually published around the world in print and aired on television, then is it not also possible that Ronald Cross was accused of having done things that were actually perpetrated by others?

All of these hidden circumstances changed the entire scope of the crisis for me—so much so that, one morning, I told myself it was all too much to be true. It was plausible, but was it true? I had my doubts. Which one of us was having delusions of persecution, Lasagna or I? Finally, it was Shaney Komulainen, photographer of the famous face-to-face shot of Private Patrick Cloutier and the misidentified Warrior, who put an end to my doubts by confirming that it was not Lasagna who appeared in that picture. So *that* was why I had not recognized Lasagna at our first meeting! I had stared at that picture of the false Lasagna for so long that I couldn't recognize the real one!

The Wonderful World of Photojournalism

The interview with Shaney Komulainen was conducted by Eric Desbiens on behalf of Les Éditions Sedes.

In January 1991, many months after the end of the Oka Crisis, Shaney Komulainen was slowly and painfully recovering from a serious car accident that had almost cost her her life. During this time, when she was hospitalized with two broken legs, and having great difficulty in getting about, she found out that she was accused of several criminal infractions: threatening an officer with a weapon (a machete); possession of a weapon (the machete); possession of a weapon (a firearm); participating in a riot; and obstructing a peace officer in the performance of his duties. All of these infractions had allegedly taken place on September 1, 1990, the same day the famous picture was taken.

Eric André Keable, a Canadian Army sergeant, claimed he had been threatened, and had three other soldiers as witnesses: Private Michel Chulak, Chief Corporal Denis Rouleau and Sergeant Gilles Paradis. These witnesses stated that Shaney had removed weapons from a pile that Sergeant Keable was guarding. She was supposed to have taken a rifle and a .357 Magnum, and threatened Keable with a machete. She had purportedly yelled at him to "get the hell out of there." Sergeant Keable said she held the machete in a threatening manner. He also claimed she had threatened him and pushed him around. The other soldiers confirmed having seen this.

It is interesting to note that Sergeant Paradis, during his testimony, said that the incident happened almost at the same time that the photo of the face-to-face encounter was taken, some three hundred feet further away. Paradis' statement, especially the words "approximately at the same time," raised doubts as to the truth behind the testimony of these events, doubts which in the end were useful in the defence. Was it possible for Komulainen to take the picture and then to run three hundred feet to pick up a weapon and threaten Keable? Not very.

The defence called on twelve witnesses, of whom all but one—a military photographer—were members of the media. They submitted their photographs and some video segments taped by CTV, CBC and TVA. In one of the CTV video segments, a black-haired Mohawk woman was clearly visible picking up weapons at Sergeant Keable's feet. She did not look the least bit like Shaney, was carrying no photography equipment and was dressed in a way that made it impossible to confuse her with the photographer. The events recorded on the video segments could have been those Sergeant Keable described. Shaney could have very well have been accused of something that had been done by someone else, the only point of resemblance being that they were both women.

However, the Army photographer, Corporal Marc Lamontagne, was a great help to Shaney Komulainen's case. Standing right next to Sergeant Keable at the time the incident was alleged to have happened, he testified that he never saw Shaney during the events under discussion. "I think," Corporal Lamontagne said, "I would have noticed a six-foot tall blonde woman brandishing a machete."

Because Shaney was not with anyone in particular on September 1, 1990, and also because of how hectic things were on that fateful day, many different witnesses had to be found so that Shaney's movements at any given time could be pieced together. The testimony of the twelve witnesses finally made it possible to reconstruct faithfully the events of September 1, 1990, demonstrating without doubt that Shaney did not take part in the activities of which she was accused.

According to Shaney Komulainen, her troubles began when, after the crisis was over, the Sûreté du Québec asked all soldiers who had been in Oka and who had been victims of or witnessed what might be considered criminal acts, to come forward and be witnesses for the Sûreté du Québec. These four soldiers went to the Sûreté with their story.

The jury trial began in November, 1991. It lasted two and a half weeks. A solid defence had to be mounted for Shaney, who had to reconstruct a nebulous day in her life. A blonde woman with a machete who might have been mistaken for Shaney had to be found, as well as witnesses, either military or civilian, or any other person present on that day, who might remember something that would help prove Shaney's innocence. Private detectives had to be hired and numerous calls made throughout Canada, to Japan, to Italy and to Washington in order to contact journalists, photographers, cameramen or anyone else who could supply some pieces of the puzzle. More than fifty photographic blow-ups and three video cassettes were presented in court, as well as many witnesses, brought in from Montreal, Toronto, Ottawa and Washington. Shaney was acquitted of all charges. The astronomical court costs of this trial—over $100,000—fortunately were paid by The Canadian Press.

Shaney says she was greatly upset for a long time at the absurdity of the situation. In the spring of 1992, she decided to make a formal complaint against the various bodies and departments that could have prevented this dramatic mix-up, especially the Sûreté du Québec for its mediocre investigation of the events described by the four soldiers. The Police Board of Ethics began to look into this case in the fall of 1992. Shaney also claims that, before the preliminary investigation got under way, a Crown prosecutor made it very difficult for her to obtain a video which he had seen and which could have helped prove her innocence. Part of this video clearly showed a Native woman grabbing the weapons that Keable was guarding. Keable had also seen this video but did not mention it to anybody. Knowing that Shaney did not appear in that footage, the Crown had no interest in presenting this cassette. Shaney's last complaint was made against the four soldiers who evidently, she says, changed the facts of the events in order to accuse her. With the integrity of its soldiers under question, the Army refused to get involved in this case, claiming the whole thing was a provincial matter.

An unknown soldier and a "Lasagna" so threatening that some soldiers have their backs turned to him as they go about their business. CANAPRESS *photo by Shaney Komulainen, taken on 11 July 1990.*

The "International Crime Cartel-Sponsored Airlift"

The story of Lasagna being beaten by Sûreté du Québec officers did not travel around the world as effortlessly as the famous photo of the face-to-face encounter with Private Cloutier. It also did not seem of interest to journalists who, for a while now, seemed more preoccupied with rumours that the Warriors had escaped by night, in Cessnas, to unknown destinations.

One morning we were told that the *real* Warriors had quietly slipped away—right under the noses of the Canadian Army and the Sûreté du Québec! A few weeks later, the crisis was over and everyone seemed relieved to start talking about other news.

The Oka Crisis was over, the Mercier Bridge was reopened, the Army had "peacefully" defeated all those rebellious Mohawks—the "Indian Summer" had come to a happy ending. On television, we heard paeans sung to our ministers and our Army, praising this peaceful conclusion to the affair. Jean Cournoyer spoke, on the air, of his *copain* Robert Bourassa, who hated to be mixed up in such potentially bloody situations. As if the Natives had enjoyed it.

And finally, the public—the White public, of course—had to be reassured that these "crimes" would not remain unpunished. The Indians who had dared to rebel against the theft of their lands, would be brought to justice. As proof of this good resolution, several Indians had been arrested—including the most visible one: Lasagna. And on television you could almost hear the applause of the viewing audience who, now safe in their homes, had just learned this bit of good news.

What a thrill to be the victors! Who, especially among the "official" media, cared about the sadness felt by the Mohawks that night? Once more we had shown them the power of the White Man. His organization, his Army. Average Quebecers saw in this crisis little more than the tax-money wasting and paycheque deductions. Every penny taken from their pockets to pay the price of putting down this rebellion made them hate Indians even more.

In this crisis everything the "official" media propagated became a cunning ruse, including the name it was given. Calling it "The Mohawk Crisis," "The Indian Crisis," "The Indian Summer Crisis," immediately put the blame for the event on the heads of Indians. After all, was it not their crisis? Had the media called it "City Hall's Crisis" or even "The Oka Golfers' Crisis," the common perception of the event would have been markedly different. Such a name would have turned the tables. The public's perceptions of the crisis would have been more on a par with: "What?! All this mess, this near-war—all this money wasted for a golf course? Let them play somewhere else!"

In all probability, had the media projected the events at Oka from this angle, in the public's perception it would no longer have been the damned Mohawks who had blocked the Mercier Bridge but, rather, the damned golfers who had started this whole quarrel with their bright idea of adding nine holes to their golf course. The people really responsible for the mess would have been those Sunday golfers who stirred up a fight between the Natives and the Whites of Oka, who had usually gotten along very well before this! It would have become the battle of the Golfers against the Warriors: armed Golfers against armed Warriors— that's what we should have seen. Armed Golfers ready to trample sacred Indian burial grounds to get the golf course of their dreams. On the other side, armed Mohawks trying to protect the remains of their ancestors and their motherland.

Had the media projected such a scene, it would have triggered entirely different public reactions. Public sympathy would have sided steadily with the Warriors. But to see the Canadian Army pitted against the Warriors implied that the Indians were the criminals; in our minds, the Army and the police are supposed to fight criminals, not "the good guys."

With modern marketing techniques you can sell anything to anyone. When you want to sell a product, you have to describe it in ways that will reach its target market. That this event was titled the "Oka Crisis," that it was said to have been fomented by the "Oka Indians" resulted in blame being laid directly on the Mohawk Warriors. The golfers were invisible throughout this conflict. Standing in for the golfers was the Army.

It still seems strange that, at the very beginning of the crisis, when Whites were asked about the golf course and the consequences of expanding it onto Mohawk lands, the majority sided with the Mohawks. White residents of Oka would say: "It's their home, it's understandable that they're upset." A few days later such comments had turned into cries of "damned Indians"; soon we heard "They're all thugs from New York"; and even later, some Whites wanted the Army to open fire on all of those "underworld-controlled, Vietnam-trained criminals."

The sight of an Army that apparently didn't budge, didn't even flinch, finally unnerved some people so much that they began clamouring for action. As for the peaceful bystanders, they had their tempers heated by continual repetitions of how much money the whole thing was costing them. They became increasingly anxious over the expenses caused by the whole affair. Once more, the right information was presented at the right time.

When we saw them on television, our Canadian Army soldiers appeared so immobile, they seemed like wooden soldiers. They allowed themselves to be pushed around and bullied by the Mohawks without batting an eye.

Julio Peris found these images amusing: "That was when the cameras were rolling! When they stopped rolling, the soldiers were beating up Indians."

That's why Randy Horne, a Mohawk, had to be brought by ambulance to the Treatment Centre after having been beaten by Canadian Army soldiers, who certainly proved to be less immobile when out of the cameras' scope. Why had the cameras stopped rolling during these incidents?

The costs were rising every day. The higher the figures climbed, the more angry became the tone of the White majority. The crisis had to be settled before the financial losses became too great. It became almost a national obsession to talk about how much the Indians were costing us, so much so that we forgot how the whole thing began in the first place. A headline such as "Warriors Obtain Secret Safe Passage" immediately suggested that the Warriors got away without paying for their actions. And that we, the good and proper White folks were suckered into letting them get away with it. Headlines like that one obviously incurred even more resentment. Had the headline read: "Warriors Forced To Leave," it would have suggested that the Army had won, making the Whites the happy victors. As for the Indians—too bad for them, and good riddance!

Both these headlines "mean" the same thing: The Warriors left Oka. Yet their wording implies two very different events. This is "slanted" news: Crucial information is downplayed or even withheld with the intent of manipulating public opinion. From the "official" media's vantage point, the public confusion, outrage or panic incited by such sensationalism give a healthy boost to ratings and advertising sales.

On September 2, 1990, the Sunday edition of *La Presse* ran this front-page article:

THE WARRIORS OBTAIN SECRET
SAFE PASSAGE

The real Warriors, the men of the hour, the thugs whose numbers included several criminals wanted in Canada as well as in the United States, benefited during these last few days from what amounts to "secret safe passage" in order to flee hastily from the Montréal area with most of their arsenal without being noticed by the army or police.

They were allowed to leave the area, bringing all the weapons which the army had publicly described on television last week.

Not only were they able to escape in the night in small planes that whisked them from the Châteauguay area to who knows where, the masked men were also able to leave the Oka region because the area was never "sealed," allowing them to depart, perhaps even in seaplanes taking off from Lake of Two-Mountains.

This confidential information was confirmed to *La Presse* yesterday by a Québec government source. "To avoid a bloodbath, the army proceeded with great prudence, never encircling an area completely and making public its every move," said our source, adding that today, all that was left were "some last-minute Warriors," a few moderates and some teenagers, even some children.

Of the 200 to 400 Warriors spotted by the army in the Oka region, only about forty were left manning the last barricade... (*La Presse* 2 Sept. 1990)

According to this article, hundreds of Warriors allegedly escaped by helicopter, others by plane, abandoning some 10% of their Native brothers, a cowardly gesture to be sure. How did these mysterious Warriors—New York thugs or ex-Vietnam vets—succeed in escaping without being noticed by either the Sûreté du Québec or the Canadian Army?

Even Reverend Jesse Jackson hadn't been able to get in, but suddenly here were all these planes and helicopters landing and taking off with the greatest of ease, their cabins filled with Warriors and their heavy artillery. Does this mean that the Reverend Jackson would have made it through the barricades more easily if he had flown in? Whatever the case, this exploit is said to have occurred without the Sûreté du Québec or the Army being able to do anything about it. How strange! And it was only the next morning that we were informed of the Warriors' "nocturnal escape."

The White majority was shocked by this "news," and started saying that the Army had purposely looked the other way, no doubt because it had received orders to do so. "Preferential treatment," some people whined, which well betrayed the fear they had of Indian reprisals. Immediately, Whites started saying "We were too good to those Indians. If a non-Native had done the same thing he would be in prison. But those Indians can flout the law with impunity."

As for me, this whole story of planes, helicopters and seaplanes had tarnished the image of the Warriors, because I could not understand how or why people so brave could have left behind one of the main figures of the entire crisis, and the focal point of all the cameras: Ronald Cross, a.k.a. Lasagna. It was as if they had traded him to the police in exchange for their escape. For people who were supposed to be Mafia hitmen, this behavior made them look pretty cowardly. To act like tough guys and then to creep away in the night while leaving Ronald Cross behind—I needled Lasagna about it.

"There were never any planes or choppers," Ronald Cross replied. I looked stunned, so he added: "There weren't any planes and nobody got away by plane, helicopter or seaplane."

"In Kahnawake they'd painted some markings on Route 138 so that a small relief plane carrying food and medicine could land on it. The pilot tried to land but the 'runway' was too short. He gave up and left.

None of us ever depended on a plane or a chopper to get away from Oka. If we'd wanted to leave, we could have at any time. The only helicopters we saw belonged to the Army.

In Kahnawake, the Army had decided to destroy our barricades; the weather was stormy and the Army choppers took off and landed several times. There were a lot of aircraft in the air. That's when the Army made this new statement that a plane had come to pick up the Warriors during the night."

According to Ronald Cross, the constant comings and goings of helicopters, easily witnessed by the media and the public at large, was an Army ruse that allowed it to construct a scenario with which to salvage its honour and to polish its image. From then on, the White majority was convinced that there had been a much more impressive number of Warriors in Oka: The Canadian Army and the Sûreté du Québec had not been mobilized to confront a mere handful of inexperienced Mohawks, but rather had locked horns with a large horde of armed and dangerous Warriors. "It was the Army's way of justifying their presence to the public," said Ronald Cross.

Was Ronald Cross making this up? I asked his lawyer, Julio Peris, who denied this categorically: "No! Ronald Cross is not a liar. If he told you there were no planes, then there weren't any. Anyway, why use a special plane when the Warriors could cross the barricades anytime they wanted and leave without the slightest problem?"

That changed things for me, and I was starting to put this puzzle together in an entirely different way. First I had to stop accepting as truth what had been said by the "official" media about the crisis so far.

In that same report in *La Presse*, there was mention of "confidential information…[from a] government source…adding that today, all that was left were 'some last-minute Warriors,' a few moderates and some teenagers, even some children."

But if that were true, if one were to believe this "government source," then one could only conclude that the three arrested Warriors—Lasagna, Noriega and Nicholas—were not quite the great captures that the authorities claimed! On the one hand we were told they had arrested the "ringleaders" of the Oka Crisis, while on the other, those men had only been "last-minute Warriors," moderates even….

Who was telling the truth in this story, and who was lying?

After having told the media that the Warriors were criminals wanted by the FBI, what could the authorities do once they discovered that their "ringleaders" Lasagna and Noriega had no criminal records?

I don't know the other Warriors in the Oka Crisis, but if they were as "bad" a bunch of criminals as Lasagna and Noriega, I can understand why the police preferred to save face and let them go. The worst crime committed by Ronald Cross before the crisis was the incident when he overturned tables in the disco. As for Gordon "Noriega" Lazore, he had no record before the crisis. Single, he was living with his handicapped mother, taking care of her with his sister. There have certainly been more impressive "criminal ringleaders." It must be embarrassing for the police to display publicly the two most notorious Warriors of the crisis, both with clean or near-spotless police records and with one of them taking care of his handicapped mother when he comes home from work.

I admit that if I were in the same position as the authorities, I would have had serious problems of conscience. This discovery would have been a great embarrassment to them. Did they decide to get out of this mess by claiming that the "real Warriors"—"the dangerous ones," the wanted ones had just disappeared? There was no better solution than to create these "other Warriors," the "dangerous ones" who had "escaped." Except that next you had to come up with a plausible explanation as to why the whole provincial police force and the Army allowed such a gang of hundreds of criminals to get away without even lifting a finger to stop them. The easy answer was: Just say they were *so* dangerous that you let them go because you wanted to avoid a bloodbath.

That night in Oka, reporters badgered police and the Army to find out what was going on, to get fresh news for their next deadlines. No one gave clear answers, which created even more suspense, but which also left the media to draw their own conclusions from what they were seeing or partially being told. Planes coming and going would suggest the Warriors were packing their bags or sending their guns to safety. Since the police and the Army were not doing anything about it, the journalists were doubly intrigued.

To justify the Army's inaction, Captain Saint-Laurent said: "Our soldiers are there for ground operations. We have no mandate to intercept planes" (Lamarche 152). But the planes had to land, at which point it would have become a land operation. As for Lieutenant Colonel Robin, he replied that "control of the airspace was not my jurisdiction" (ibid.).

Are we to understand that if that whole merry crew had seen a plane landing or taking off with 1000 kilos of heroin, nobody would have intervened since no one had the proper authority or jurisdiction?

Lieutenant Colonel Robin had previously admitted "not having yet seen weapons or armed people on the reservation" (Lamarche 152). Finally, neither the Sûreté du Québec nor the Army had clearly stated having seen the Warriors escape in the night or use planes to ferry out their guns. But the rumour was left floating because it was convenient. And the media eagerly and repeatedly embellished and spread this bit of "news" which came from an unidentified "Québec government source"!

Did the media make up this scoop? Was it the police? Was it the Army? The fact remains that none of them denied it, knowing that silence is the best form of assent.

Everything about this whole affair was fishy. Many conflicting statements were made, events were shrouded in unnecessary mystery, then three Mohawks were handcuffed, and we were told, in effect, "The crisis is over, go home and don't ask for more."

But when a case is closed too quickly, it is because someone somewhere has an interest in not letting the matter remain open: Someone else just might discover its flaws.

Top: Gordon "Noriega" Lazore with Ronald Cross.
Bottom: Gordon Lazore. Photos by Francine Dufresne.

Claiming that the people wearing masks were criminals wanted by some police force somewhere was too easy. In order to know that the person behind the mask is wanted, you first must know the identity of the person behind the mask. So why had the government and the media not named those men? Why spare them if they were wanted?

Wearing a mask in a crisis does not automatically turn a person into a criminal wanted by the FBI. Lasagna was not sought by any police force. He wore a mask simply because he did not want to be arrested at the end of the stand-off. As soon as his name was made public, he removed his mask, and we could all see who he was: a Mohawk from Kahnawake whose job had taken him to New York.

Many other Warriors had left during the crisis. By choice, by fear of reprisals—who knows. Among them was Francis Jacobs, who left Oka on August 31 to become an SQ informer. He was not wanted by the FBI, either.

Innocent or guilty, no one involved in the crisis had anything to gain by taking off his mask. In either case, those who were not identified at the start would have become so rather quickly. If those in power knew the names and criminal records of those Warriors, why did they not go public with that information, in the interests of both the White and the Mohawk populations? So that the Mohawks might know, once and for all, the identities of these people who were protecting them, where they came from and what they wanted to accomplish.

Some might say that the police did not dare risk getting sued by divulging those names without proper evidence. But would criminals wanted by the FBI sue the police? And risk being collared by the police?

The whole Warrior-Mafia rumour had only one aim: to terrorize the Mohawks so that they would not feel safe around the Warriors and so that they might chase away those of their own people who might help them.

For what possible reason would the Army and the Sûreté du Québec allow the escape—during the crisis—of dangerous criminals, only to capture three Indians with no criminal records at the very end of it? These three Indians, by the fact of their capture, became more guilty than those absent. Yet had not *La Presse* described those Mohawks who had not "escaped" as "last-minute Warriors,...moderates,...even some children?" People demanded a guilty party. A satisfactory one was found in the person of Lasagna, whose name was now famous and inspired fear.

What bothers me most about this whole rigmarole about airplanes is that, from the very beginning, Ronald Cross knew that after his capture, he would pay dearly for his few hours of fame. If there really had been planes that came to take the Warriors to some unknown destination, why hadn't Lasagna taken advantage of them to escape?

The "International Observers"

Why was Cross held at Parthenais, right next to Montreal's Palais de Justice, when his trial was taking place in Saint-Jérôme? The round trip between Saint-Jerôme and Montreal is 90 kilometres. Was this situation a question of security? Of availability? Or was this just another harassment tactic cooked up by the authorities, perhaps to make him crack at last under the strain, to provoke him into violence, to push him into taking drugs...so that proof could be offered to the Mohawk people that the hero of the crisis, the idol of their cause, was nothing more than a dangerous delinquent?

It does not matter how this trial will end, whether or not the Court of Appeals finds him guilty. In the eyes of the legal community, and in my eyes, Ronald Cross has no criminal record. He has a political record. The media did not insist enough on this point.

Even though Ronald Cross has never expressed a single regret at having been involved in the Oka Crisis, the fact remains that, while he bears the weight of most of the blame for this incident, many things still confuse him, or are very difficult for him to understand—especially concerning the political help he is getting, or, more to the point, is not getting.

"There could have been a lot more Indians supporting us and helping our lawyers fight in court to turn this whole story into a constitutional issue. This case should have taken a political direction instead of a criminal one. How could the court consider the fact of protecting and defending one's own land a criminal act? Our lawyers tried to give this case a political slant and the judge wouldn't hear of it.

I don't understand what happened. There were negotiations going on between the Mohawks and the government. So the incident was political, not criminal. During the crisis, there were international observers there, from the League of Human Rights and the Geneva Convention. What happened to them once my trial got under way? Why wasn't I protected by these conventions? Why have we received almost no help from these observers?"

I almost feel like telling him that they only came for show, that they were paper-shufflers who went back home as soon as the TV cameras left and who will pop up again at the next scene of injustice in order to broadcast their concerned faces to the world. They'll be there again when taking pity becomes a job. Do they act this way to soothe their consciences, to justify the salaries they get from their sponsoring organizations? To take advantage of the travelling opportunities such cases allow?

From our first meeting, I knew that Ronald Cross was being abused; that somewhere inside, he felt he had been duped, trapped. How could he possibly have seen himself as a criminal when, during the crisis, so many educated people coming from so many different countries were voicing their support for the Mohawks? How could he have foreseen their silence after his incarceration?

How could all these people who talked about the justice of the Indian cause simply disappear after the police had their hands on him? Evidently, Lasagna did not know that observers simply observe! They do not campaign, they do not become spokespeople; they watch and take notes. And they "do as they are told." At the Quebec government's request, twenty-four observers from the International Human Rights Federation had to leave Oka and Kahnawake on August 27, 1990 (Lamarche 137).

Ronald Cross fought just like the other Mohawks and ended up imprisoned in a maximum security facility. As if he could read my mind, he adds: "I did what I had to do and I have no regrets. The governments' abuse of the Native people has been going on for long enough and it's time it stopped."

During the crisis, the Mohawks were often accused of negotiating in bad faith. But in the past, have the Whites ever negotiated in good faith with them? In what or whom could they have put their trust? It is true that, with so many parties sticking their noses in the conflict, it was easier to confound things, to complicate what was already confused. It would have been easier to sort things out had there been fewer people involved.

What is the point of having all those international observers—United Nations, Geneva Convention—present at such a conflict if the victim is then left alone to serve his sentence? What, then, is the point of their speeches, or their involvement at all? Why do they present themselves to the oppressed as if they have great influence on the countries involved, when in fact they just pack their bags and leave as soon as they are requested to go elsewhere?

Today, Ronald Cross is alone. The global sympathy machine that supported the Mohawks' claims has withdrawn to its air-conditioned, plush-carpeted offices while he awaits his appeal, "free" on a $50,000 bail bond, with his human rights—including his freedom of speech—curtailed.

Finally, so few people are aware of this other version of the Oka Crisis that we can sum up these "hidden facts of the Oka Crisis" as follows: no criminal records, no Vietnam, no FBI, no Cessna airplanes ferrying out Warriors in the middle of the night; Randy Horne *was* beaten by the Army, Lasagna *was* beaten by the police.

On the other hand, too few Natives know that a number of police officers supported them but, for professional reasons, could not allow their personal feelings to interfere with their work. Among them was an RCMP officer who sympathized with the Indians and their claims. He had come to Châteauguay from Toronto, on one day's notice, with orders to help relieve the Sûreté du Québec. Commenting on the anger of the local Quebecers, which had been intensifying daily since the blockade of the Mercier Bridge, he told a reporter:

> "It'll get worse tonight. A lot more of them will come down here, especially since it's Friday night. A lot of 'em will be drinking, too." He suddenly seemed to remember that he was talking with a member of the press; the professional, detached, public-servant manner returned. (Coleman 43)

What Does It All Mean?

In the course of editing and updating this book for its publication in English in 1994 at Talonbooks, Hélène Sévigny talked to Karl Siegler about how her original French language book had been received in Quebec. Her description of the publication of her book by Les Éditions Sedes in April of 1993 is astonishing, in that it reveals elements of francophone Quebec's aspirations to become a "distinct society" that are not well-known, much less well-understood by Quebec's anglophone neighbours in North America.

First of all, I have to say that I did not expect a bad reaction to the book in French. Countless popular books have been written and films have been made on the lives of vicious criminals in our society: Bonnie and Clyde, Al Capone, Lucky Luciano, Jacques Mesrine—how many murders have been ordered or committed by these individuals? With *Lasagne: L'homme derrière le masque*, I had not even set out to do a biography of a notorious criminal, but had intended instead to show that Ronald Cross' "criminalization" had essentially been a creation of the media. In retrospect, I should have realized that the same media which had so effectively misrepresented Cross to their public as a "common criminal" both during and after the events at Oka would be less than inclined to accept a book in which "Lasagna" was presented from an entirely different point of view, and in which their own responsibility for socially constructing this misrepresentation was so thoroughly questioned. But I was so wrapped up in the justice of the cause I had taken on that I hadn't paid attention to the early warning signals which should have alerted me to my naïveté, the most obvious of which occurred when my editor informed me, before publication, that he did not want his name associated with the book.

When we launched the book, we had given an exclusive to the television interview program, "Ad Lib." No one had seen Ronald Cross in civilian dress on French television before, and of course many people tuned in to the program, more for the sake of curiosity than anything else. Ronald Cross was the perfect interview: He answered all the questions, no matter how difficult and confrontational, calmly and reasonably. For the first time, the people of Quebec were given an opportunity to see and hear him talk about his version of these significant historical events. Viewers' reactions to this popular program were spectacular. Hundreds of callers after the broadcast telephoned to say how impressed they were with the interview. It was immediately obvious that, given the opportunity to speak for himself, Cross would have no difficulty turning the tide of public opinion in Quebec, despite the fact that he speaks English, not French. The next morning, the media campaign against Cross got under way.

I believe that the francophone media had expected that Cross would make a fool of himself on television, and when they saw him speaking like an intelligent, articulate individual that night, they understood that they would have to discredit him quickly. All the classic tricks were used: short clips from long interviews were quoted out of context by Claude Poirier on Channel 35; open line radio hosts had callers suggest long lists of derogatory alternate titles for the book amid gales of sardonic laughter which the host actually encouraged; we were invited to appear on a live-at-noon television program, by the award-winning host, Jean Luc Mongrain, without adequate notice—it was physically impossible for us to arrive on time, and he knew it—and he spent the first fifty-five minutes of his show badgering the audience with his allegations that we had been invited, but had been too afraid to appear on his show. But the worst was Gilles Proulx from CJMS radio, whose vitriolic diatribes against the First Nations people of Quebec finally culminated in his screaming at me on air, "You go to bed with terrorists." Alleging he was reading from a fan letter addressed to him, he also said: "You are a prostitute to the Warriors." This is the same open line Quebec nationalist who several years before had opened a rally in an arena with the particularly constructive and intelligent remark: "English people...Eat shit!" The racist reaction of the electronic media became so overwhelmingly strident that I finally had to write to Judge Dusault, presiding over the Royal Commission on Aboriginal Peoples, with specific reference to Proulx, asking him to invoke the Charter of Rights to stop the open line host from inciting racism and hatred among the people who were calling in, and listening to, his show.

All the French women's magazines refused an exclusive on the book, despite the fact that many of them had covered both my career as a lawyer and journalist, and my previous books. *Elle* Quebec refused; *Chatelaine* refused; one of them hung up after screaming at my press agent, "I will never write a line about a killer!" After the book was published, only one French magazine, *Seven Days*, approached us for an interview. While their story was excellent, they felt it necessary to protect themselves by beginning their article with the question: "Ronald Cross, some people consider it immoral that I'm sitting here interviewing you. Does that surprise you?"

Ironically, it was only the anglophone journal, *Maclean's*, that jumped at the chance of doing a major article on the book before I had even finished explaining to them what it was about, and even though, at the time, it was only available in French.

Despite the strident opposition to the book from some sectors of the media, what surprised me most is the position of silent "neutrality" that many of my fellow journalists, colleagues and even my friends have adopted since I published this biography. I began to realize, over the past year, that the negative public reaction to this book in Quebec had to be based on something more than a simple attempt by the francophone media to cover up its misrepresentation of the events at Oka in 1990. The larger dimension of my increasing alienation from my former colleagues in journalism, the legal community, the conference circuit, and even my social circle, began to give me pause for considerable thought. I began to realize that the overwhelming majority of people who had criticized the book had not even bothered to read it. Indeed, the most common reaction from people I spoke to, both publicly and privately, as soon as they heard I had written a book like this, but before they had read it, was to accuse me of "being on the side of the Mohawks, of 'justifying their violence' and of 'having no sympathy for White Quebecers'." No statement brings this into sharper focus than the first question I was asked by the journalist covering my launch of the book in Trois-Rivières: "Do you know that Quebecers see you as a traitor to your own race?"

Clearly, the publication of *Lasagne* had touched a raw cultural nerve within the rapidly growing popular nationalist movement within Quebec: By legitimizing the sovereigntist aspirations of the First Nations peoples of Quebec, the book had begged some very important questions of the Quebec sovereigntist movement itself. How, for example, would an independent Quebec deal with the hundreds of unresolved Native land claims issues, particularly given the behavior of the provincial government during the Oka Crisis? Would an independent Quebec consider these issues with a greater sense of fairness, justice and humanity than either the provincial or the federal governments had done over the past centuries of conflict? Indeed, would an independent Quebec deal with the aspirations of "the inherent right to self-government" among the "distinct societies" of its Native population in a manner more just and humane than the manner in which Canada had dealt with similar aspirations on the part of francophone Quebec? Or would an independent Quebec ruthlessly suppress all cultural differences in its new sovereign state, in the manner in which they had suppressed English as one of Canada's two official languages with its provincial language laws? Was it these larger issues which the book had raised, no matter how obliquely, that appeared to stand behind and fuel the virulent, irrational and uninformed reactions to *Lasagne* in the strident populist reaction to the book in my own society, my own community and my own country?

In the beginning, I did not ask these questions rhetorically, but rather in all innocence. I had always thanked God for giving me the grace to be born in Quebec, with its French culture and its Catholic religion. I had always perceived my community to be a democratic, non-violent society in which a writer's views could be freely and openly expressed and discussed. I had never seen the question of bilingualism as a political question, but rather as a cultural one. I come from an exclusively French-speaking town, Cap-de-la-Madeleine (near Trois-Rivières), and it wasn't until a long time after I had completed university that I taught myself to speak English. I am now learning Spanish and intend to learn Italian. I have always believed that it is important for people to understand many languages, because it is through an understanding of different languages that cultural differences are most thoroughly recognized and understood. Despite all of my cultural biases, I have also never been afraid of the possibility of Quebec attaining sovereignty and separating from Canada, at least not until I wrote Ronald Cross' biography. Now I am no longer sure. I always understood, and we can see from his memoirs, that René Lévesque was a democrat who always respected the majority, and that he disapproved of the radical faction among Quebec nationalists, even if it meant that his personal dreams were occasionally delayed or disappointed.

However, after the experience of publishing *Lasagne*, I am beginning to have an inkling of how Salman Rushdie must feel. Under the current leadership of the Quebec separatist movement (whose children invariably attend the best English schools), there exists a cultural imperative, perhaps more accurately described as a dogma, that Catholic White French Quebecers be seen as righteous and perfect: "We are generous. We give too much to the English and the Natives. We are an oppressed minority in Canada. Our cause is just." If, however, as a White French Quebec woman you write a book in which you attempt to demonstrate that we Catholic White French Quebecers may not be perfect, and that the Mohawk nation in our midst has a political and a cultural claim which is also just, you are perceived to be a traitor, to have undermined the fundamental tenets of belief within your own culture.

After my book was published in French, I found that I would never be the same person again. The reception the book got in Quebec has irrevocably changed my life. It was as if I had been dreaming, and I'd been awakened or reborn in a different world. I suddenly saw so many things wrong with my community—I saw an image of my society that I had never expected to confront. The world I see now is ugly. Mean. Narrow-minded. I have discovered that I live in a world I never really knew. When I began this book, I embarked on it with a naïve faith that I might contribute, through its publication, to the reconciliation of two peoples. In one of my earlier books, I had asked a whimsical question, the full import of which I never really understood until today: If we cannot any longer cherish our dreams, what is left for us to do on this earth?

HÉLÈNE SÉVIGNY AND THE WHITE WAY

"In the Name of the King of France...

...and in the name of Christ whom he represents, we take possession of these lands."

One fine day, a stranger, speaking a foreign language, lands in what is now called Quebec and starts planting crosses all over the place. "If that's how he gets his kicks..." the Natives probably thought, not understanding anything of the man's affectations. They must have thought he was nuts! For the moment, his crosses are not hurting anyone and all those incantations in the name of the King of France leave the Natives perplexed. How could they have guessed that planting a cross or a flag could make this stranger the owner of the land that he touched?

What would we say if, one fine morning, some weirdo walked into our backyards with his flag and said that, in the name of some king, this was now his home?! You might think a lot of different things about that nutcase—except that he was *seriously* taking possession of your land and that people elsewhere would think he had a right to do so. As outlandish as this story may seem, it is the basis for the white version of the "discovery" of New France and of how we established ourselves on this continent.

Of course, back then notaries were rather scarce. The story of Cartier sticking his flags all over the place and claiming ownership of these lands dazzled generations of school children. And the Holy Church was teaching us how to steal from our brothers without it being a sin. Louis Hall, the great Mohawk painter and philosopher of Kahnawake, put it this way: "History is written in such a way that the Europeans appear as the heroes. There they are, plundering and pillaging the Indian lands, but it's their God-given right to do so and the Indians shouldn't try to stop them, they're supposed to like it..." (Sioui 56).

The great European discoverers survived winds and tides, storms and scurvy, to the astonishment of their kings. And their seduction of the "savage nations" was glorified as much as their courage.

How could those "good" Indians who had devoted themselves to saving Cartier's crew from scurvy—when it would have been so easy to poison them instead—how could these same Indians, from one day to the next, suddenly start yanking out those sailors' fingernails? How could the "neighbourly" Indian so quickly transform himself into the "evil" Indian? In our history books, the Indians are generous and hospitable on page 50 and suddenly, on page 70, they have turned into complete savages, devoted to a cult of massacre. Perhaps we have not been told the whole story....

●

What is left of the Red Man whom we came to convert to Christianity a few centuries ago? At that time it seemed so important to save his soul and to work for his salvation. A great many missionaries and nuns, some more exalted than others, came here truly intending to convert the "pagans," and for them this mission represented so many challenges and so much love that they were ready to give it their lives. It would be dishonest not to speak of all those who came here at the risk of their lives in the real—and naïve—hope of "saving the world." They wanted to serve God and committed themselves to His ends.

There were also all the others, all those citizens of France who were fleeing indescribable misery and who dreamed of a paradise where they could live, hunt, fish, have all they could eat—as long as they had courage. The year 1653 was the time of France's greatest recruitment. Almost 5,000 French immigrated to North America in the 17th century. On June 20, 1653, a hundred of them waited at the port of St-Nazaire for the boat that would take them to the unknown land of the New World. They had been told of the cruel ways of the Natives, of the risks involved in their journey across the ocean, and yet there they were, ready to face the storms and the ice floes on such rickety ships. How they must have believed in that New World!

And how miserable and hopeless they must have been in their Old World! If we are to believe the writings from that time, "the poor could be seen crawling on manure like lizards, others on straw, stilled by the exhaustion of all their strength, while others in cesspools and in stables, like people who had already been seized and rendered so insensible by the duration and the extremity of their pain, that they could barely listen to the word of God, more like dumb animals than human creatures.... They retired into pits or shacks, where they lay on bare earth, naked save for a few miserable tatters, with which they covered themselves" (*Nos racines*). Such was the misery of France at that time.

Obsessed with the salvation of their souls and ready to brave any peril to save their skins, most of them went to confession before embarking on the great journey. In forsaken, rotting boats that leaked, they were forced to return to St-Nazaire. And Marguerite Bourgeoys wrote: "I was greatly saddened to see us in such straits; we were almost one hundred and twenty passengers without a priest, and our people were ill-prepared to die..." (*Nos racines*). So their greatest worry was not the condition of the boat but rather the fact of not having priests with them at such a time. Who on that boat thought then of coming to pillage the Natives? Many among them saw in this New World the hope for their own survival, nothing more.

Others came here to do good deeds. Among them, the Jesuits, healers of bodies and souls. The first surgeons in Quebec were—and wore—black robes. The Jesuits arrived here with the Bible in one hand and their medical treatises in the other. They used their medicine to gain entry to the "savage" lands. In 1642, the Jesuit René Goupil was murdered, supposedly by a suspicious Mohawk (*Le courrier Médical*). Simon Baron cared for those ravaged by the smallpox epidemic which at the time was decimating the Hurons. His successes earned him the trust of the Natives, who were henceforth more open to accepting the Christian faith.

During the 18th century, 5,000 more French citizens arrived in Nouvelle-France. This immigration of unfortunate colonists swelled the already extant French population here to the point where their numbers exceeded those of the Native population—or, rather, what was left of the Native population after the decimation of their numbers by murder, smallpox and other imported diseases. Our French ancestors came here with their traditions, their mores, their customs, bringing with them and their thin baggage a certain homesickness for their lost France. Like all other unhappy and nostalgic immigrants, they attempted to recreate the country of their origin, in this case, a new France. Over the years, they took root in this area to the point where this land became "their" land. They cut down its trees, pulled out its stumps, plowed it, cultivated it, seeded it until it began to look like the land they had left behind. They loved it to the point that, hundreds of years later, none of them want to leave. Did they really wish to obliterate the Native people? Their fight with the English occupied them so much. Each side fought in the name of a king who wanted to expand his kingdom and neither the English nor the French seemed to recognize they were fighting over land that belonged to the Natives!

There is a common complaint among many Quebecers that "Indians make nothing of themselves." It is too easy to resort to name-calling and label an entire people as lazy drunkards. In our Canadian history classes, didn't we find the English and the French agreeing on this one point: Get the Indians drunk, the better to rob them! Their alcoholism was convenient to the White colonists back then, as they could make a profit from it.

> For just a few pints, Indians would trade whole bales of beaver pelts. Alcohol attracted them and blinded them. Greedy and unscrupulous traders took advantage of the uncontrollable passion Indians had for the stuff. Indifferent to the physical and mental ravages caused by intoxicating spirits, they would give booze to Indian hunters and get rich quick and easy.
>
> The civil authorities admitted to the inconveniences of this miserable custom, but they thought of it as being a necessary evil. "If we don't give the Indians what they crave the most," the traders would say, "they'll simply take their furs to the less scrupulous English dealers." Even the usually wise Jean Talon thought it best to maintain this commerce, considered as indispensable for the prosperity of the colony. (Tessier 154)

A great many churchmen tried to stop the firewater trade. A letter by Monseigneur Pontbriand dated 22 August, 1742, testifies vividly to his disapproval: "It is notorious...that the savages do not know at all how to drink moderately and that, when they are masters, they always or almost always drink to the point of drunkenness, and even then, instead of sharing, they willingly deprive themselves so that someone else can put himself in this pitiful state" (O'Neil, n.p.). Very upset by this commerce, Monseigneur Pontbriand advocated denying absolution to those who engaged in this trade.

It was during the French regime, Jean O'Neil continues, that the worst stories concerning Indian drunkenness are heard. For his part, O'Neil prefers to believe that, when it comes to alcohol, Indians are no better or worse than anybody else. "The problem is identical to when hash or cocaine were introduced to society. Who are the most frequent users of these drugs? Mostly those who are poorly adapted to the culture of their society." He concludes: "When the whole of society and when every cell of society is governed by notions of profit and of gross national product, those who are not interested in such ideals drop out sooner or later."

Since the Natives are a perfect example of a people whom Whites have stripped of their culture and, moreover, since they had no concepts of things like money or taxes before we arrived here, we can draw our own conclusions concerning their legendary problems with alcohol.

As for Ronald Cross, he does not hesitate to admit that he has a drug and alcohol problem. "It's happened before," he says, "that I've been involved in situations of violence because I drank too much. A nice guy when sober, I become a terror when drunk. Then my father would tell me: 'You don't have to go looking for trouble, it'll come to you. And when it does, you'll be a better man for being able to turn your back on it and walk away.'"

"I always want to negotiate to the very end but if it's not happening and the last alternative is violence, I'll defend myself."

As for Natives in general, they are very much aware that on reservations, alcohol has become a veritable plague. Most have their own detox centres. What we have referred to throughout this book as the Treatment Centre is the Oka Detoxification Centre. During the 1990 crisis, this building became the rallying point of the Oka Warriors.

Kanehsatake, Akwesasne, Kahnawake...

To think that, just a few months earlier, I felt sorry for—and envied—those journalists who had to pronounce, without stumbling and all in one sentence the Indian names of Kanehsatake, Akwesasne and Kahnawake. They sounded as if they had been saying these words all their lives, but I suspected that they had practised for hours before facing the cameras.

The crisis at Oka was certainly not the first time in history that the White Man has gone back on his word. What Ronald Cross and other Natives have come to learn is that White society builds and demolishes, according to the tastes of a generation, to the whims of current fashion and, most especially, according to the biggest profit margin.

The White man commits this injustice regularly in his own communities, as well. How many times have communities been dislodged, or agricultural and wilderness lands been disrupted or lost, just to build a highway, an airport? Take Mirabel, for one Quebec example: An international airport, north of Montreal, used only to 25% of capacity, it is a tremendously expensive white elephant. There were strong objections to its construction. But eventually, those individuals who objected to it, bowed to the strength of the authorities and their laws, and succumbed without retaliating. So often the individual just assumes that his cries of hopelessness may postpone things for a while, but finally will not succeed in changing the location of the strip mall or highway or airport.

The White man in power is a stranger to sentiment. For centuries, the Indian did not know this. All he knew was that the land that belonged to him had been taken away, only to be lent back to him—with an eye-dropper, yet—and then taken away yet again at the whim of the White powers. He lived peacefully on his land and did not want any trouble, as long as trouble did not go looking for him. He had already succumbed once to the White man—too much so—and lived to regret it. But that is in the past. The Native peoples have reconquered certain rights and have no intention of ever letting themselves be robbed again; they are ready to fight back. And now, at a time when Mohawks have reclaimed certain rights and finally feel at peace with the White man, there is again talk of stripping them of their security: their land.

The Whites have become masters in the art of signing papers that purportedly bind and protect both parties, later only to demonstrate that these same papers protect only one side. It is only after the papers are signed that the White man's true intent appears. And far from becoming an owner, or even a co-owner, the other party realizes it has even less than before.

According to a certain treaty, say the experts, the Oka territory belonged to the Order of St-Sulpice who tolerated the presence of the Indians on their lands so that, today, everything could be taken back without anything being owed to them. So for all those years the Natives were merely being "tolerated"!

For their part, the Mohawks have finally begun to understand. So now their presence is merely "tolerated"...*when they are on their own land?!* Where *are* those papers that their ancestors allegedly signed when they allegedly handed over their lands? Nowhere. Those lands were a gift from the British King to the Sulpicians. A gift from the King? *What king?* Where did *he* come from?

The answer to these questions are ultimately to be found in a series of Papal bulls, like the "Inter Cetera" bull, issued right at the beginning of the "age of discovery." The *intent* of these bulls was to give the "discoverors of new lands" the power to claim title to those lands for either the Catholic Church or the "Christian monarchs" (European Kings) within its sphere of influence. These bulls, while allowing for continued *residency* on those lands by indigenous peoples, cancelled any claim to *sovereignty* over those lands by those indigenous peoples. These Papal bulls have determined—and continue to determine—the questions of jurisprudence impinging upon claims of sovereignty by all indigenous peoples "discovered" by Europeans since the 15th century:

> Five hundred years ago, on May 3rd and 4th, 1493, Pope Alexander VI issued several documents, known as "papal bulls," from the Vatican. Those documents expressed the pope's desire that what he called "barbarous nations" should be militarily overthrown and placed under foreign control ("subjugated"), and reduced to "the Catholic faith and Christian religion." The pope said that by subjugating the nations that Cristobal Colon (Columbus) had recently "discovered," the "Christian Empire" would be increased.
>
> While the Alexandrine bulls seriously call into question the presumption that the Catholic Church is historically an institution of peace and justice, other such documents make the point as well. In 1452, for example, Pope Nicholas V issued a bull to King Alfonso of Portugal. Pope Nicholas called on the king to "seek out" (meaning "to locate and attack") "all Saracens, pagans, and other enemies of Christ," to "put them into perpetual slavery," and to take away and "convert" all their lands and property. The word "convert," as used by the [Pope], means "to wrongfully take away the property of another." (Newcomb A6)

Regardless of where he lived, the good King of France originally came into "possession" of these lands through the actions of a ship's captain who, during a voyage sponsored by His Majesty, was dazzled by the Indians' hospitality and by a river that went on till it disappeared from sight. Back at home, this captain ran to the king and gave him a fantastic description of these lands that "belonged to no one" and, to prove his gratitude, made a gift of them to the king. It was his way of thanking the king for having paid for the voyage.

Since that day, White people—both francophones and anglophones—have killed themselves and each other in the hopes of becoming the dominant power, free to impose their customs, their religion and their traditions on the conquered.

The bitterness of the defeat on the Plains of Abraham and of the end of the Patriotes' rebellion has been handed down from one generation to the next. Since that day, White children fight each other in schoolyards because one's father is English or another's mother is French. Feeble attempts to avenge one's great-grandfather. Hundreds of years later, the French and the English of this land still scorn one another, and look to quarrel with each other at the slightest provocation. While elsewhere others die of misery and of hunger, in this country millions of dollars are swallowed up each year in endless constitutional and language debates. In Quebec, local wars are waged over signs. Under one regime, they are bilingual. Under another other, they revert to one language, i.e. French. After all, this is *our* home, say the francophone nationalists.

Why not signs in "Mohawk," then, while we are at it? I am surprised that the Mohawks have not entered this debate in order to affirm their language rights on this—their own—territory!

When White people are expropriated, they move out. That the White man suffers the White man's law is the lesser evil. The greater evil is the imposition of White law on the Native population. Natives have been here long before us, and they could have passed laws ordering our dismissal from their lands, had they the advantage of foresight, and of Warriors who would have rallied together against their colonial "masters," rather than exterminating each other in territorial wars or for the fur trade—engineered by the very people who exploited them in these endeavours.

What pressures were brought to bear on the mayor of Oka that he agreed to the expansion of a golf course on land whose ownership was contested by the Mohawks, thereby provoking—naïvely or intentionally—these people whose presence was still merely "tolerated"?

Throughout this affair the Oka authorities have taken refuge behind a judgment of the London Privy Council, rendered in 1912, which confirms the ownership of the estate by the Order of St-Sulpice and thus nullifies the Mohawks' claims. This information led Gilles Boileau to ask: "Would it be out of place to believe that, at that time, the Oka Indians were no match for the Order of St-Sulpice and that the dice were loaded from the start?" (Boileau 251).Writing about the events of the year 1735, Boileau asks an even more embarrassing question: "The Sulpicians had requested an expansion of their original estate in order 'to better serve the Indians' needs, whose activities required a large territory'. If the increase was awarded for that reason, how then can one explain that the lands obtained through this expansion have, through the years, all been ceded to Whites?" (247). And further: "At Oka, the clergy of the Séminaire de Montréal...used every means possible and imaginable to retain the exclusive ownership of their estate. They have never bowed to threats, blackmail, dispossession, prison, exile, lawsuits or even excommunication in order not to grant the slightest speck of land to the Indians" (266).

The proposal to expand the golf course onto sacred Mohawk Territory rekindled old animosities. What was still not openly declared a war became one. The Whites were becoming more intolerant than ever. "The Indians have everything," they were saying, when it wasn't "The Indians want everything." For their part, the Natives said: "The Whites have always stolen everything from us and they still want to take all we have."

●

In 1994, for most people, the Oka Crisis is over. Only Lasagna and a few others have had to pay for the failed ambitions of His Honour the Mayor. But, behind His Honour the Mayor, who was there?

A quick look at the past informs us that the Mohawks have never been able to live in peace on their lands and that, in the end, they have always ended up hunted, pushed out, expropriated. Their territories have constantly been redefined and reclaimed.

In 1889 in Kahnawake, Canadian Pacific built a bridge across the St. Lawrence river; in 1930, the Quebec government built the Mercier Bridge there as well as highways that went through the reservation; in 1955, the Canadian government built the St. Lawrence Seaway there. Not only was the best farmland sacrificed to these projects, but once the

Seaway was built, it was understood that, unfortunately, this was the end for the Indians of the well-known Lachine Rapids (see *Nations autochtones du Québec*).

At Oka-Kanehsatake, the Mohawks constantly had to fend off the Order of St-Sulpice who claimed the Indians' lands as their own. These were the claims from men of God who had taken vows of poverty! The Kingdom of Heaven which they have been promised has not kept them from hungering for earthly goods and it seems obvious they might have some trouble convincing St. Peter that they were not corrupted by the materialism rampant down here.

How often have Natives been accused of being lazy because they did not cultivate the land that they were "given"? How can you give a piece of land to the person who already owns it? And once given, how can it then be claimed by any number of non-Native third parties? How can the Mohawks instill in themselves a desire to cultivate a plot of land which might be taken away from them at any moment? Why should they expend the effort and energy of clearing and cultivating land only to have that land taken away from them once it starts looking rich and promising? In such a context, they would not appear to be lazy ingrates so much as voluntary stoop labour. In other instances, their best farmland has been repeatedly expropriated for the creation of large building projects. Who could possibly be interested in cultivating lesser land, that is hard or sterile?

This is not the entire history of the Mohawks' problems, but it can help to explain why the following comment made by Mr. Justice Benjamin Greenberg in his decision at the Cross-Lazore trial can seem naïve: "The land claims of the Mohawks at Oka-Kanehsatake are perhaps well founded in law or, perhaps not. The present case has not required that I make any inquiry into that issue" (see Appendix 1, below).

The problem is precisely there—that the judge in the Cross-Lazore case can actually claim, with *any* credibility at all, that "the present ['criminal'] case *has not required* I make any inquiry into that ['political'] issue!" Because if the Mohawks' cause is well-founded in law, this absolutely changes the entire case. And if time had been spent debating this very topic, then Cross and Lazore would have been acquitted of the criminal accusations against them, just as the other Mohawks were acquitted in Montreal's Palais de Justice. If the Mohawks' claims are well-founded in law, it then becomes extremely difficult, odious even, to speak of banditry in such circumstances, and to dare try the case as a criminal offence.

The Judge continued as follows: "Yet, those claims are not to be settled at the point of a gun, but rather by negotiation in good faith between, on the one hand, the natives, acting through properly constituted and legitimate representatives, and, on the other hand, the affected persons or groups and the Governments, and, failing agreement, by recourse to the courts" (see Appendix 1, below). I would have liked, in the interest of clarifying his decision, for this Honourable Judge to have gone further in his statement. That he list, for example, all the cases in which Natives have gone before the courts, and the number of times that they have won. Of the trials that they have won—if any—I would also have liked to know how many years all the procedures and legal wranglings had lasted.

Take Ronald Cross' case as an example: He was arrested in September 1990, and the case is still pending in 1994. And if the Court of Appeals renders its judgment in 1995, this does not mean necessarily that the case is over. The prosecutors may go to the Supreme Court if they so choose, meaning that Ronald Cross could see his ordeal end sometime toward the end of this century.

Is it normal for someone to stop working for five or ten years merely to insure his constant presence in court? If this person is guilty, then this is simply the just consequence of his actions; but what if he or she is not guilty? What will it give Ronald Cross to find out in five years that he is innocent?

I would also have liked for the judge to list all the money that the Natives have had to invest to fight for their rights, whether it be through the Band Council or other agencies; in short, what it has cost them in legal fees, including the salaries they have lost in order to testify in court, and the remaining finances at their disposal with which they may have to continue defending themselves in the event of future litigation. Then and only then would I feel confident in judging whether or not the Oka Crisis had been "justified."

It is easy to say that the Native peoples can always go to court. That is what you call thinking White. Since most of these land claims come from either of two levels of government or else from big corporations, the White side has no need to worry about legal costs. Who among the Native peoples is as financially well-off as Canadian Pacific or the Environment Department? I am not saying the White conglomerates *buy* the law. They do not have to: They simply have the means to pursue their legal proceedings to the very end and, in so doing, to exhaust the resources of their adversaries.

I would also have liked for the judge—or anyone else involved in this case—to be informed that "...only 38 of the 506 land claims appearing on the federal roster have been resolved. Many among them have been languishing or are simply waiting their turn since the beginning of the century.... At Oka, for example, the Mohawks have been waiting their turn to negotiate with the federal government for more than fifteen years...." (Boisseau 12). Knowing this, how can people retain their confidence in obtaining justice legally in their lifetimes?

Would not this slowness of the courts in providing justice understandably give one the urge to take back one's property, at the barrel of a gun? Is this not a more expedient form of justice? Frustration often forms the basis of a population's violence. Do we have the right to demand such extraordinary patience from the Natives? The patience to wait for the endless decisions of all these judgments, of all these Honourable Courts?

When I think of Justice, I ask myself, what is Justice? What is freedom? Whom does the Charter of Rights and Freedoms protect?

The meaning of the word "freedom" has so widened that sometimes it seems to favour criminals more than the innocent. And because of this, honest people feel they have no more recourse, no more justice. They go to Court only to leave there humiliated, for having lost both face and their noble causes. There is no justice, there are only good lawyers, some say with bitterness. There are no good causes, there are only points of law and petitions. Individuals do not matter anymore, and neither do the actions they take.

I say all this because I do not understand Ronald Cross' present legal situation. Of course, during the crisis, Cross made death threats. But in the course of this affair, everyone made death threats—even the "victims." Some have been brought to court for having made such threats. Others have not. Did Dr. Mongeon not go into his house for a gun to threaten Roger Lazore who was sitting on his tractor, peacefully mowing his lawn? But the Court was lenient towards Dr. Mongeon— first because he was a Crown witness and second, because his property had been badly damaged. In his case, apparently, the provocation justified his anger and his threats.

But if property damage becomes a sufficient reason for the law to overlook someone making threats, then one wonders why the Mohawks, whose Pines and ancestral cemetery were about to be ravaged, did not benefit from the same sort of legal tolerance. This unbalanced dispensation of justice is what Julio Peris tried to establish when he questioned Dr. Mongeon. He did not want to make a criminal of him, or to make the doctor feel guilty for his threatened violence. He wanted to demonstrate that any individual, Native or White, as peaceful as his nature might be, can become violent if pushed too far.

Mr. Peris: You...yourself Sir...at that point in time...just before leaving... you could feel the tension as well?

Dr. Mongeon: That's why I left. I couldn't endure it anymore or put up with it anymore.

Q: On the 27th, when you left with your wife, you also thought the end was coming?

A: Yes.

Q: And you didn't want to be in your house when the assault tanks and...when the war breaks out, if you like?

A: I could no longer stay there.

Q: The tension, I believe, became too much?

A: Correct.

Q: The tension that you had in front of your living room window for the past two (2) months?

A: Not only the tension from a Warrior standpoint or because of the Warriors, but also the tension mounting between my wife and myself.

Q: O.K. So there was a number of factors and a number of considerations and tension that was building within you throughout this period of time?

A: Yes.

Q: When you attempt to come back, that increases the tension when you can't?

A: Yes.

Q: They hold you from coming back to your house. You have heard about your alarm going off?

A: Yes.

Q: And you have got the horses as well on the farm?

A: Yes.

Q: So you come back finally. You get into your property. And what you see is the damage that is done to your property?

A: Correct.

Q: And Roger Lazore is on the lawnmower cutting the grass?

A: Correct.

Q: Now…you have stated, Sir, in your testimony…and we'll leave the "asshole" and the rest of that apart, but you stated to him "I'm going to kill you"?

A: Yes.

Q: And you said that also to the other Mohawk Warriors that were there?

A: Yes.

Q: But you are not…you are not a violent man, Sir, I know that.

A: No.

Q: But the tension was just too much?

A: Yes.

Q: And if you had a gun, you would have killed him?

A: I don't know.

Q: O.K. But if you had had one, you went to get one? Because Sir, you couldn't take it any longer. The pressure was so intense. Your property was occupied by others. And under all those circumstances, you uttered words which are in themselves a criminal offence?

A: I do not know.

Q: Now under all that pressure, Sir, and under everything that you…that had happened to you, you threatened to kill someone who you didn't see do anything really? Because the pressure was so…is that a fact?

A: Yes.

Q: And the others that were around there as well?

A: Yes.

Q: Because the pressure was so intense?

A: If one could say.

Q: And you were never charged with any criminal offence or anything?

A: No.

By the Defence: (Mr. Peris): I thank you, Sir.

Emotions were running so high that Roger Lazore, who was getting ready to repair the damage caused by others, found himself the target of death threats from Dr. Mongeon, and was later accused by the Crown prosecutor of wanting to steal the tractor!

If a peaceful doctor can be pushed to uttering death threats at the sight of his damaged house, how should the Mohawks have reacted when bulldozers showed up on their lands? Is the violence of one side more excusable than that of the other?

During the Oka Crisis, all of us witnessed a spectacle of stunning violence on TV. Unarmed Native children and elderly people were stoned by angry Whites. Their cars were ravaged. This was a barbaric demonstration whose only purpose was the venting of public anger. And one of those Mohawks, Joseph Armstrong, died of a heart attack at the hospital. The Whites pleaded guilty. Their sentences? Bail, fines... The harshest sentence was one of twenty days in jail...staggered! A "staggered" sentence means that the guilty party keeps his day job and serves his meagre sentence in jail on weekends.

Why does Ronald Cross' violent behavior deserve so much more severe a sentence? How can anyone justify such a disparity in sentencing? To this day, Ronald Cross has been in jail for eleven months, six of which were spent in Parthenais, the "Guilty House." And it isn't over yet! He is appealing a fifty-two month sentence. As far as I know, Ronald Cross did not attack defenceless old Whites who had nothing to do with the crisis. He did not act for the simple thrill of venting his anger; his violence in this affair was always tied in with his political action.

Justice: What can one think of it?

During the October Crisis in 1970, the FLQ heroes, guilty of kidnapping, were given safe passage to Cuba which, in the end, turned into a trip to Paris, as Communist Cuba was too constraining! In the name of who knows what worthy motive, they were declared patriots and came back to Quebec during the Parti Québécois regime.

What does this precedent suggest? If Lasagna had taken hostages would he have been given a plane ticket to Cuba or Paris? And then he could have hoped to come back a few years later, accused of nothing at all?

It is often said that there is never any excuse for violence. But if not for the violence that erupted in the summer of 1990, would the Mohawks have retained their land? Ronald Cross still awaits the end of the story, but other Mohawks have remained on their land and the plans concerning the expansion of the golf course have been shelved. Even though it seems the Native people lost their fight, they nevertheless kept their land. For now. Had they been quiet and reasonable and passively sat down to discuss things, the government would have delayed debating this immediate issue until it had talked about other Native issues which, as we have seen, have been languishing for fifteen or twenty years.

When the time comes to see and listen to other long-suffering minorities, nobody gives a damn. It is as if the only thing that matters is the anguish of the complainer. And that is why, as far as the governments are concerned, the people are nothing. When each minority isolates itself from every other minority instead of joining forces, in the eyes of the government it becomes little more than a grain of sand on the bargaining table. But if all the minorities joined together in a common approach, there would be so many more grains of sand clogging up the works that the government would finally see the necessity of sitting down and resolving their claims.

To the people of Canada, including the Native people, Quebec francophones lost the war against the English on the Plains of Abraham. There is a sort of rough justice in the colonialism that they now have to endure. Those are the rules of the game. The winner and the loser. Why be a winner if there is no advantage in being one? Had the francophones won that war, would they have told the English: "We've won but we'll behave as if we had lost. Keep all your privileges." Would we have been such a generous people?

Between the Iroquois Confederacy and the Whites there has never been such a war by which one could determine who won and who lost. Had the Native people lost, they would at least have had their defeat to comfort them. But both the English and the French never even bothered waging open warfare on them. We just moved in on them, threw them out, stole their land and then said: "What are you complaining about? You were the first ones here? So what?" It is as if two burglars had broken into a home and were locked in a never-ending struggle about how they were going to divide the booty once inside.

The history of the world is filled with injustice and barbarism. There is no need to look as far back as Caesar. Right here at home, the story of how the Acadians were deported seems like the world's greatest tragedy; the revolt of the Patriotes can still make some hearts beat a little faster, the stories of the White settlers tortured and scalped by the Natives are tragic. But the Englishman facing me today is not the one who sent the francophone patriots to the gallows, no more than Lasagna is the Indian who tortured Brébeuf and Lallemant, no more than I am the one who exterminated the buffalo herds in order to drive the Native population to starvation.

If the Native people rail against injustices that occurred on their land four hundred years ago, if Quebecers alive today wish to avenge the Patriotes of 1837, then we will never see an end to it. Some bad memories need to be buried and forgotten. That was another time, another world: "Let the dead bury the dead." How can we hope to solve the problems of previous centuries when we cannot even solve the problems of the last ten years while our governments let everything get worse?

As for the politicians, what would they not do to get elected? Do they really care for the people they claim to serve?

When they have fits in the Quebec National Assembly over power bills unpaid by Natives, are they really convinced that they are claiming justice in the name of the Whites? Or, instead, have they understood that the best way to win an election is to pay their staff to be constantly on the lookout for a juicy scandal among people who, in the main, do not vote for them anyway? Do they not know that a nation can rise up in the name of Justice—that the nation lacks discernment when faced with a noble cause? Why is it that politicians do not have the guts to say openly that Justice is on the side of whomever votes for them?

●

I agonize over so many aspects of this crisis. I have never understood by what system of classification the guilty were separated from the non-guilty. How were they selected? Were they not all armed during the crisis? Why Dennis Nicholas, Gordon Lazore, Roger Lazore and Ronald Cross as opposed to the thirty-nine other Mohawks? What happened to all the others? There were only around forty-three Mohawks standing-off against the Sûreté du Québec and the Canadian Army.

As far as determining whether the incident was of a criminal or a political nature, we only have to think of how we would want to be judged as Québécois if a foreign government decided to throw us off our own lands. What would the hours following such a decision be like? They would be like the political debates held in the square to stir up all the injustices inflicted on the French people since the founding of the colony. And would the leaders have any other choice than to incite the nation to take up arms? What would the Québécois do about other Quebecers who would be opposed to such a rebellion and who were seen as supporting the English? Who would feel sorry for them? Would they not see them as traitors and would they not have them suffer the fate of traitors? This is how one must look at Ronald Cross' violence towards Francis Jacobs, the Crown witness.

Having said this, I do not condone violence. I am only trying to understand in what way the violence of one nation is more excusable than that of another. Why did the violence of the Whites on the night of August 27, 1990, go unpunished and practically unnoticed, while that of Ronald Cross and Gordon Lazore was described in the smallest detail, the better to paint them as irredeemable killers?

Francis Jacobs has a right to his opinions and his political choices. He had a right to express his dissent; he should not have been beaten for that. His actions, which to Ronald Cross represented treason, would be perceived by those who accept the Canadian and American governments as being truly democratic, as a demonstration of simple political free choice, an inalienable right of expression. Ronald Cross reacted brutally, impulsively. No more impulsively, however, than those Whites who stoned the Mohawk women, children and elderly people. Ronald Cross did not beat up Jacobs because the latter was a dissident but because Jacobs was a Sûreté du Québec informant and because Cross thought Jacobs was responsible for a series of break-ins and incidents of vandalism that he then blamed on the Warriors.

Being comfortably ensconced in a juror's chair, listening passively to the description of a war or some larger public drama, is not the setting in which you can honestly judge what you might have done had you been in the shoes of the soldier in the witness box. It is in the thick of battle that emotions escalate, that decisions are made, that the ultimate political actions are taken.

CONCLUSION

You will believe me, I hope, if I tell you: I love my country. Have I loved it wisely? Have I loved it madly?... On the outside, opinions can be divided. Nevertheless, having conscientiously consulted both my heart and my mind, I think I can decide that I have loved it as it ought to be loved.

> —Louis-Joseph Papineau,from his last speech, at the
> Canadian Institute in Montreal

Every country in the world has its conflicts, its wars, its heroes, its sacrifices. Yes, I say "sacrifices" because in every conflict, some pay more dearly than others.

Hero, victim, scapegoat? I don't know anymore. One thing is certain, of all the First Nations people involved in the Oka Crisis, only a few have paid the bill. Why precisely *those* individuals? What did they do that was greater or lesser than the others? Were they not all armed?

Referring to Lasagna, an officer of the Sûreté du Québec told me: "He was the most visible one. He was always in front of the cameras." *There* is his real crime: He became a star, so the bill was higher.

I expected a rebel, a killer. Most of all, someone violent. Perhaps a psychopath. What I had seen on television, and what had been said of the Warriors, had terrified me. I think back now on my fears as I waited to meet him for the first time: "If I were smart, I'd leave." But I stayed. And I made the right choice. In retrospect, the whole thing looks like a sham to me, a frame-up.

There are those for whom Ronald Cross will never be anything but a crook. Faced with such contempt, Ronald Cross can only follow his father's advice: "Turn around and walk away." There is no enemy for whom it is worth spending time in jail.

The history of political events creates legends, and those manipulated by the victorious authors of history follow the received wisdom. "Riel was crazy." "Cross was a crook." Is it better to be remembered as a madman or as a criminal?

For me, Ronald Cross is more than merely innocent. He is a soldier. A Warrior. Seen in this light, his actions no longer surprise us; instead they take on a whole other meaning. He needled one soldier, pushed another around, yes. But who, in war-time, would consider these incidents "crimes"?

The camera showed us the scene of the terrible face-to-face encounter between Cloutier and the Warrior purported to be "Lasagna" over and over, until *we* were the ones who became the victims of the terror. We were manipulated by the media to put ourselves in that soldier's boots. No one, on that day, would have traded places with that soldier. That image, repeated endlessly in extreme closeups on all the screens of the world, gave us the chills. What we forget and what the cameras did not show sufficiently, were all the other soldiers ready to open fire on the person the media alleged to be Ronald Cross if he showed the slightest sign of becoming physically aggressive. If the Warrior had touched that soldier with his weapon, he would have been a dead man. Did Ronald Cross want to die? From this other, invisible camera angle, it was not so much the soldier who was risking his life, but rather the Warrior who was taking all the risks.

•

During the trial, the Crown prosecutor referred to Cross as a "commonplace criminal" (*La Presse* 23 Apr. 1992), when the only crime he had ever been guilty of before the events of the Oka Crisis was a drinking spree that had cost him a $250 fine. He had, the prosecutor added, broken Canadian law. And what about us? Have we not broken Mohawk law? Have we not provoked this violence by telling ourselves that, however the Indians chose to retaliate, we had the Canadian Army and the Sûreté du Québec on our side? Did we not know from the very start that we were on the stronger side? Does that lessen our crime?

Was it not obvious to any White person of average intelligence, from the first day of the crisis, that the Indians did not stand a chance other than that of showing us their courage? And that, sooner or later, they would be forced to lay down their guns?

Sometimes, what is perceived as a crime is nothing more than a contest of strength. The victor writes the history, said Jacques Vergès.

Will someone one day explain to us why the other Native people involved in this same crisis were acquitted—as Ronald Cross had predicted—while those whom the politicians and the media claimed were the ringleaders were judged and found guilty of criminal charges? Is it because Cross and the Lazores dealt with Mr. Justice Greenberg, while the others faced Mr. Justice Tannenbaum? Is it because Cross and the Lazores were judged in Saint-Jérôme, near Oka, while the others were tried in Montreal?

Some have said Ronald Cross is a gangster, a punk. Others have claimed that the Warriors were criminals, possibly even linked to the Mafia—as if, through this fabricated guilt by association alone, the justice of the Mohawk cause could or should be diminished.

And even if it were true: Since when does a government at war withdraw a good soldier from its troops, a good warrior defending his country, simply because he once committed a hold-up, or because he has a criminal record, or even because he is allegedly a member of the Mafia? Since when do you have to be pure to fight a war? In virtue of which law should we be more demanding of Native soldiers than we are of American or Canadian ones? When an American wins a war and returns home as a hero, is he stripped of his medals because he once had "bad" friends, because he once took cocaine? Do we celebrate his arrival with less pomp, or do we see him in that moment as nothing less than the victor? If those alleged to be crooks and thieves are no longer allowed to defend their country, someone had better tell us. The next time we go to war, men will no longer have to hurry through shotgun weddings to avoid the draft, they will simply have to rob a bank and try to get caught!

If we want to judge this affair objectively, we need to do it from the perspective of the rules of war. Instantly we see the drama in a different way. Ronald Cross' involvement becomes that of a soldier. And what, in criminal law, normally becomes a criminal act—a death threat, a disciplinary action—now becomes a legitimate public act by the fact of the declaration of, or the state of, war.

Everything in this case resembles a comedy by Molière. The most touching accusation of all, by virtue of its naïveté or its hypocrisy, simultaneously the most laughable and the most dramatic charge laid against

Ronald Cross, was "the possession of firearms with harmful intent." Since when do people go to war without guns?

After the jury had rendered its verdict, Ronald Cross is said to have turned to Roger Lazore, who had just been acquitted, and said: "Roger, we did it for the Nation and we'll do it again." These patriotic words were used by the prosecutor as "proof" that Cross had no regrets about his actions and thus deserved a harsher sentence. But Ronald Cross tried to defend Mohawk lands, hoping to make the whole world understand the extent to which his people were oppressed. And if it had not been for his media image and the fear it inspired, who would have bothered with this crisis?

Ronald Cross is not the terrifying character we have been shown by the media. In the end, Ronald Cross is not "Lasagna."

By writing this biography, I hope to have shown the world that, in the case of Ronald Cross, justice ceased to be a right but rather became a privilege, meted out at the pleasure of the Crown. I have shown you Ronald Cross as I came to know him. I have not tried to hide his less appealing sides. Nor do I think that I have embellished him.

Several decades from now, people will want to have an answer to the historical question, "Who was Ronald Cross?" Some will portray him as a saviour. Others will say he was a criminal, because what they will recall is that he used drugs and that he exploited this cause to vent his violent nature and inclinations. But that version of history will also conveniently forget to mention that the brave Canadian Army soldier, so applauded during this crisis, also had problems with drugs, alcohol and violent personal tendencies.

In the end, even Julio Peris' statement that, "If it hadn't been for that business with Francis Jacobs, Ronald Cross would have been aquitted a long time ago," does not adequately serve to explain the severity of the sentence the courts have imposed on Cross. In the spring of 1994, a Canadian soldier on "peacekeeping" duty in Somalia was convicted for his role in the torturing and beating to death of a Somalian teenager, a member of the community which the Canadian Army had been sent to protect in that country. The Canadian public has heard and read the reports of a photograph showing the Canadian soldier posing with his foot on the broken body of the victim. His sentence? Five years, currently under appeal. The same sentence imposed by the courts on Ronald Cross, primarily for his alleged "criminal assault" on Francis Jacobs. Yet Francis Jacobs was, despite the ruthlessness of Cross' "disciplinary action," neither tortured nor beaten to death. I am reminded of

Ronald Cross' repeated assertions that his sentence has more to do with an attempt by the governments of Canada and Quebec to find a scapegoat for their own violence against minorities in this country and abroad than with their attempt to see that justice was finally done in the interests of the defenders of the Pines. How much longer will the people of North America continue to accept our governments' historic inclination to blame the victims of their own violence against minorities in our society?

After all the time spent in jail, Ronald Cross has consoled himself with the thought that his actions have made a small contribution to furthering the Mohawk cause. As I leave him in the Oka Pines, he seems preoccupied: "Nothing's been solved, finally."

In finishing this book, he has gone back to take his place in the pages of the larger book from which he sprang.

Now there is talk of building condominiums. If there are to be more fights, I have trouble imagining Ronald Cross far from the firing line. No sentence will make him back down from what he considers to be a just cause. *This* is the explanation behind his apparent lack of remorse.

Hero or Scapegoat?

A rebellious hero is always alone, because a nation, once its hatred or its rebellion has been sated, rejects its heroes as much as it needs them or has used them. To forgive itself for having come back home, to forget its defeat, its shame, the nation needs to exile its heroes, to destroy the monument which might remind it of defeat. To forget all this, the people need to kill their idols.

After having sparked in them the taste for battle, after having stoked their anger by reminding them of the injustices done to their people, their heroes are scolded for being incapable of fading away, of reentering their previous molds and forgetting.

The hero with his medals, decorations and front-page pictures, also excites the jealousy of the other combatants. Far from being a reward, this stardom sometimes becomes his worst punishment. Looking at him, everyone thinks: "He's no more a hero than I am."

War always initiates, at the level of the individual, a struggle with— and sometimes a delusion of—one's self. Often we know little of those for whom we fight. If only we knew whose interests we really serve when we risk our lives and our freedom. Faced with Cross' sincerity, I have often thought that his fatal flaw was that he had not lost enough wars to know those who made them.

Where are those who organize war in the shadows, plan it and prepare every detail and consequence of it, from beginning to end? Where are those who consciously plan to risk the lives of others? Ronald Cross will never be one of them. He will not wage his battles from behind a computer and send pawns to fight in his place. But in the end, heroes are puppets of the people, of their fantasies, of their moods and of their whims. The people decide when a hero is born and when he dies. Unfortunately, the people also decide when a hero dies and a scapegoat is born.

Ronal Cross endures a fate different from most. And if he could do it all over again, he would. Because of all he has learned, he would do it differently, yes. But his hunger for justice has not been stilled.

With this book I wanted to show what Justice has become in this country. After the outcome of the events at Oka, I am tempted to say that Justice no longer exists, that for the cause of Native North Americans, there is only Fate.

APPENDIX 1

WHEN THE COURT SPEAKS

CANADA
PROVINCE OF QUEBEC

SUPERIOR COURT
(CRIMINAL DIVISION)

DISTRICT OF TERREBONNE
No. 700-01-000009-913

PRESIDING:
THE HONOURABLE MR. JUSTICE
BENJAMIN J. GREENBERG

St. Jérôme, February 19th, 1992

HER MAJESTY THE QUEEN

vs

RONALD CROSS and
GORDON LAZORE

(ORALLY)

S E N T E N C E

After a lengthy and complex trial, the Jury has spoken! The two remaining accused, no less than the presiding Judge, are bound by its verdicts.

It is now my duty to impose Sentence. In my view, that duty is manifestly the most difficult and delicate one which a Judge can be called upon to perform.

There were originally three accused in this dossier, RONALD CROSS, GORDON LAZORE and ROGER LAZORE. In a Direct Indictment signed on January 30th, 1991 by the Deputy Attorney-General of Quebec, those three accused were jointly charged with a total of fifty-nine counts, all concerning events and incidents which had occurred within the context of the disturbances at Oka, Quebec during the summer and early Autumn of 1990, commonly known and sometimes herein referred to as the "Oka Crisis".

Originally, each of those three persons was, variously, either named alone in certain counts or together with one or both of his co-accused in others, such that, had all the counts remained extant, the Jury would have been called upon to render 85 verdicts, 50 in the case of Ronald Cross, 20 concerning Gordon Lazore and 15 for Roger Lazore.

However, after giving effect to the permanent stay of proceedings ordered by the undersigned on November 28th, 1991 with respect to counts 57 and 59, the nolle prosequi on count 56 deposited by the Crown prosecutor on December

17th last and my decisions thereafter to direct verdicts of not-guilty on counts 1, 33, 35, 42, 44, 45 and 58, in favour of only Roger Lazore on count 18, with respect to only Ronald Cross on count 19 and regarding only Gordon Lazore on count 25, there finally remained for decision by the Jury 66 contested verdicts affecting the various accused, such that Ronald Cross remained in jeopardy in 40, Gordon Lazore in 16 and Roger Lazore in 10.

By their verdicts rendered on January 22nd, 1992 the Jury acquitted Ronald Cross on twenty of those counts and found him guilty on the twenty others, found Gordon Lazore not guilty in seven and guilty in nine, and acquitted Roger Lazore on all ten counts remaining out-standing against him.

Thereafter, pursuant to the application of the principle first enunciated by the Supreme Court of Canada in <u>Kienapple vs The Queen</u> ([1975] 1 S.C.R., 729), the undersigned ordered a conditional stay of proceedings in respect of the convictions of Ronald Cross by the Jury on counts 20, 23 and 28 and the same regarding Gordon Lazore on counts 19, 20, 23 and 30.

There accordingly now remain for Sentencing seventeen counts in the case of Ronald Cross and five counts for Gordon Lazore. They are:

<u>(A) FOR RONALD CROSS</u>:
Counts 21, 22, 24, 25, 26, 27, 31, 32, 38, 40, 43, 46, 48, 49, 50, 52 and 55;
<u>(B) FOR GORDON LAZORE</u>:
Counts 21, 22, 24, 26 and 29.

— — — — — — — — —

Even though, as will be seen below, I will be recalling events of the Oka Crisis by way of the background to the incidents for which the two accused have been found guilty by the Jury, I must and shall guard myself against indirectly Sentencing them for events in respect of which the Jury acquitted them.

In the Indictment as originally preferred, counts 1 to 36 inclusive (sometimes herein referred to as the "first group of counts") indicated as victims various civilians, native and non-native, whereas counts 37 to 59 inclusive (sometimes herein referred to as the "second group of counts") related to crimes committed against members of the Canadian Armed Forces.

The various offences on which Ronald Cross is to be Sentenced are scattered through both groups of counts, whereas those on which Gordon Lazore is to be Sentenced are limited to the first group.

The underlying facts which resulted in the Oka Crisis are generally well-known. However, in order for the present Sentence to be coherent and stand on its own, it is necessary to review some of the history and background to the whole affair.

Long before the first arrival of the Europeans on this Continent, it was already inhabited by native peoples, both Indian and Innuit. As to the former, they were able to live and move freely about the land as their needs dictated.

Their culture and society were structured and developed.

The accused are Mohawks and the Mohawks, an ancient and proud people, comprise one nation of what was originally a grouping of five Indian nations. Later, by the adoption of the Tuscarora nation from the Cherokees, that grouping became the "Six Nations Iroquois Confederacy." The other four nations which, together with the Mohawks formed that original Five Nations Confederacy before the arrival here of the white man, are the Seneca, the Oneida the Onondaga and the Kayuga.

Those nations developed structured relations among themselves, as well as between the Confederacy and other Indian nations.

Even before the Confederation of Canada as a Nation in 1867, the British Sovereigns, and the Sovereigns of France before them, dealt with the Indians here as though they were quasi-sovereign nations themselves. That recognition has been incorporated into the dicta of the highest Court of our Country.

In R. vs Sioui ([1990] 1 S.C.R., 1025), probing the legal effects of a Document signed by General Murray on behalf of the King of England in 1760 and addressed to the Chief of the Hurons, Lamer J., as he then was, wrote:

"At the time with which we are concerned relations with Indian tribes fell somewhere between the kind of relations conducted between sovereign states and the relations that such states had with their own citizens." (At page 1038)

And further, by Lamer J.:

"I consider that, instead, we can conclude from the historical documents that both Great Britain and France felt that the Indian nations had sufficient independence and played a large enough role in North America for it to be good policy to maintain relations with them very close to those maintained between sovereign nations.

The mother countries did everything in their power to secure the alliance of each Indian nation and to encourage nations allied with the enemy to change sides. When these efforts met with success, they were incorporated in treaties of alliance or neutrality. This clearly indicates that the Indian nations were regarded in their relations with the European nations which occupied North America as independent nations. The papers of Sir William Johnson (*The Papers of Sir William Johnson*, 14 vol.), who was in charge of Indian affairs in British North America, demonstrate the recognition by Great Britain that nation-to-nation relations had to be conducted with the North American Indians. As an example, I cite an extract from a speech by Sir Johnson at the Onondaga Conference held in April 1748, attended by the Five Nations:" (At pages 1052-53).

Then, Lamer J. again:

"The British Crown recognized that the Indians had certain ownership rights over their land, it sought to establish trade with them which would rise above the level of exploitation and give them a fair return. It also allowed them autonomy in their internal affairs, intervening in this area as little as possible." (At page 1055)

And, finally, still Lamer J.:

"The colonial powers recognized that the Indians had the capacity to sign treaties directly with the European nations occupying North American territory. The sui generis situation in which the Indians were placed had forced the European mother countries to acknowledge that they had sufficient autonomy for the valid creation of solemn agreements which were called "treaties," regardless of the strict meaning given to that word then and now by international law." (At page 1056)

That recognition of the North American Indian nations is not limited to Canada, for the highest Court of the United States of America has also spoken in very similar terms, by the then Chief Justice of the U.S.A. in <u>Worcester vs State of Georgia</u> (31 U.S. [6 Pet.], 515 [1832], at pages 548-49):

"Such was the policy of Great Britain towards the Indian nations inhabiting the territory from which she excluded all other Europeans; such her claims, and such her practical exposition of the charters she had granted: <u>she considered them as nations capable of maintaining the relations of peace and war; of governing themselves, under her protection; and she made treaties with them, the obligation of which she acknowledged.</u> (Emphasis added.)

In the early eighteenth century a community of Mohawks was living near Mount Royal in the centre of what is now Montreal, under the spiritual guidance of the Ecclesiastics of the Seminary of St. Sulpice of Montreal. Wishing to move that Indian community away from what those Ecclesiastics considered to be "certain temptations," they had done so in 1717 to Sault-aux-Récollets, to what is now part of the north-east sector of Montreal.

Deciding soon that this was not far enough, the Ecclesiastics petitioned the Governor, Vaudreuil, and the Intendant, Bégon, to obtain a concession on the north-west shore of the Lake of Two Mountains. It was granted to them and, in 1718, the King of France confirmed that grant of what became known as the "Seigniory of the Lake of Two Mountains." Those grants conveyed the land in question to the Ecclesiastics, and here I quote from the Privy Council in Corinthe et al. vs Ecclesiastics of the Seminary of St. Sulpice of Montreal:

"... on the condition that they should alter the situation of a certain mission they had founded among the Indians in the neighbourhood, and build a church and a fort for the security of the latter." (1912 A.C., 872, at page 877)

In its Judgment, the Privy Council spoke of a controversy which had then existed for upwards of a century concerning the title to the Seigniory of the Lake of Two Mountains. The Lord Chancellor, Viscount Haldane, continued:

"The ecclesiastics of the Seminary of St. Sulpice of Montreal, on the one hand, have claimed it under grants from the King of France, and under statutes passed later on by the Canadian Legislature. Their assertion has been that they hold the seigniory in the full proprietary title, and that the Indians residing within the limits of the seigniory have no individual title to it, nor any right, competent to them as individual beneficiaries, to control the administration of the land. The Indians belonging to the band resident upon the seigniory have, on the other hand, contended that they possessed proprietary rights, or at all events indefeasible rights of occupation, by virtue of either an unextinguished aboriginal title, or occupation sufficient on which to found a prescriptive title, or by virtue of an obligation created by the grants, statutes, and other documents relating to the seigniory." (At page 877)

Their Lordships decided that the Ecclesiastics had legal title to the Seigniory, but appeared to keep the door open a bit by adding:

"(Their Lordships) desire, however, to guard themselves against being supposed to express an opinion that there are no means of securing for the Indians in the seigniory benefits which s. 2 of the Act shews they were intended to have. If this were a case which the practice of the English Courts governed, their Lordships might not improbably think that there was a charitable trust which the Attorney General, as representing the public, could enforce, if not in terms, at all events cyprès by means of a scheme, or, if necessary, by invoking the assistance of the Legislature. Whether an analogous procedure exists in Quebec, and whether in that sense the matter is one for the Government of the Dominion or of that of the Province, are questions which have not been, and could not have been, discussed in proceedings such as the present. All their Lordships intend to decide is that, in the action in which the present appeal arises, the plaintiffs' claim was based on a supposed individual title which their Lordships hold not to exist. If in some different form of proceeding the Crown, as representing the interest of the public, puts the law in motion, or if negotiations are initiated for the settlement of a question as to the location of these Indians which may be of importance to the general interests of Canada, their Lordships desire to make it clear that nothing they have now decided is intended to prejudice the questions which may then arise." (At pages 878, 879)

It is against that background that one must try to understand the attitude of the Mohawks to the proposal approved by the Municipal Council of the Village of Oka in March 1990 to enlarge the Oka golf course, which they feared would disturb "the Pines" and the ancient Mohawk cemetery located there.

It must be recalled that the Mohawks had opposed, unsuccessfully, the building of the original golf course some thirty years earlier.

As was explained to me during the evidence presented at the pre-Sentence hearings, Indians do not perceive land, trees, and nature generally, as do non-natives. Chief Billy Two Rivers of Kahnawake and Grand Chiefs Joe Norton of Kahnawake and Jerry Peltier of Kanehsatake testified that for Mohawks, land is everything; it is all encompassing. They consider it to be a gift from the creator, their "maker," which provides all their needs and ensures their survival as a people. They pass on from generation to generation the teachings of the duty to take care of and preserve the land.

They spoke of their responsibility for the stewardship of the land, to take care of it for future generations.

As to the Pines, Grand Chief Peltier described it as "very precious, spiritual, a sacred place, the heart and soul of my people." The elders use it to gather medicines. Also, he explained that the pine trees in the Pines have to hold down the soil, which is sandy and fine and had, before the planting of those pine trees, a tendency to erode and blow away.

This is confirmed in an affidavit and Report by Michel F. Girard, an expert in History of the Environment, which Report is entitled "Étude Historique sur la Forêt du Village d'Oka" and is produced in the Court file of the Injunction referred to below. There, that expert explained as follows:

"Les pages qui suivent résument l'histoire de la plus vieille forêt plantée par l'homme au Québec. Il sera tout d'abord question de la problématique entourant sa préservation. Ensuite, un tableau de la situation du reboisement au tournant du XXe siècle sera brossé à grands traits afin de mettre l'expérience d'Oka dans son contexte historique plus large. Enfin, les documents et cartes trouvés dans le cadre de cette recherche seront étudiés. Ils sont présentés en annexe.

[...]

Mais au delà des considérations des écologistes et des Amérindiens, la décision d'agrandir le golf dans cette forêt surprit les anciens du village et ceux qui connaissaient l'histoire de la région. Car fondamentalement, la forêt d'Oka protège ses habitants de l'ensablement. Avant le boom forestier des années 1850, la plupart des rives de la rivière Outaouais étaient recouvertes de forêts de conifères, notamment du pin blanc. Dans la région d'Oka, où les arbres étaient d'accès facile, la coupe a été particulièrement sévère. Les Sulpiciens, qui ont pris possession du territoire grâce à un don du Roi en 1719, désiraient y établir des fermes pour enseigner l'agriculture aux Amérindiens de la mission Mohawk du Lac-des-Deux-Montagnes. Mais les sols à l'ouest du village étaient tout à fait impropres à l'agriculture. Ce vaste dépôt de Quaternaire des Basses terres du Saint-Laurent, constitué de sable fin et instable, mesure près de 30 mètres de haut. Il repose sur une couche imperméable d'argile de la Mer de Champlain et est traversé d'une douzaine de sources importantes. La nappe phréatique est à un mètre sous le niveau du sol. Cet escarpement est donc très sensible aux mouvements de sol en profondeur."

I can discern echoes of the Mohawk thinking in that regard in the convictions of environmentalists. The protection and preservation of the environment looms large on Canada's agenda for the nineties. Perhaps we have here an example of the wider society, the non-natives, taking a lesson from their native fellow-citizens.

It was the concerns and fears of the Mohawks at Kanehsatake regarding the proposed expansion of the golf course which resulted in the first barricade which they erected, near Route 344, on Chemin du Mil, which leads through the Pines; that led to the Injunction in dossier no. 700-05-000950-901 of the Superior Court for the district of Terrebonne, issued by my brother Bergeron J. on June 29th, 1990, ordering the removal of that barricade; which led to negotiations between representatives of the Government of Quebec and the Mohawks; which negotiations were interrupted by the Sûreté du Québec raid on that barricade on July 11th, 1990, with the tragic loss of the life of an S.Q. Officer; which led to more barricades; which led to more violence and criminal acts, including widespread vandalism, assaults, break-ins and thefts; which led to the evacuation from the Municipality of Oka Parish of 346 non-native families—970 people out of a total non-native population of 1,600—and the evacuation from the Municipality of the Village of Oka of 677 non-native families—1,520 people out of a total non-native population of 1,800; as to the natives, from the Oka Parish and Oka Village combined, there were evacuated 299 families, comprising 604 people out of a total native population of about 1,000 people; let us remember also the crippling of the economy and tourist industry of the Oka region, with the attendant losses sustained by numerous business enterprises there; all of which which was accompanied by the blockade of the Mercier Bridge by the Mohawks of Kahnawake, seriously inconveniencing many thousands of people who live on the south shore of Montreal and particularly in Châteauguay, requiring them to spend many hours and drive many, many miles out of their way over a relatively long period of time in order to get to work each day (similar inconveniences were caused to many people who lived in the Oka area); that blockade of the Mercier Bridge was followed some time later by the stoning carried out by an unruly mob of non-natives against a group of Mohawks, including women, children and old persons, trying to leave that reserve by motorcade. Most of the foregoing litany of events constituted criminal acts, which must be condemned, no matter from which side of the dispute they emanated!

All that being said and even though the actions of the two accused here have to be evaluated against that backdrop, it must be remembered that it would be patently unfair to visit the entire consequences of the Oka Crisis on them and that is not what Crown counsel pleaded.

It is indeed an important aggravating factor, but it must be kept in mind that the accused here were but a small part of the Oka Crisis. Many, many others were involved.

I cannot close the present chapter of this Sentence without also mentioning the many tens of millions of dollars which this entire episode has cost the Government of the Province of Quebec and, hence, its tax-payers, you and me!

In regard to their actions of opposition to the wider non-native community, which, in the case of Ronald Cross resulted in the convictions enumerated above in the second group of counts, I am satisfied that he was not motivated by greed or reasons of personal gain.* He acted out of a deep anger, rage, desperation and a sense of hopelessness, all the result of the systematic discrimination and racism against his people over several centuries.

Also, if the media featured him prominently—as "Lasagna"—during the Oka Crisis, his public image as such is purely a creation of the media. Although he was prominent, was aggressive and, yes, was often violent, there was absolutely no evidence adduced before me to suggest that he was the leader or even a leader of the militant Warrior Society at Kanehsatake during the crisis.

In fact, the evidence was to the effect that, prior to the Oka Crisis, he was not

---

* In R. vs Switlishoff et al., (1950) 97 C.C.C. 132, see at page 137: "It is plain that the Assize Judge did not look upon these respondents as six individuals who had committed these offences for personal ends."

even active or involved in the Warrior Society. It appears that he was galvanized into action by the fear of the Mohawks regarding the proposed expansion of the golf course.

For years, decades, even centuries, the aboriginal people of this country have endured, at best, indifference, neglect and unfairness and, at worst, open hostility, contempt, discrimination and racism.

The aboriginal peoples occupy a special place in the firmament of Canadian society. They were the original inhabitants of this country; this continent!

The white man, the European settlers, came here and, by dint of their superior numbers, state of technological development and, hence by force of arms, took the land from the natives.

The Queen (symbolically as the titular embodiment of the State) owes a special duty to the aboriginal peoples. In <u>R. vs Sparrow</u> ([1990] 1 S.C.R., 1075), the Supreme Court of Canada spoke of "...the unique contemporary relationship between the Crown and Canada's aboriginal peoples."

The land claims of the Mohawks at Oka Kanehsatake are perhaps well founded in law or, perhaps not. The present case has not required that I make any inquiry into that issue.

Yet, those claims are not be settled at the point of a gun, but rather by negotiation in good faith between, on the one hand, the natives, acting through properly constituted and legitimate representatives, and, on the other hand, the affected persons or groups and the Governments, and, failing agreement, by recourse to the Courts.

Against that historical background which I have traced, it nonetheless remains abundantly clear that the Courts must continue to perform their role of instrument of social peace by the orderly and peaceful settlement of disputes, according to the Rule of Law.

It is, however, indeed gratifying to observe that, with the First Report issued last Thursday by the Royal Commission on Aboriginal Peoples, entitled "The Right of Aboriginal Self-Government and the Constitution: A Commentary," as well as the current round of Constitutional Consultative Regional Conferences and Constitutional Negotiations, aboriginal issues are finally being addressed by Government in a meaningful way.

The accused here and their compatriots were no doubt motivated by a sincere and honest belief in the legitimacy of the natives' land claims and the frustration, bitterness and intense anger which are the legacy of centuries of neglect, indifference, unfairness, hostility, contempt, discrimination and racism.

Some will say that there is no place for such comments in a Sentence pronounced by a Court. I do not agree with such views. The criminal acts committed during the Oka Crisis, try as one might, cannot be entirely dissociated from the historical and political origins and background of that Crisis.

Even in my Directives to the Jury, I included a chapter entitled "History, Politics and the Law."

The Judgment of the Privy Council in Corinthe, referred to above, was by way of appeal from the Judgment ([1912] 21 K.B., 316) in that matter of The Quebec Court of King's Bench (the then title of the appeal court of Quebec).

In examining that Judgment, I was struck by the fact that the Judge who wrote for the Bench there used the term "sauvages" (English translation, "savages") many, many times in referring to the natives of Oka-Kanehsatake. That is in today's context clearly a pejorative term, and probably was so as well in 1911.

While it was one thing to have quoted that term from official documents and correspondence dated back in the 17th and 18th centuries, that Judge used the term "sauvages" in his own text no less than 41 times. If the terms "natives" and "aboriginals" (French equivalent, "autochtones" or "aborigènes") were not then in current usage, it might have been preferable to refer to the natives of Oka-Kanehsatake as "Indiens," rather than as "sauvages."

That is but one example of the contempt, discrimination and racism which the native peoples of Canada have endured over the centuries, and it came there not from an uneducated man on the street, but from a Judge of the highest Court of Quebec.

Let me make clear, however, that I do not intend to belittle the tragedies which befell the Lemay and Mongeon families during the Oka Crisis. Whoever ransacked their homes, be they native or non-native, truly acted like savages. If the accused were acquitted on the counts relating to those incidents, it was because the Crown was not able to prove their participation beyond a reasonable doubt.

All that I have written above concerning the experience of Canada's native peoples most probably explains what motivated the behavior of the two accused before me here at Oka-Kanehsatake during the summer and early autumn of 1990. That being said, such motivation behind Ronald Cross' acts is a mitigating factor, but only as it relates to the second group of counts.

However, I cannot emphasize enough that it does not justify or excuse such behavior.

Canada, and of course Quebec, operate under the Rule of Law and it is my sworn duty to apply and uphold the Law. We live here in an open, free and democratic society; probably one of the most free countries in the world. Yet, no one can take the law into his own hands. To allow this to happen, even for the most worthy cause, would be the first step towards anarchy. All persons present within the borders of Canada, be they natives, non-natives, citizens, non-citizen immigrants, visitors or tourists, are subject to and bound by the Criminal Law of Canada.

I turn now to the facts of the incidents which underlie the convictions among the first group of counts.

The Mongeon home and farm had been vandalized between August 27th and 31st, 1990 and this was discovered by the Mongeons when they returned home during the afternoon of August 31st.

Francis Jacobs, a former chief on Council and Ronald Bonspille, who operated the Kanehsatake Mobile Services (ambulances and medical transport), were in the area at the time, heard the commotion and came there at about the same time as the Mongeons arrived.

The same applied to Dennis Nicholas of Warrior Security. Present there, moreover, when the Mongeons, Nicholas, Jacobs and Bonspille arrived, were Roger Lazore and Gordon Lazore, but not Ronald Cross.

Francis Jacobs and Ronald Bonspille had been instrumental in setting up and organizing the house patrols, in which about 30 Mohawks patrolled daily and nightly, in order to deter break-ins, thefts and vandalism. That group of patrollers operated out of the community gymnasium, which also served as the food-bank. They covered a part of the territory which had been blocked off by the Mohawk barricades, whereas Warrior Security, operating out of the Treatment Centre, patrolled the remainder of that territory.

Notwithstanding those patrols, many houses which had been abandoned by their owners or occupants were broken into and vandalized during the Oka Crisis, the most notable among them being the Lemay home and the Mongeon home. There were moreover many other break-ins and thefts, for a total of over forty.

Although the Sûreté du Québec had no reason to suspect and in fact did not suspect Francis Jacobs or Ronald Bonspille, the accused here did believe that the former were guilty of some of the break-ins and vandalism and were blaming it on the Warriors. Moreover, the media showed up at the Mongeons very shortly after the return home of the Mongeon family on August 31st. The accused believed that Francis Jacobs had called in the media. However, the evidence at trial here revealed that the accused were wrong and that it was Dennis Nicholas, of Warrior Security, who had in fact called them in.

Also, as seen on the TV that evening, Ronald Cross' motorbike was thrown off a truck at the Mongeon farm, doused with gasoline and set alight. Francis Jacobs' name was then mentioned in that TV report, although he was no longer there at the time of the filming.

Later that night, in the early hours of September 1st, two Mohawks, Angus Nelson and Maurice Binette, friendly to the warriors although not themselves warriors, having seen that TV report referred to above and then, for want of something better to do, just driving around in the pick-up truck of Angus Nelson, passed by the home of Ronald Cross' brother, Glenn, on Pine Road and, seeing the lights on, went in, as they put it: "just to talk to the boys."

Present there at that time were Ronald Cross, Gordon Lazore and two other persons. The topics of Francis Jacobs and Ronald Bonspille, Ronald Cross' bike, the break-ins and the media, all came up and Ronald Cross and/or Maurice Binette suggested that they all go find Francis Jacobs, in order to, as they put it: "talk to him"!

The six of them left there in Nelson's pick-up truck, Nelson and Binette in the cab and the four others in the open box at the back.

Ronald Cross took along a firearm, an M-16.

After about 15 minutes of searching they found Francis Jacobs in his car with his son Cory, then aged 20, parked near the intersection of Route 344 and Rang Ste. Germaine, talking to Ronald Bonspille, there in his own vehicle with some others.

When Nelson's pick-up truck came to a stop there near the Jacobs car, Ronald Bonspille took off up Ste. Germaine Road towards the barricade manned a bit further away by the Army.

The four in the back of the pick-up and Maurice Binette jumped out and approached the Jacobs automobile. Nelson also came out, but stood near the back of his truck and observed, without getting involved in the fracas which followed.

Ronald Cross, gun in hand, ran towards the Jacobs car and shouted: "We're gonna fix you tonight." Francis Jacobs put his car into reverse gear and was starting to back up, obviously with the intention to get away. Ronald Cross then said, while pointing his gun at both Jacobs in the car: "If you don't stop, I'll shoot." Francis Jacobs then heard a "click" from Ronald Cross' weapon and Cory ducked in the car as the rifle was then pointed at him.

The Crown suggests that the "click" heard was a misfire of the rifle, which would mean that Ronald Cross intended to shoot Cory Jacobs. Ronald Cross then raised his rifle up towards the sky and fired three shots in rapid succession.

I am convinced, rather than that "click" having been a misfire, drawing on the evidence which heard relative to the second group of counts, that what Ronald Cross had in fact done there is to arm, or cock his weapon. That "click" was the noise made when a cartridge is moved from the magazine into the firing chamber, ready for firing.

The two Jacobs, in the meanwhile, had rolled up their windows and locked the doors. This was to no avail. Ronald Cross broke the windows with his rifle butt and Ronald Cross, Gordon Lazore and Maurice Binette, together with the two other persons unknown to me, proceeded to administer beatings to Francis Jacobs and Cory Jacobs.

Ronald Cross hit Francis Jacobs with his fists and with his rifle butt. Francis Jacobs and Cory Jacobs had reached for two baseball bats which they kept in their car for protection, but the assailants took the bats away from them. Gordon Lazore got one of those bats in his possession and used it to poke at Francis Jacobs' face and head, causing him a gash over his left eye which bled profusely and later needed three or four stitches to close. Gordon Lazore also beat Cory Jacobs.

With respect to the two firearm offences, Counts 22 and 24, it is abundantly clear that Ronald Cross' responsibility is far heavier than that of Gordon Lazore. Ronald Cross brought along and directly used the firearm. Gordon Lazore never touched it. He was found guilty on those two counts solely via Section 21 Cr. C., by aiding or abetting.

The baseball bats were also used to damage the Jacobs' car and the aggressors also caused damage to that vehicle by jumping on the hood, trunk and roof. In all, that car was damaged to the extent of approximately $4,500.

Someone among the group of aggressors then heard on a two-way radio that Warrior Security was coming, whereupon they all left, taking the baseball bats with them, and proceeded to the house of Ronald Bonspille, at which property was also located the business premises of Kanehsatake Mobile Services. More about the Bonspille incident in a few moments.

Ronald Bonspille's son Robert, then age 19, saw Francis Jacobs and Cory Jacobs later that night at the food-bank. He testified at the trial and, among other things, described Francis Jacobs as "a mess." Apart from the gash over his eye, Jacobs' face was bruised and swollen to twice its normal size. Cory Jacobs, although less badly hurt physically, was in a state of shock. He had clearly been traumatized. He had a blank look and did not respond when spoken to. Both father and son were treated at hospital emergency and released. Two photos of each of them taken later that day were produced by the prosecution as Exhibits P-8 and P-9 and are revealing as to their physical injuries.

Some months later both had to see a psychologist. Cory Jacobs did not testify at the trial, apparently because the incident had severely traumatized him. Francis Jacobs, when he testified, seemed to me to be depressed.

When the group of six arrived at Ronald Bonspille's place, the latter's son, Robert, had already gotten out of the house. He had been sleeping and was told phoned by his father and told to get out at once as the group, "they," were coming there.

He did that, wearing only his underwear shorts and hid in the nearby bushes, observing what later went on at that property. Although he did not include that comment in his testimony before the Jury, in his statement given to the police later that same day, Robert recounted how he was so frightened that night that he got over the 15-foot high fence to get to the bushes and thinks he never even touched the fence in doing so.

Two ambulances were parked on the driveway there, one owned by Kanehsatake Mobile Services and the other one on loan from Ambulances Joliette. Robert Bonspille could see Ronald Cross break the windows and roof lights of one of them, using the butt of his rifle and then stoop down and slash a tire. There was a double spotlight on a tree nearby which shone directly on the driveway, thus enabling Robert Bonspille to see and identify Ronald Cross.

The Kanehsatake Mobile Services ambulance was damaged to the extent of approximately $8,000. The other one was towed away and later repaired by its owner. However, witnesses here confirmed that the damages to it were similar to those caused to the Kanehsatake Mobile Services ambulance.

In respect of the Jacobs and Bonspille incidents, the victims being fellow-Mohawks, the comments which I made above concerning the mistreatment over the years of the native peoples by the wider society can play no mitigating role whatsoever.

Turning now to the second group of counts, the incidents there were part and parcel of a military-type confrontation, the Army on one side and the warriors on the other.

It must be mentioned that when the Quebec Government called in the Army at Oka, as the <u>National Defence Act</u> (R.C.S., c. N-5) permits them to do in very special circumstances, Section 282 of that law decrees:

"Officers and non-commissioned members when called out for service in aid of the civil power shall, without further authority or appointment and without taking oath of office, be held to have, in addition to their powers and duties as officers and non-commissioned members, all of the powers and duties of constables, so long as they remain so called out, but they shall act only as a military body and are individually liable to obey the orders of their superior officers."

Hence, at Oka, the soldiers were acting as police officers.

On September 1st, "C" Company of the Second Battalion of the Royal 22nd Regiment of the Canadian Armed Forces, which Regiment is often referred to as the "Van Doos," led by Major Alain Tremblay, a young but an experienced, highly-competent and professional military officer, received its orders to advance on Annunciation Road, past the Mongeon Farm, to take the Pines and to push the warriors into a defined perimeter.

One cannot but be impressed with the cool, careful, moderate and professional manner in which he, his officers and troops proceeded, past the Mohawk barricades, through the bunkers, trenches and booby-traps which the Mohawks had prepared as defensive positions, and into the clearing in the Pines near the lacrosse rink. Their orders were, if at all possible, to avoid a shoot-out; not to shoot first, but to fire only if fired upon.

As one might expect, the soldiers were well-armed in preparation for their mission. The Army used Grizzlies, which are armoured personnel carriers, and had available to it field artillery, machine guns, both light and heavy, grenades, sniper rifles, a Canadian version of the U.S. M-16A2 automatic rifle, pistols and knives.

Although not nearly as well-endowed in terms of heavy equipment, the Mohawks were nevertheless also well armed, with M-16A2s, AK-47s, a Barrett machine gun, shot-guns, pistols and knives.

The first three of those categories are weapons of war and quite lethal. They were pointed outward from the Pines in a defensive formation. The M-16 and AK-47 have a range of 3.3 kms, and the Barrett has a range of 8 kms. That 3.3 kms range was such that, for example, if a shoot-out had occurred, besides soldiers and Mohawks dying, people walking in the streets of Hudson, across the Lake of Two Mountains from Oka, could have been killed or seriously wounded if struck by a stray bullet.

The munitions used in the M-16 and the AK-47 were designed to cause maximum damage with the smallest possible calibre or size; that is, to wound as grievously as possible and, if at all possible, to kill. The M-16 munition 5.56 mm x 45 mm, was designed so that, after it hits a human body and enters ten cms, it will fragment and explode. It will cause a very serious injury at between 15 and 25 cms of the point of entry, that is, at about the centre of a person's mass.

That weapon, in its automatic mode, which means continuous fire as long as the trigger is held, will empty its 30-cartridge magazine in 2.3 seconds. An experienced user, changing magazines rapidly, can fire it at a cyclical rate of 150 rounds per minute. Even in its semi-automatic firing mode, which requires a separate pull of the trigger for each shot, an experienced user can fire up to 100 rounds in a minute.

As to the AK-47, its munition of 7.62 mm x 39 mm calibre was designed with its centre of gravity at the back of the bullet, so that, once it hits and enters the human body, it starts to rotate on itself, again in order to cause maximum injury and, if at all possible, death.

That weapon is manufactured to fire semi-automatically, but not automatically. However, with a minor modification, it too can be rendered automatic. Even in its semi-automatic mode, an experienced user can fire up to 100 rounds in a minute.

As to the Barrett machine gun, it is semi-automatic and is designed to be an anti-tank-weapon. Its munition, 12.7 mm x 99 mm, is very large. The complete cartridge measures approximately 5.5 inches in length and is fed into the gun through an 11-bullet charger. When fired, its projectile will go through three compacted automobile motor blocks at 500 metres. It will, as well, pierce the side of a tank at 100 to 150 metres. Clearly, it is not a toy!

Seeing the weapons arrayed on both sides on September 1st, 1990 in the Pines, at Oka, what we had there was clearly a tinderbox. If shooting had erupted, it would have been a blood bath!

Credit must therefore be given to Major Tremblay and his men that this did not happen. They were disciplined and acted with moderation, coolness and control.

It must also be mentioned that, although there were some hot-heads on the Mohawk side, cooler heads prevailed. We can see on the video-cassette exhibits, an older Mohawk, whose real name is Robert Skidders but who was known by the sobriquet "Mad Jap," exerting a calming influence on the warriors.

Mr. Skidders and Major Tremblay had two conversations that day. Each gave the other the assurance that his side would not shoot first. This went a long way towards defusing the situation.

However, it still left Major Tremblay apprehensive. Even though he had complete control of his troops, Mad Jap did not have complete control of all the warriors, nor were the latter as disciplined as the Army personnel.

The undersigned also noted on the video-cassette exhibits two Mohawk women, one of then scooting around on an all-terrain vehicle, also exerting a moderating influence on the warriors.

With regard to the seven Section 87 Cr. C. offences of which Ronald Cross was found guilty, namely having in his possession a weapon for a purpose dangerous to the public peace, in six of them the weapon he carried was a U.S. M-16A2 and in one a Ruger 44 Magnum pistol.

Moreover, at many times during the Oka Crisis, Ronald Cross was observed carrying an AK-47, a "Remington 870" 12-Gauge shotgun (which is quite a dangerous weapon at a distance of up to 60 metres) and an M-9 U.S. army combat knife held on his chest in the webbing of his camouflage gear.

As such, he represented a constant danger to his adversaries.

A general goal of every Sentence is the protection of the public, and this is sought by the application of several general principles, including specific and general deterrence, stigmatizing the behaviour of the delinquent, punishment (in its philosophical sense and not as vengeance or retribution) and the rehabilitation of the offender.

The behavior and conduct of an accused after he is charged, and until he is Sentenced, is also to be considered.

Gordon Lazore's behavior in that regard has been good. He has not exhibited continued defiance, as has Ronald Cross. Gordon Lazore attended at his trial when required to do so and, moreover, I sense in him some element of remorse.

On the other hand, the same cannot be said for Mr. Cross. Twice during the trial, he did not attend at Court when required, obliging the Court to issue arrest warrants in each case. The first such occasion was on July 5th, 1991, prior to the selection of the Jury, when the undersigned was conducting hearings relating to his bail status. In my Judgment of July 11th, last at the end of those hearings, I wrote the following at page 7:

"The evidence heard prior to July 5th had convinced me by a balance of probabilities that Ronald Cross is a person who is prone to violence, both physical and verbal. He has only defiance, disdain and contempt for constituted authority. Even before the evidence heard on July 9th, it was clear that in regard to certain incidents involving him during the Oka Crisis, as well as the Kahnawake Incident, the excessive consumption of alcohol was a salient feature.

His testimony before me on July 9th clearly established that, for some time now, he has had a problem of substance abuse, both as to alcohol and non-prescription drugs. His failure to be present at Court on Friday, July 5th last, was the result of a two and one-half day binge on alcohol (including beer, wine and hard liquor) as well as cocaine. That binge, during much of which he was either sleeping or in black-outs, started during the late afternoon of Thursday, July 4th and continued until the early morning hours of Sunday, July 7th."

The "Kahnawake Incident" referred to there concerns an occurrence of May 11th, 1991 in respect of which Ronald Cross still faces three criminal charges before the Court of Quebec, Criminal Division, in the District of Longueuil. The Crown has asked that this Court take that incident into account in formulating the Sentence herein. Such a request is totally unfounded. As Kaufman, J.A. wrote in <u>Chartier vs R.</u> ([1980] 13 C.R. [3d], 194, at page 199):

"..., as we said in R. vs Paradis ([1976] 38 [2d], 455, at page 462), an accused should not be sentenced, **nor should he appear to be sentenced**, for an offence for which he has not yet been convicted.... [T]he principle remains, and care should be taken to avoid any suggestions that an accused may be punished twice—for that is what it comes to—for any offence, let alone one which has not yet been established."

The second time when Ronald Cross did not attend at his trial when required to do so, which was more serious than the first time because the Jury was in function and present, was on January 8th, 1992, the morning when Mtre Brière was to deliver his summation to the Jury. An arrest warrant being issued, he was arrested at about 4 a.m. the next morning in a residence in Lasalle, which is closely connected in the minds of the police authorities to the traffic of cocaine and crack.

It should be remembered that when he failed to appear last July 5th, he explained in his subsequent testimony at that hearing that his alcohol-cocaine binge took place at a house in Lasalle.

———————————

What does the jurisprudence teach us about the effect to be given to an accused's behavior during his trial?

In R. vs Chartier, cited above, Kaufman J.A. stated as well:

"I should add that, in my view, a judge is perfectly entitled to draw a conclusion from an accused's behavior—both good and bad—after conviction and before sentence...." (Also at page 199)

However, in R. vs Di Sensi, we read, again from the pen of Kaufman J.A.:

"The learned trial judge placed heavy emphasis on the fact that for 30 months preceding the sentence the accused had not committed any crime. This is, perhaps, a factor to be weighed, but, with greatest respect, I am not impressed by the fact that an accused, after arrest and before sentence, is of good behavior. It would be utterly foolish to do otherwise, and while misconduct in that crucial period may be an aggravating factor—as is misconduct while on bail or probation—the reverse is not necessarily true." ([1978] 2 C.R. [3d], pages S-4 and 5)

———————————

In our case, there was also an incident involving Ronald Cross during the afternoon of January 22nd, last following the Jury's verdicts earlier that day.

Right after I had finally left the Courtroom that day, after deciding on the status of Mr. Gordon Lazore pending Sentence, the detention constables were putting handcuffs on Gordon Lazore while Ronald Cross stood, handcuffed, just outside the box and near the exit door.

Umberto Tucci, an officer of the Sûreté du Québec, who was present in the Courtroom at that time, testified at the pre-Sentence hearings that he saw Ronald Cross raise his fists aloft, held together by the handcuffs, and he heard him say, addressing himself to Roger Lazore who had been acquitted of all charges pending against him, and who was standing outside the box at about fifteen feet from Mr. Cross:"Roger, we did it for the nation and we'll do it again!"

This, Crown counsel argued, shows that Ronald Cross is unrepentant and feels no remorse for his actions during the Oka Crisis. Crown Counsel may well be right.

As to the effects of remorse or the absence of same, genuine remorse should be taken into account as a mitigating factor, reflecting on the character of an accused and providing hope for reformation.

Lack of remorse, however, should not be used against an accused as he is not punished because of his character per se. In R. vs. Campbell ([1977] 18 N.S.R. [2d], 547 [N.S.A.C.]), Nova Scotia's then Chief Justice McKeigan wrote:

"Remorse should, in my view, carry more weight on the positive side than on the negative side. If a person shows genuine remorse, it indicates rehabilitation. The converse is not necessarily true."

Insofar as both accused with respect to the Jacobs and Bonspille incidents, the absence of planning and long premeditation is an attenuating circumstance, whereas acting in concert with others as a group is an aggravating one: R. vs Lévesque ([1981] 19 C.R. [3d], 43 [Que. Sup. Ct.]).

As relates to Ronald Cross and the second group of counts, acting in concert with others, long planning and premeditation, and the duration of the events over a period of 78 days, are all aggravating factors.

Several cases have stated that recognition of cultural differences between an accused and society in general may also be a relevant factor in determining an appropriate punishment. Cases dealing with the native people of Canada reflect this principle, as do cases in British Columbia relating to the Doukhobors (R. vs Switlishoff et al.: see footnote 11, **supra**; R. vs Ayalik, [1960] 33 W.W.R., 377 [N.W.T.C.A.].

In a collection of essays entitled *New Directions in Sentencing*, edited by Brian A. Grosman, Butterworths, Toronto, 1980, Chapter 17 is one entitled "Sentencing in the North." Mr. Justice C.F. Tallis, then of the Supreme Court of the North West Territories, now of the Court of Appeal of Saskatchewan, wrote:

"The Northwest Territories are characterized by a small population scattered over vast tracts of land. The population can be broken down into one-third Indian, one-third Innuit and one-third white.

(…)

In dealing with the question of Sentencing, courts in the Northwest Territories cannot overlook the fact that society has the basic roots of these three cultures. When the common law was transplanted into Canada, it proved to be very flexible, but native people, whether Innuit or Indian, had their own system of laws, tribunals, penalties, and, in effect, their own justice system. Furthermore, such cultures did not have jails. This was a new concept introduced from the white man's world. It continues to be little understood by many of the elders in the Indian and Innuit communities."

That, too, is a factor to consider here.

As required by Section 668 Cr. C., at the termination of the pre-Sentence hearings on February 6th last, I asked each of Ronald Cross and Gordon Lazore if he had anything to say to the Court before Sentence was imposed on him. After consulting with counsel, each of them informed me that he had nothing to say.

In all crimes except for those for which a minimum Sentence is fixed, as we shall see below, a very wide discretion in the matter of fixing the degree of punishment is allowed to the Judge who presides the case. The policy of the Law in such cases is to fix a maximum penalty, which is intended only for the worst cases and the worst offenders, and to leave it to the discretion of the Judge to determine to what extent in a particular case the punishment fixed should approach to or recede from the maximum limit.

In fixing the Sentence for any particular crime, and every Sentence must be fit and appropriate taking into account the crime and the offender, the Court will take into consideration the nature of the offence, the circumstances in which it was committed, the degree of deliberation and planning shown by the offender, the duration of the offence, whether violence was involved, all attenuating and aggravating circumstances surrounding the commission of the offence, and, on the subjective side, the rehabilitation of the accused, his previous criminal record, if any, and his age, character and previous experiences.

With respect to the quality of fitness which every Sentence must have, the dictum of Marchand J.A. in R. vs Lemire et Gosselin is often quoted in reasons for Sentence, where he said:

"On peut dire qu'une sentence a cette qualité de convenance quand elle est proportionnée à la fois à la gravité objective de l'infraction et sa gravité subjective pour le délinquant; et que de plus, elle a les qualités nécessaires d'exemplarité protectrice et de la correction curative. La gravité objective du crime [...] est écrite dans le code. [...] La gravité subjective d'un acte peut varier suivant le degré de l'intelligence et de la détermination de la volonté d'un délinquant." ([1948] 5 C.R. 181, at pages 186-87 [Que. C.A.])

Finally, in Droit Pénal canadien (2nd ed. 1974. Vol. 2, at page 1574) Judge Irénée Lagarde reminded us that under the objective aspect, one should consider the gravity of the crime with respect to the provisions of the Criminal Code, the deterrent effect of the Sentence and, under the subjective aspect, the attenuating or aggravating circumstances, the possibility of rehabilitation of the guilty person, his background and circumstances.

In the matter of indictable offences, Parliament has established five categories or levels of maximum punishment, namely 2, 5, 10 and 14 years and life imprisonment. It is obvious that those offences for which a greater maximum punishment is provided are objectively more serious than those for which a lesser maximum punishment is provided.

———————————————

In the case of Gordon Lazore, with respect to counts 26 (mischief) and 29 (assault while carrying a weapon), the maximum provided is ten years. In the case of the count 21 (aggravated assault), the maximum provided is 14 years. As regards counts 22 and 24 (the use of a firearm while committing an indictable offence), the maximum provided is 14 years and since this is a first offence for him, there is a minimum sentence of one year imprisonment.

With regard to Ronald Cross, in the cases of counts 25 and 50 (uttering threat) and 49 (simple assault), the maximum term of imprisonment is five years. As regards counts 26, 31 and 32 (mischief), 27 (assault while carrying, using or threatening to use a weapon), and 38, 40, 43, 46, 48, 52 and 55 (having in possession a weapon for a purpose dangerous to the public peace), the maximum penalty in each case is ten years imprisonment. As relates to count 21 (aggravated assault), the maximum punishment is 14 years imprisonment, whereas for counts 22 and 24 (use of a firearm while committing an indictable offence), the maximum in each case is 14 years and there is, of course, the same minimum of one year.

— — — — — — — — — —

With respect to the objective gravity, there is also the question of deterrence, both subjective with respect to each accused himself, and objective, that is to deter others from committing the same acts. However, one must not accord to the deterrent aspect of a Sentence such a great weight that it renders the Sentence unjust towards an accused.

On the subjective level, it is appropriate to say a few words on the background and history of each of the two accused.

Mr. Gordon Lazore is 32 years old and is a high school graduate. He is single. He has had a fairly constant work history and is known in his community as a hard-working person.

He is one of five children and the only one who lives at home with his 75-year-old handicapped mother. With the help of his sister, he looked after his mother. His father died in 1977.

His criminal record consists of a conviction for the possession of illegal tobacco products, for which he was fined $2,800 in September of last year.

Ronald Cross is 34 years of age and is also a high school graduate. He is one of seven children. His father died tragically in a drowning accident in 1967, and his mother is still alive. He is married and has an infant son, born December 5th last, while this trial was in progress.

His work history has been constant. He has been an iron worker since 1977. His criminal record consists of a conviction for assault of a peace officer which occurred on April 13th, 1990. He was fined $250.

He was described by Grand Chief Joe Norton as "a regular person," "a happy-go-lucky fellow."

With respect to the aspect of the rehabilitation of each of the accused, it has often been held in recent years that the existence of administrative boards working for the rehabilitation of prisoners and their parole reduces the importance of the criterion of rehabilitation in fixing the length of Sentences.

The issue of the principle of the "parity" of Sentences has also been discussed during the hearings. I have been made aware by counsel of the Sentences imposed by the Courts on others involved in various incidents relating to the Oka Crisis. Of course, the nature of each incident and the extent of the participation of each accused person will necessarily vary and must be weighed and considered.

In determining the Sentences of the present accused, I shall keep the parity principle in mind, together with all the other applicable principles, criteria, rules, concepts and factors which affect Sentencing.

Since the Oka Crisis occurred, each of the two accused has been detained for a period prior to the trial, during the trial and since the Jury's verdicts. In the case of Mr. Cross, the total of his pre-Sentence detention has been seven months and twenty-two days, while in the case of Mr. Lazore, it has been six months and sixteen days.

Section 721(3) Cr. C. declares:

"In determining the sentence to be imposed on a person convicted of an offence, a justice, provincial court judge or judge **may** take into account any time spent in custody by the person as a result of the offence." (Emphasis added.)

Although the Interpretation Act* provides that 'may' is permissive, within the context of the foregoing Section it has become almost imperative.

In R. vs Gravino, Montgomery J.A. stated:

"It is a recognized rule of thumb that imprisonment while awaiting trial is the equivalent of a sentence of twice that length." ([1970-71] 13 C.L.Q., 434 [Que. C.A.])

The Courts of Alberta have refused to accept such a "rule of thumb." In R. vs Regan et al., we read:

"In imposing sentence, the learned Judge adopted what he referred to as a 'rule of thumb' by which imprisonment awaiting trial is said to be equivalent to a sentence of twice that length. In other words, he equated the five months spent in custody awaiting trial to a sentence of 10 months' imprisonment imposed by the Court. That would mean that in the view of the learned Judge a fit sentence on the counts of assault causing bodily harm would be 12 months, and as to Regan's sentence for the attempted extortion, 22 months, if we understand his theory correctly.

In our view, no such rule of thumb has ever been recognized by the Courts of this Province, and, furthermore, such a rule ought not to be recognized in the future. Each instance of sentencing has to be considered on its own merits, and, no doubt, in proper cases time already spent in custody, and the circumstances thereof, may be taken into account as provided by the Criminal Code. Beyond that, we do not believe any rule in this regard can be laid down." ([1976] 24 C.C.C. [2d], 225, at page 226)

Again, in R. vs Tallman ([1989] 48 C.C.C. [3d], 81), that same Court of Appeal said that while there is no automatic formula for taking into account pre-trial custody, the usual practice is to give credit against Sentence which is somewhat more than the actual time spent in such custody.

The British Columbia Court of Appeal has also recognized that a credit

---

* R.S.C., c. I-21, Section 11: "The expression 'shall' is to be construed as imperative and the expression 'may' as permissive."

which is greater than actual time of detention should be given. In Ko vs R., we may read:

"Counsel for the Crown, who was counsel at trial, told us that on the sentencing proceedings he had taken the position that the sentence should be in the 14-year range, with some appropriate reduction for the 15 to 16 months the appellant spent in gaol. With scrupulous fairness, counsel took the same position before this court. The 15 to 16 months spent in prison is colloquially called 'dead time,' because, in my understanding, it does not attract any benefit by way of remission for a prisoner. Thus, in respect of such time, credit is usually given which is greater than the actual time of imprisonment." ([1980] 11 C.R. [3d], 298, at page 309)

The position on that issue taken by the Ontario Appeal Court is illustrated by its Judgment in R. vs Meilleur, by Martin J.A.:

"Section 649(2.1) of the Criminal Code [now 721(3)] provides that in determining the sentence to be imposed on a person convicted of an offence the court may take into account any time spent in custody by the person as a result of the offence. It was, accordingly, clearly appropriate for the learned trial judge to take into account the period of pre-trial custody in arriving at an appropriate sentence. We are all of the opinion, however, that he erred in applying a mathematical formula by multiplying the months spent in pre-trial custody by three, so as to arrive at a deduction of 42 months. It is apparent that had it not been for this error in principle O'Leary J. would have imposed a larger sentence than a sentence of four years." ([1981] 22 C.R. [3d], 185, at page 188)

It is clear that the time which each of Gordon Lazore and Ronald Cross has spent detained until today is time which will not be calculated towards statutory remission, nor towards parole. Also, it is spent in a place of detention which does not have programmes of recreation nor of work which, on the other hand, exist in penal institutions where persons actually serve their Sentences.

Accordingly, that pre-Sentence detention is often called, as we noted above, "dead time" or "hard time." In keeping with those **dicta**, without applying any automatic formula or rule of thumb, I consider it to be just and fitting that I calculate with respect to Ronald Cross a credit or reduction of fifteen months from each Sentence which I would otherwise have imposed and, in the case of Gordon Lazore that period will be thirteen months.

———————————

I now turn to the question of the relationship of Sentences among themselves, that is as to whether they are or should be concurrent or consecutive.

In that regard, it is opportune to refer back to two Judgments previously rendered in this case. In the first one, dated September 26th, 1991, prior to the selection of the Jury, the undersigned dismissed a defence Motion to Sever for separate trials the first group of counts from the second group of counts, stating the following at pages 6 and 7 of that Judgment:

"...where one or more accused are faced with numerous counts which all arise from one connnected series of incidents closely related as to time and place, so that, as here, there is a clear nexus among the offences charged, again saving the overriding rule that each accused is entitled to a fair trial, the general rule is that all such counts are to be tried together if the Crown frames its indictment accordingly."

Moreover, after the Crown had declared its case closed and before defence counsel were required to declare before the Jury if any of the accused intended to call witnesses, a further Motion was presented by Ronald Cross requesting the Court to sever for separate trials the first group of counts from the second group of counts. In that Motion, as in the prior one, the first two grounds read as follows:

"1. Insufficient factual **nexus** between the incidents or transactions comprised in the two groups of counts;

2. Insufficient legal **nexus** as between the incidents or transactions comprised in the two groups of counts."

In dismissing that Application, the undersigned wrote at page 19 of the Judgment dated December 30th, 1991:

"Those are the same arguments raised in a Motion to Sever Counts presented by the three accused in September 1991, prior to the selection of the Jury. All those grounds were addressed and disposed of in my Judgment of September 26th last. The reasons given therein are hereby incorporated into the present reasons by reference as though repeated here, with the following additional comments.

My determination of those grounds Nos. 1, 3, and 4 was then based solely on the contents of the Indictment. I have now had the benefit of hearing the Crown's evidence and am of the view that my earlier conclusions still apply, **a fortiori**."

— — — — — — — — — —

Hence, it is clear that my opinion throughout the trial has been that there was a sufficient factual and legal **nexus** between the incidents or transactions comprising the two groups of counts in order to try them before the same Jury.

However, the criteria to be applied in order to determine whether Sentences on various counts in the same indictment are to be concurrent or consecutive, although they are similar, are not the same as those which are **ad rem** on the question of severing counts for trial.

———————————————

It has long been settled law that, unless the Sentencing Judge states otherwise, all Sentences imposed are deemed to be concurrent.

The statutory authority which permits a Judge to impose consecutive Sentences in the case of more than one term of imprisonment being decreed on a multiple-count indictment is Section 717(4) (c)(ii), which declares:

"Where an accused

(a) ....

(b) ....

(c) is convicted of more offences than one before the same court at the same settings, and

(i) ....

(ii) terms of imprisonment for the respective offences are imposed,

(iii) ....

the court that convicts the accused may direct that the terms of imprisonment shall be served one after the other."

Concurrent Sentences are generally imposed where the multiple convictions arise out of a single transaction or are nearly contemporaneous in time: See R. vs Chisholm ([1965] 4 C.C.C., 289 [Ont. C.A.]).

On the other hand, where the multiple convictions relate to a number of counts which are diverse as to the type of offence and relate to different transactions, the offences should be grouped into categories by type of offence or by transaction. Concurrent Sentences should then be imposed with respect to each offence within the same category or group.

However, although the Sentences for each category or group should be concurrent among themselves, they should run consecutively as between or among the other categories or groups, providing that the total Sentence so arrived at is not excessive, having regard to all the facts and circumstances: See R. vs Haines ([1975] 29 C.R.N.S., 239 [Ont. C.A.]).

The latter notion to the effect that the total Sentence so arrived at should not be excessive is known as the "totality principle." Where it is called into play, the Court must give priority to that principle over the ordinary rule that each Sentence must be appropriate to its offence. It will do so by reducing one or more of the consecutive Sentences to the point where the total Sentence is not excessive and is appropriate and fit for the overall incidents or transactions.

———————————————

Hence, I have decided that, as regards Ronald Cross, all the Sentences to be imposed upon him within the second group of counts will run concurrently among themselves, but as a group they will run consecutively to those imposed against him on the first group of counts.

As to that first group of counts, for both Mr. Cross and Mr. Lazore, leaving aside for the moment the issue of the two firearm counts, numbers 22 and 24, the Sentences on all the other counts within the first group of counts will run concurrently among themselves.

However, as regards Mr. Cross only, the Sentences on those other offences within the first group of counts will run consecutively as a group to the Sentences imposed for the offences comprising the second group of counts.

———————————————

Counts 22 and 24, what I have referred to as the "firearm offences," are infractions under Section 85 of the Criminal Code. The relevant portions of that Section read as follows:

"(1)   Every one who uses a firearm

(a) while committing...an indictable offence,...

(b) ...,

whether or not he causes or means to cause bodily harm to any person as a result thereof, is guilty of an indictable offence and liable to imprisonment

(c) in the case of a first offence,...for not more than fourteen years and not less than one year, and

(d) in the case of a second or subsequent offence,...for not more than fourteen years and not less than three years.

(2) A sentence imposed on a person for an offence under subsection (1) shall be served consecutively to any other punishment imposed on him for an offence arising out of the same event or series of events and to any other sentence to which he is subject at the time the sentence is imposed on him for an offence under subsection (1)."

Since this is the first such offence for both accused, the Court must impose on each of them on each of counts 22 and 24 a Sentence of no less than one year and no more than fourteen years imprisonment. Whatever that Sentence is it is clear and undisputed that it must run consecutively to the Sentence on its underlying or prerequisite offence.

For both Mr. Cross and Mr. Lazore the underlying offence relative to count 22 is count 21, the aggravated assault on Francis Jacobs. With respect to count 24, for Ronald Cross the underlying offence is count 27 (assault on Cory Jacobs while carrying a weapon) and for Gordon Lazore the underlying offence is count 29 (carrying a baseball bat while assaulting Cory Jacobs.).

Hence, for Mr. Ronald Cross, the Sentence against him on count 22 must be served consecutively to that against him on count 21, and the Sentence against him on count 24 must be served consecutively to that against him on count 27.

For Gordon Lazore, the Sentence against him on count 22 must be served consecutively to that against him on count 21, and the Sentence against him on count 24 must be served consecutively to that against him on count 29.

Moreover, the legal issue has arisen as to whether, with respect to each of the accused, the Sentence against him on count 22 must or need not be served consecutively to that against him on count 24.

The position of the Crown is that it must, whereas the defence's position is that it need not and is subject to the general and ordinary principles governing of the question of whether Sentences are served consecutively or concurrently.

In MacLean vs R. ([1980] 13 C.R. [3d], 1), the Nova Scotia Court of Appeal ruled that, in imposing Sentence for a second offence under the then Section 83 Cr. C. (identical to the present Section 85), the court was obliged to make the Sentence for that offence consecutive to any other Sentence to which the accused was subject at the time that Sentence was imposed. It held that, in the result, all Sentences under Section 83 Cr. C. had to be consecutive to each other, as well as each one having to be consecutive to that on its own underlying offence.

Subsequently, the Alberta Court of Appeal refused to follow that of Nova Scotia in R. vs Jensen et al. ([1983] 3 C.C.C. [3d], 46), where it held that when an accused was convicted of a number of offences contrary to the then Section 83 Cr. C. of using a firearm while committing an indictable offence, each Sentence for an offence under the then Section 83 must be consecutive to that imposed for its underlying offence, but they need not be consecutive to each other.

Kerans, J.A., writing for the Court, ruled that the expression "…an offence arising out of the same event or series of events…" found in the then section 83(2) Cr. C., necessarily and only referred to the underlying or prerequisite offence in each case.

There then remained to consider the wording "…and to any other sentence to which he is subject at the time the sentence is imposed on him for an offence under subsection (1)."

That Court held that the latter phrase was ambiguous and, accordingly, the reasoning of <u>Paul vs R.</u> ([1982] 1 S.C.R., 621) would apply and cited (at page 49) the following extract from that case:

"The ordinary rules of interpretation would have us then look to discover Parliament's purpose and give those words whatever meaning within reasonable limits that would best serve the object Parliament set out to attain. But when dealing with a penal statute the rule is that, if in construing a statute there appears any reasonable ambiguity, it be resolved by giving the statute the meaning most favorable to the persons liable to penalty."

As to the ambiguous phrase in then Section 83(2), he felt it was reasonably capable of several meanings, declaring:

"The phrase under consideration is ambiguous: the expression 'to which he is subject' reasonably is capable of several meanings. A sentence to which a prisoner is 'subject' could mean only a sentence which he is actually serving, or also a sentence which he is not yet actually serving but which he has been ordered to serve, or also one which he has not yet been ordered to serve but which he might be ordered to serve because he has already pled guilty and sentence is pending, or also one which he might receive because he has been charged and the charge is pending and he might be convicted and he might be sentenced.

In <u>R. vs Martin (1911) 2 K.B. 450</u>, the English court made the point that a prisoner does not commence to serve a consecutive sentence until the future date set for its commencement, which is the day after the expiry of the sentence to which it is ordered to be consecutive. When, therefore, the sentencing judges in the cases at bar each came to sentence on the second firearm count, the sentence on the first firearm count arguably was not a sentence to which the accused was at that moment 'subject' because he had not yet begun to serve it because its commencement had been postponed. This construction is not exceptional and appears to be the one most favourable to persons liable to penalty." (At pages 49, 50)

He then concluded:

"In my view, s. 83(2) does not require a sentencing judge to impose a sentence consecutive to other consecutive sentences which the prisoner has not yet begun to serve." (At page 50)

— — — — — — — — — —

With respect, although I agree with his conclusion, I do not subscribe to the application of that English case in our Canadian criminal law in the light of Section 20(1) of the <u>Parole Act</u>, which decrees:

"Where, either before, on or after the coming into force of this section, a person sentenced to a term of imprisonment that has not expired is sentenced to an additional term of imprisonment, the terms of imprisonment to which the person has been sentenced <u>shall, for all purposes of the Criminal Code</u>, the Penitentiary Act, the Prison and Reformatories Act and this Act, except subsections (1.1), and (1.2), <u>be deemed to constitute one sentence consisting of a term of imprisonment commencing on the</u> earliest day on which any of the sentences of imprisonment commences and ending on the expiration of the last to expire of those terms of imprisonment." (R.S.C., c. P-2; underlining added.)

In <u>R. vs Goforth</u> ([1986] 24 C.C.C. [3d], 573), the British Columbia Court of Appeal aligned itself with that of Nova Scotia on this issue. Macdonald, J.A., writing for the Bench, discussed both MacLean and Jensen, and then stated as regards the last conclusion of Kerans, J.A., cited above:

"I am in respectful disagreement. There is no ambiguity in s. 83(2). A person is subject to a sentence which has been imposed upon him whether or not he has actually begun to serve it. It follows that in my view <u>R. vs MacLean</u> was correctly decided." (At page 576)

———————————————

Closer to home, in <u>Joly vs R.</u> (unreported; File No. 500-10-000409-803, Judgment of September 12th, 1983), the Quebec Court of Appeal seemed to also align itself on this issue with the view expressed in <u>MacLean</u> and later approved in <u>Goforth</u>.

That case concerned an accused who, in a single incident, had shot five people, none of whom died. He was charged with five counts of attempted murder and five counts under the then section 83 Cr. C.

At trial (unreported; Quebec Court of Sessions of the Peace, File No. 500-01-000690-807, Judgment dated November 3rd, 1980; Judge Marc Choquette), he was found guilty on all counts and the Judge sentenced him to twenty years on each count of attempted murder, all concurrent with each other, and then to one year consecutive on each of the five Section 83 offences.

The Appeal was only against Sentence and the Appeal Court diminished it, declaring.

"CONSIDÉRANT à l'égard des accusations relatives à l'usage d'une arme à feu, que le juge était tenu par l'article 83(2) du Code Criminel d'imposer une peine consécutive pour chacune des offenses distinctes;

CONSIDÉRANT que cette question a été considérée par la Cour d'appel d'Ontario dans R. vs. Woods and Feuerstein (65 C.C.C.(2)554) en ces termes (p.562):

'In our opinion, this submission is unsound. The wording of s. 83(1)(a) makes it abundantly clear <u>that a separate offence is committed</u> by a person under that section <u>each time that he uses a firearm in the commission of a separate indictable offence involving a separate transaction</u>. It is immaterial that the separate indictable offences are committed by such person within a short period of time or space of each other or that the same firearm is used by him in the

223

commission of each such separate offence.

CONSIDÉRANT qu'il y a eu tentative de meurtre à l'égard de cinq personnes différentes, chacune d'elles ayant été atteinte par un projectile tiré avec une arme à feu utilisée par l'appelant;

CONSIDÉRANT que ces tentatives de meurtre ont donné lieu à des condamnations différentes dans chaque cas;

CONSIDÉRANT qu'il devait par conséquent y avoir une peine consécutive sur chacun des chefs d'accusation;"(I have underlined)

Because it was not absolutely clear there if the five Sentences of one year pursuant to Section 83 were consecutive each to the others in addition to being consecutive each to its own underlying attempted murder charge, I obtained and examined the files in that case of both the Court of Sessions and of the Appeal Court.

In fact, the five one-year Sentences under then Section 83 were each consecutive to the others, as well as to the five concurrent twenty-year Sentences, so that the total Sentence there was twenty-five years.

However, the legal question being considered here was not invoked in the Inscription in Appeal nor pleaded there. Except for six lines, the fifteen-page Factum produced on behalf of the accused-appellant there discusses only the evidence of the various witnesses in respect of the facts of the case. Surprisingly, even though it was not an appeal against conviction, the legal argument there was restricted to the following:

(a) At page 12:

"Le droit: La poursuite prétend qu'elle a prouvé hors de tout doute raisonnable tous les éléments essentiels des infractions reprochées à l'appelant."

(b) At page 15:

"Le droit: L'appelant soumet que la poursuite n'a pas prouvé hors de tout doute raisonnable les éléments essentiels des crimes reprochés."

With respect, not a very profound argument in law even if the Appeal has been against conviction, let alone where it was only against Sentence.

Again, with the utmost deference for the Court of Appeal, the Woods Case cited by it does not stand for the question in issue here.

The issue there was expressed as follows:

"It was the submission of counsel for the appellant that the trial Judge should have left it to the jury as a question of fact whether there was one continuing use of a firearm. We understand his argument to be that it was open to the jury to so find and accordingly only one conviction should have been registered under s. 83(1)(a) of the Criminal Code of Canada." (At page 562)

The paragraph in the Woods Judgment which follows the one I have cited immediately above is the one quoted by the Quebec Appeal Court in its Judgment in Joly, and merely states that there can be multiple convictions under Section 83: (now Section 85 Cr. C.) where there are separate transactions, as in our case there are two separate victims.

Hence, even though in the Woods Case the Ontario Court of Appeal confirmed Sentences under the then Section 83 which were to be served consecutively to each other as well as to each one's underlying offence, no one questions in the present case that multiple Sentences under Section 85 Cr. C. **may** be consecutive to each other. The question is, **must** they be?

In R. vs Cheetham ([1980] 53 C.C.C. [2d], 109), the Ontario Court of Appeal ruled that the provision for a three-year minimum for subsequent offences under then Section 83 applied only to an offence committed subsequent to a prior conviction on such an offence, not to multiple Section 83 Cr. C. offences under the same indictment, as here.

There, however, defence counsel argued that not only was it not required to do so, but that one could not impose consecutive Sentences for multiple Section 83 offences in the same indictment.

We read there:

"I do not accept Mr. Gold's additional argument that s. 83(2) does not permit sentences imposed under s. 83(1) to be consecutive to each other. The submission is answered by the recent decision of the Appeal Division of the Supreme Court of Nova Scotia in **R. vs MacLean** (1979) 49 C.C.C. (2d) 552, 12 C.R. (3d) 1, 32 N.S.R. (2d) 650, whose conclusion and reasons I adopt on this point." (At page 118; my underlining).

———————————————

Now, in analysing Section 85(2) Cr. C., it seems that all agree that the phrase "...shall be served consecutively to any other punishment imposed on him for an offence arising out of the same event or series of events..." means, for each Section 85 offence, its own underlying or prerequisite offence.

The real issue here is the meaning of the following phrase, which reads:

"...and to any other sentence to which he is subject at the time the sentence is imposed on him for an offence under subsection (1)."

———————————————

Pursuant to Section 721(1) Cr. C., a Sentence commences when it is imposed. Therefore, contrary to the view of Kerans, J.A., an accused is subject to a Sentence the moment it is imposed upon him.

Clearly, one is also subject to any Sentence which one is already actually serving. However, it is my view that one is not necessarily yet serving a Sentence to which one is subject because it has just been imposed upon one.

In the opinion of the undersigned, when a Sentence is imposed, one only starts to actually serve it when one is delivered over to the Director of a Penal Institution together with a Warrant of Committal.

Thus, the French version of Section 85(2) Cr. C. is of great importance here because the equivalent phrase speaks of any other Sentence which the accused **is serving** at that time and not of any other Sentence to which he is subject at that time. The French version declares:

"La sentence imposée à une personne pour une infraction prévue au paragraphe (1) est purgée consécutivement à toute autre peine imposée pour une autre infraction basée sur les mêmes faits et **à toute autre sentence qu'elle purge à ce moment-là.**" (Emphasis added.)

To "purger" a Sentence is to be actually serving it. None of the cases I have mentioned above from the Provinces of Nova Scotia, Ontario, Alberta and British Columbia discussed or inquired into the French version of that subsection.

————————————

Now, pursuant to the following constitutional and statutory texts, the French and English versions of all Laws of Canada are each equally official, authentic and authoritative.

Section 16(1) of the <u>Canadian Charter of Rights and Freedom</u> decrees:

"English and French are the official languages of Canada and have equality of status and equal rights and privileges as to their use in all institutions of the Parliament and government of Canada."

The first paragraph of the Preamble to the <u>Official Languages Act</u> (R.S.C., c. 0-3.01) declares:

"Whereas the Constitution of Canada provides that English and French are the official languages of Canada and have equality of status and equal rights and privileges as to their use in all institutions of the Parliament and government of Canada."

Then, Sections 2(a), 6 and 13 of that <u>Act</u> state:

"2. The purpose of this Act is to

(a) ensure respect for English and French as the official languages of Canada and ensure equality of status and equal rights and privileges as to their use in all federal institutions, in particular with respect to their use in parliamentary proceedings, <u>in legislative and other instruments,</u> in the administration of justice, in communicating with or providing services to the public and in carrying out the work of federal institutions.

6. All Acts of Parliament shall be enacted, printed and published in <u>both official languages</u>.

13. Any journal, record, <u>Act of Parliament</u>, instrument, document, rule, order, regulation, treaty, convention, agreement, notice, advertisement or other matter referred to in this Part that is <u>made, enacted, printed, published or tabled in both official languages</u> shall be made, enacted, printed, published or tabled simultaneously in both languages, and <u>both language versions are equally authoritative</u>." (Underlining added)

It is commonly accepted that, when the French and English texts of a Section of the Criminal Code have different meanings, since both versions are equally authoritative, the rule enunciated by the Supreme Court of Canada in <u>Paul</u> is triggered and the Court must apply the version which is more favorable to an accused, being the French version in the present case.

Hence, although by a different path of reasoning, I reach the same conclusion as <u>Kerans, J.A.</u> did in <u>Jensen</u>. It is my view that once I impose the Sentences on the accused here this morning, they are immediately "subject to them," but at the moment I will leave this Courtroom, they will not yet have begun to "serve them."

Hence, with deference to those who hold the contrary view, it is my opinion that it is not obligatory that multiple Sentences under Section 85 Cr. C. be served consecutively to each other, but only for each one to be served consecutively to its underlying or prerequisite offence.

Of course, a Judge always has the discretion to declare whether more than one Section 85 Cr. C. offence in the same indictment shall be served either consecutively or concurrently with each other, based upon the general principles which govern that question.

In the present case, since it was one incident, albeit that two victims were involved, and since one firearm was used at the same time and in the same way for each of the two victims together, the Sentences for both accused under counts 22 and 24 will each be served concurrently with the other, although consecutively each to its underlying or prerequisite offence.

Having decided this, the third and constitutional issue raised by Mtre Peris in his written Motion dated January 29th, 1992 is now moot.

— — — — — — — — — —

Perhaps the irony will not be lost on the accused and their counsel. After the bitter struggle which they waged last April on the language issue and the question of whether or not the Crown prosecutors had the right to use French in this trial, it is the French version of Section 85(2) Cr. C. which saves each of the accused from at least one more consecutive year of imprisonment!

———————————————

Although none of the attorneys mentioned during the representations on Sentence, the law obliges me in the present case to impose on each of the accused an order pursuant to Section 100(1) Cr. C. Section 100(1) and (2) declare the following:

"100(1) Where an offender is convicted or discharged under section 736 of an indictable offence in the commission of which violence against a person is used, threatened or attempted and for which the offender may be sentenced to imprisonment for ten years or more or of an offence under section 85, the court that sentences the offender **shall**, in addition to any other punishment that may be imposed for that offence, make an order prohibiting the offender from having in his possession any firearm or any ammunition or explosive substance for any period of time specified in the order that commences on the day the order is made and **expires not earlier** than

(a) in the case of a first conviction for such an offence, **five years**, and

b) in any other case, ten years,

after the time of the offender's release from imprisonment after conviction for the offence or, if the offender is not then imprisoned or subject to imprisonment, after the time of the offender's conviction or discharge for that offence.

(2) Where an offender is convicted or discharged under section 736 of an offence involving the use, carriage, possession, handling, shipping or storage of any firearm or ammunition or any offence, other than an offence referred to in subsection (1), in the commission of which violence against a person was used, threatened or attempted, the court that sentences the offender **may**, in addition to any other punishment that may be

imposed for that offence, make an order prohibiting the offender from having in his possession any firearm or any ammunition or explosive substance for any period of time specified in the order that commences on the day the order is made and **expires not later than five years** after the time of the offender's release from imprisonment after conviction for the offence or, if the offender is not then imprisoned or subject to imprisonment, after the time of the offender's conviction or discharge from that offence." (My emphasis)

It will be noted that under subsection (2), the maximum duration of such an order is from the time of its imposition until a date **not later** than five years after the offender's release from imprisonment, whereas under subsection (1), for a first offence, the minimum period is to expire **not earlier** than five years after the time of the offender's release from imprisonment. Subsection (1) does not fix any maximum duration for such an order.

Moreover, under subsection (2) the Court **may** make such an order, whereas under subsection (1) the Court **shall** make such an order.

In the present instance, although subsection (2) can apply to Ronald Cross but not to Gordon Lazore, it is for the purpose of such orders superseded by subsection (1). Each of the accused has been convicted of two offences under Section 85 Cr. C. and, as well, of other indictable offences in the commission of which violence against a person was used and which are punishable by imprisonment for 10 years or more.

I will therefore be issuing an order against each accused under Section 100(1) Cr. C.

Moreover, Section 100(13) Cr. C. declares:

"An order made pursuant to subsection (1), (2), (6) or (7) **shall** specify therein a reasonable period of time within which the person against whom the order is made may surrender to a police officer or firearms officer or otherwise lawfully dispose of any firearm or any ammunition or explosive substance lawfully possessed by him prior to the making of the order, and subsection (12) does not apply to him during that period of time." (Emphasis added)

In fixing the Sentence under each count against each accused, I must weigh, balance and apply all the principles, criteria, rules, concepts and all mitigating and aggravating factors, and moreover, in the light of all the facts and circumstances of the case.

As Mackay J.A. put it so well in R. vs Willaert ([1953] 105 C.C.C., 172 [Ont. C.A.]), a fit and just Sentence requires a "wise blending" of all those principles, criteria, rules and concepts.

In doing so, leaving aside for the moment the credits or reductions for the pre-Sentence detention of both accused, which will be fifteen months in the case of Ronald Cross and thirteen months in the case of Gordon Lazore, the following are the Sentences which I would have imposed for each accused on all the counts, had there not been any pre-Sentence detention:

A: GORDON LAZORE:

Count 21: Aggravated assault against Francis Jacobs—2 years imprisonment;

Count 22: Use of firearm while committing an aggravated assault against Francis Jacobs—1 year imprisonment;

Count 24: Use of firearm while committing an assault on Cory Jacobs—1 year imprisonment;

Count 26: Mischief in relation to Francis Jacobs' automobile—nine months imprisonment;

Count 29: Assault against Cory Jacobs while carrying a weapon, to wit a baseball bat—eighteen months imprisonment.

Since in the case of two of those counts, the pre-reduction terms of imprisonment exceed thirteen months, the second issue raised by Mtre Peris in his January 29th Motion in relation to Gordon Lazore is also moot.

B: RONALD CROSS:

Count 21: Aggravated assault against Francis Jacobs—three years and four months imprisonment;

Count 22: Use of firearm while committing an aggravated assault against Francis Jacobs—eighteen months imprisonment;

Count 24: Use of firearm while committing an assault on Cory Jacobs—one year imprisonment;

Count 25: Uttering threat to Cory Jacobs—one year imprisonment;

Count 26: Mischief in relation to the automobile of Francis Jacobs—nine months imprisonment;

Count 27: Assault on Cory Jacobs while carrying a weapon—eighteen months imprisonment;

Count 31: Mischief in relation to ambulance, owned by Kanehsatake Mobile Services—eighteen months imprisonment;

Count 32: Mischief in relation to ambulance owned by Ambulances Joliette—eighteen months imprisonment

--- --- --- --- ---

Count 38: Having in possession a weapon for a purpose dangerous to the public peace while in the presence of Patrick Cloutier—two years imprisonment;

Count 40: Having in possession a weapon for a purpose dangerous to the public peace while in the presence of Jacques Brault—two years imprisonment;

Count 43: Having in possession a weapon for a purpose dangerous to the public peace, while in the presence of Michel Chulak—two years imprisonment;

Count 46: Having in possession a weapon for a purpose dangerous to the public peace while in the presence of Stéphane Tremblay—two years imprisonment;

Count 48: Having in possession a weapon for a purpose dangerous to the public peace while in the presence of Stéphane Desgagné—two years imprisonment;

Count 49: Simple assault against Michel Roy—six months imprisonment;

Count 50: Uttering threat to Michel Roy—six months imprisonment;

Count 52: Having in possession a weapon for a purpose dangerous to the public peace while in the presence of Sabin Renaud—eighteen months imprisonment;

Count 55: Having in possession a weapon for a purpose dangerous to the public peace while in the presence of Mario De Mariano— two years imprisonment;

Since in 11 of those counts, specifically counts 21, 27, 31, 32, 38, 40, 43, 46, 48, 52 and 55, the pre-reduction terms of imprisonment exceed fifteen months, the second issue raised by Mtre Peris in his January 29th Motion in relation to Ronald Cross is also moot.

FOR ALL THE FOREGOING REASONS, GORDON LAZORE, THE COURT HEREBY SENTENCES YOU AS FOLLOWS:

ON COUNT 21: to eleven months imprisonment;

ON COUNT 22: to twelve months imprisonment;

ON COUNT 24: to twelve months imprisonment;

ON COUNT 26: to the time already served in detention; and

ON COUNT 29: to five months imprisonment.

The Sentences on Counts 21 and 29 shall be served concurrently with each other;

The Sentences on Counts 22 and 24 shall be served concurrently with each other;

The Sentence on Count 22 shall be served consecutively to that on Count 21;

The Sentence on Count 24 shall be served consecutively to that on Count 29.

Hence, for the purpose of evaluating the "totality principle", the total Sentence for Gordon Lazore is **TWENTY-THREE MONTHS** imprisonment, which I find to be fit and just in the circumstances and thus that total Sentence meets the requirements of the totality principle.

GORDON LAZORE, pursuant to Section 100(1) Cr. C., the Court hereby makes an Order against you prohibiting you from having in your possession any firearm or any ammunition or explosive substance for a period commencing today and **expiring five years** after you will be released from imprisonment.

Pursuant to Section 100(13) Cr. C., the Court hereby fixes at 30 days the period of time within which you may surrender to a police officer or firearms officer or otherwise lawfully dispose of any firearm or any ammunition or

230

explosive substance lawfully possessed by you prior to the making of the fore-going Order under Section 100(1.) Cr. C.

——————————————

Moreover, <u>GORDON LAZORE</u>, the Court orders you to pay within 30 days a Victim Fine Surcharge as provided for in Section 727.9(1) Cr. C. and the Regulations adopted pursuant thereto.

————————————

FOR ALL THE FOREGOING REASONS, RONALD CROSS, THE COURT HEREBY SENTENCES YOU AS FOLLOWS:
<u>ON COUNT 21:</u> to twenty-five months imprisonment;
<u>ON COUNT 22:</u> to eighteen months imprisonment;
<u>ON COUNT 24:</u> to twelve months imprisonment;
<u>ON COUNT 25:</u> to the time already served in detention;
<u>ON COUNT 26:</u> to the time already served in detention;
<u>ON COUNT 27:</u> to three months imprisonment;
<u>ON COUNT 31:</u> to three months imprisonment;
<u>ON COUNT 32:</u> to three months imprisonment;

——————————————

<u>ON COUNT 38:</u> to nine months imprisonment;
<u>ON COUNT 40:</u> to nine months imprisonment;
<u>ON COUNT 43:</u> to nine months imprisonment;
<u>ON COUNT 46:</u> to nine months imprisonment;
<u>ON COUNT 48:</u> to nine months imprisonment;
<u>ON COUNT 49:</u> to the time already served in detention;
<u>ON COUNT 50:</u> to the time already served in detention;
<u>ON COUNT 52:</u> to three months imprisonment; and
<u>ON COUNT 55:</u> to nine months imprisonment.

——————————————

The Sentences on Counts 21, 27, 31 and 32 shall be served concurrently, each with the others;
The Sentences on Counts 22 and 24 shall be served concurrently with each other;
The Sentence on Count 22 shall be served consecutively to that on Count 21;
The Sentence on Count 24 shall be served consecutively to that on Count 27;
The Sentences on Counts 38, 40, 43, 46, 48, 52 and 55 shall be served concurrently as among themselves, but consecutively to the Sentences on Counts 21, 22, 24, 27, 31 and 32.

——————————————

Hence, for the purpose of evaluating the "totality principle," the total Sentence for RONALD CROSS is **FIFTY-TWO MONTHS** imprisonment, which I find to be fit and just in the circumstances and thus that total Sentence meets the requirements of the totality principle.

RONALD CROSS, Pursuant to Section 100(1) Cr. C., the Court hereby makes an Order against you prohibiting you from having in your possession any firearm or any ammunition or explosive substance for a period commencing today and **expiring ten years** after you will be released from imprisonment.

Pursuant to Section 100(13) Cr. C., the Court hereby fixes at 30 days the period of time within which you may surrender to a police officer or firearms officer or otherwise lawfully dispose of any firearm or any ammunition or explosive substance lawfully possessed by you prior to the making of the foregoing Order under Section 100(1) Cr. C.

Moreover, RONALD CROSS, the Court orders you to pay within 30 days a Victim Fine Surcharge as provided for in Section 727.9(1) Cr. C. and the Regulations adopted pursuant thereto.

(S) Benjamin J. Greenberg, J.S.C.
BENJAMIN J. GREENBERG, J.S.C.

Mr. François Brière
Crown Counsel,

Mr. Jocelyne Provost
Special Counsel for the Attorney-General of Quebec,

Mr. Julio Péris
Counsel for Ronald Cross,

Mr. Owen Young
Counsel for Gordon Lazore.

CANADA
PROVINCE OF QUEBEC
DISTRICT OF MONTREAL

C O U R T   O F   A P P E A L

No: 700-01-000009-913

RONALD CROSS
GORDON LAZORE

Appellants-accused

—vs—

HER MAJESTY THE QUEEN

Respondent

N O T I C E   O F   A P P E A L
(s. 675(1)a)i), Criminal Code)

1.— On January 22, 1992, the appellants were found guilty at St. Jérôme, District of Terrebonne by the Superior Court composed of a judge and jury and presided over by The Honourable Mr. Justice Benjamin Greenberg.

2.— Further on January 22, 1992, the appellant Ronald Cross was found guilty on the following counts:

20. That Ronald Cross (57-11-09) and Gordon Lazore (59-02-02), on or about September, the 1st 1990, at Oka district of Terrebonne, did in committing an assault upon Francis Jacobs, cause bodily harm to him contrary to section 267 (1)b) of the Criminal Code.

21. That Ronald Cross (57-11-09) and Gordon Lazore (59-02-02), on or about September, the 1st, 1990, at Oka district of Terrebonne, did wound Francis Jacobs, thereby committing an aggravated assault contrary to section 268(1) of the Criminal Code.

22. That Ronald Cross (57-11-09) and Gordon Lazore (59-02-02), on or about September, the 1st, 1990, at Oka district of Terrebonne, did use a firearm while committing an indictable offence, to wit an assault on Francis Jacobs, contrary to section 85(1)a) of the Criminal Code.

23. That Ronald Cross (57-11-09) and Gordon Lazore (59-02-02), on or about September, the 1st, 1990, at Oka district of Terrebonne, did without lawful excuse point a firearm at Cory Jacobs, contrary to section 86(1)a) of the Criminal Code.

24. That Ronald Cross (57-11-09) and Gordon Lazore (59-02-02), on or about September, the 1st, 1990, at Oka district of Terrebonne, did use a firearm while committing an indictable offence, to wit an assault on Cory Jacobs, contrary to section 85(1)a) of the Criminal Code.

25. That Ronald Cross (57-11-09) and Gordon Lazore (59-02-02), on or about September, the 1st, 1990, at Oka district of Terrebonne, did knowingly utter a threat to Cory Jacobs to cause serious bodily harm to the said Cory Jacobs, contrary to section 264 (1)a)(2) of the Criminal Code.

26. That Ronald Cross (57-11-09) and Gordon Lazore (59-02-02), on or about September, the 1st, 1990, at Oka district of Terrebonne, did commit mischief by wilfully damaging without legal justification or excuse and without colour of right, property to wit the automobile of Francis Jacobs, the value of which exceeded one thousand dollars, contrary to section 430(1)a) of the Criminal Code.

27. That Ronald Cross (57-11-09), on or about September, the 1st, 1990, at Oka district of Terrebonne, did in committing an assault on Cory Jacobs carry an imitation of a firearm, contrary to section 267(1)a) of the Criminal Code.

28. That Ronald Cross (57-11-09), on or about September, the 1st, 1990, at Oka district of Terrebonne, did have in his possession an imitation of a weapon, for a purpose dangerous to the public peace, while in the presence of Cory and Francis Jacobs, contrary to section 87 of the Criminal Code.

31. That Ronald Cross (57-11-09), on or about September, the 1st, 1990, at Oka district of Terrebonne, did commit mischief by wilfully damaging without legal justification or excuse and without colour of right property to wit an ambulance vehicle, Dodge 1986 of Ronald Bonspille, the value of which exceeded one thousand dollars, contrary to section 430(1)a) of the Criminal Code.

32. That Ronald Cross (57-11-09), on or about September, the 1st, 1990, at Oka district of Terrebonne, did commit mischief by wilfully damaging without legal justification or excuse and without colour of right property to wit an ambulance vehicle, Chevrolet 1985 of Ambulance Joliette, the value of which exceeded one thousand dollars, contrary to section 430(1)a) of the Criminal Code.

38. That Ronald Cross (57-11-09), on or about September, the 1st, 1990, at Oka district of Terrebonne, did have in his possession a weapon or an imitation of a weapon, for a purpose dangerous to the public peace, while in the presence of Patrick Cloutier, contrary to section 87 of the Criminal Code.

40. That Ronald Cross (57-11-09), on or about September, the 1st, 1990, at Oka district of Terrebonne, did have in his possession a weapon or an imitation of a weapon, for a purpose dangerous to the public peace, while in the presence of Jacques Brault, contrary to section 87 of the Criminal Code.

43. That Ronald Cross (57-11-09), on or about September, the 1st, 1990, at Oka district of Terrebonne, did have in his possession a weapon or an imitation of a weapon, for a purpose dangerous to the public peace, while in the presence of Michel Chulak, contrary to section 87 of the Criminal Code.

46. That Ronald Cross (57-11-09), on or about September, the 1st, 1990,

at Oka district of Terrebonne, did have in his possession a weapon or an imitation of a weapon, for a purpose dangerous to the public peace, while in the presence of Stéphane Tremblay, Contrary to section 87 of the Criminal Code.

48. That Ronald Cross (57-11-09), on or about September, the 2nd, 1990, at Oka district of Terrebonne, did have in his possession a weapon or an imitation of a weapon, for a purpose dangerous to the public peace, while in the presence of Stéphane Desgagné, contrary to section 87 of the Criminal Code.

49. That Ronald Cross (57-11-09), on or about September, the 6th, 1990, at Oka district of Terrebonne, did commit an assault on Michel Roy, member of the Canadian Armed Forces, contrary to section 266(a) of the Criminal Code.

50. That Ronald Cross (57-11-09), on or about September, the 6th, 1990, at Oka district of Terrebonne, did knowingly utter a threat to Michel Roy, member of the Canadian Armed Forces, to cause death or serious bodily harm, to the said Michel Roy, contrary to section 264 (1)a) of the Criminal Code.

52. That Ronald Cross (57-11-09), on or about September, the 25th, 1990, at Oka district of Terrebonne, did have in his possession a weapon or an imitation of a weapon, for a purpose dangerous to the public peace, while in the presence of Sabin Renaud, member of the Canadian Armed Forces, contrary to section 87 of the Criminal Code.

55. That Ronald Cross (57-11-09), on or about September, the 25th, 1990, at Oka district of Terrebonne, did have in his possession a weapon or an imitation of a weapon, for a purpose dangerous to the public peace, while in the presence of Mario De Mariano, member of the Canadian Armed Forces, contrary to section 87 of the Criminal Code.

3. — Further of January 22, 1992, the appellant Gordon Lazore was found guilty on the following counts:

19 That Gordon Lazore (59-02-02), on or about September, the 1st, 1990, at Oka district of Terrebonne, did in committing an assault on Francis Jacobs carry a weapon, to wit a baseball bat, contrary to section 267(1)a) of the Criminal Code.

20. That Ronald Cross (57-11-09) and Gordon Lazore (59-02-02), on or about September, the 1st, 1990, at Oka district of Terrebonne, did in committing an assault upon Francis Jacobs, cause bodily harm to him contrary to section 267(1)b) of the Criminal Code.

21. That Ronald Cross (57-11-09) and Gordon Lazore (59-02-02), on or about September, the 1st, 1990, at Oka district of Terrebonne, did wound Francis Jacobs, thereby committing an aggravated assault contrary to section 268(1) of the Criminal Code.

22. That Ronald Cross (57-11-09) and Gordon Lazore (59-02-02), on or about September, the 1st, 1990, at Oka district of Terrebonne, did use a firearm while committing a indictable offence, to wit an assault on Francis Jacobs, contrary to section 85(1)a) of the Criminal Code.

23. That Ronald Cross (57-11-09) and Gordon Lazore (59-02-02), on or

about September, the 1st, 1990, at Oka district of Terrebonne, did without lawful excuse point a firearm at Cory Jacobs, contrary to section 86(1)a) of the Criminal Code.

24. That Ronald Cross (57-11-09) and Gordon Lazore (59-02-02), on or about September, the 1st, 1990, at Oka district of Terrebonne, did use a firearm while committing an indictable offence, to wit an assault on Cory Jacobs, contrary to section 85(1)a) of the Criminal Code.

26. That Ronald Cross (57-11-09) and Gordon Lazore (59-02-02), on or about September, the 1st, 1990, at Oka district of Terrebonne, did commit mischief by wilfully damaging without legal justification or excuse and without colour of right, property to wit the automobile of Francis Jacobs, the value of which exceeded one thousand dollars, contrary to section 430(1)a) of the Criminal Code.

29. That Gordon Lazore (59-02-02), on or about September, the 1st, 1990, at Oka district of Terrebonne, did in committing an assault on Cory Jacobs carry a weapon, to wit a baseball bat, contrary to section 267(1)a) of the Criminal Code.

30. That Gordon Lazore (59-02-02), on or about September, the 1st, 1990, at Oka district of Terrebonne, did have in his possession a weapon, to wit a baseball bat, for a purpose dangerous to the public peace, contrary to section 87 of the Criminal Code.

4. — Pursuant to the application of the principles in Kienapple vs. The Queen, Mr. Justice Benjamin Greenberg ordered a conditional stay of proceedings in respect of the convictions of Ronald Cross by the jury on counts 20, 23, 28 and regarding Gordon Lazore on counts 19, 20, 23, 30.

5. — The appellants appeal against their conviction on the following grounds:

.1 The learned trial judge erred by failing to stay proceedings in respect of all of the counts in the indictment in order to protect the right of the accused to a fair trial and their right to make full answer and defence in the face of the failure by the prosecution to meet its obligations to the accused to give full, candid and timely disclosure.

.2 The learned trial judge erred by failing to stay proceedings in respect of counts 19 to 30 of the indictment in order to protect the right of the accused to a fair trial and their right to make full answer and defence in the face of the failure or refusal of the prosecution to call Cory Jacobs and Maurice Binette, material witnesses to the events that were the subject of these counts of the indictment.

.3 The learned trial judge erred by failing to stay proceedings in respect of counts 19 to 30 of the indictment in order to protect the right of the accused to a fair trial and their right to make full answer and defence in the face of the untimely disclosure by the prosecution of the evidence to be given by Angus Nelson, a material witnesses to the events that were the subject of these counts of the indictment.

.4 The learned trial judge erred in failing to compel the prosecution to give full, candid and timely disclosure to the defence electing instead to grant inadequate and insufficient remedies only after the failures of the prosecution had come to light, thereby compromising the defence of the appellants and depriving them of their right to make full answer and defence.

.5 The learned trial judge erred by failing to order a stay of proceedings in the face of the failure of the prosecution to honour its obligation to place before the jury all material information that could reasonably be expected to assist them in arriving at a verdict.

.6 The learned trial judge erred in failing to order that the accused Ronald Cross be tried separately in respect of the two groups of counts:

— Group 1: Counts 1-36
— Group 2: Counts 37-59

.7 The learned trial judge erred in failing to order that the accused Ronald Cross be tried separately in respect of the two groups of counts particularized in sub-paragraph 6, supra, thereby prejudicing Gordon Lazore.

.8 The learned trial judge erred in concluding that the right against self-incrimination enjoyed by the accused Ronald Cross did not merit or warrant protection thereby compromising the defence of the appellants and depriving them of their right to make full answer and defence.

.9 The learned trial judge erred in precluding defence counsel from explaining to the jury in the course of their addresses the true reasons, as expressed to the court in the absence of the jury, why no witnesses had been called on behalf of Ronald Cross or Gordon Lazore, thereby compromising the defence of the appellants and depriving them of their right to make full answer and defence.

.10 The learned trial judge erred by failing to explain to the jury the legal principles applicable to the essential element of mens rea as it applied to every count in the indictment, an error rendered all the more prejudicial to the accused because of the trial judge's having forbidden defence counsel from explaining principles of law in the course of their addresses to the jury.

.11 The learned trial judge misdirected the jury as to the operation of s. 21 of the Criminal Code and its application to Gordon Lazore in respect of counts 20, 21, 22, 23, 24, 27 of the indictment.

.12 The learned trial judge misdirected the jury on the principles of self-defence as the applied to Gordon Lazore in respect of counts 20, 21, 24, 29, 30 in the indictment.

.13 The learned trial judge erred by offering the jury his speculations, unsupported by the evidence, as to the events underlying and surrounding counts 19 to 30 of the indictment.

.14 The learned trial judge erred in failing to instruct the jury that they could draw adverse inferences as a result of the failure of the prosecution to call Cory Jacobs, Maurice Binette and Stéphane Tremblay material witnesses to the events that were the subject of counts 19 to 30 and 46, and by failing to explain and to particularize the nature of the adverse inference that was open to the jury to draw.

.15 The learned trial judge erred in charging the jury be using only selective references to the evidence and otherwise generally in a manner that favoured the prosecution to the prejudice and detriment of the accused appellants.

.16 The learned trial judge erred by selectively reviewing the evidence in such a way as to dismantle systematically the defences that had been raised by was of cross-examination.

.17 The learned trial judge misdirected the jury to the effect that the proceedings were solely adversarial in nature without explaining the obligations of the prosecution to place before the jury all material information that could reasonably be expected to assist them in arriving at a verdict thereby leaving the jury with the inference and impression that the accused had an obligation to present evidence not called by the prosecution.

.18 The learned trial judge erred in concluding that the Optional Protocols to the Geneva Convention did not apply to the circumstances of the Oka crisis and to the events that were the subject of the indictment generally.

.19 The learned trial judge erred in concluding that the direct indictment was not overloaded and as such the inclusions of all these offences against the appellants could show a propensity to violence on their part thereby prejudicing them in their defence.

6. — The appellants ask to plead orally and in writing.

FOR ALL OF THESE GROUNDS, MAY IT PLEASE THIS HONOURABLE COURT:

TO SET ASIDE THE VERDICTS OF GUILTY

TO ORDER NEW SEPARATE TRIALS

TO ORDER A PERMANENT STAY ON THE DIRECT INDICTMENT.

Montreal, February 20, 1992

(S) JULIO PERIS

PERIS GOLDENBERG

(Julio Peris)

Attorney for the Appellants

APPENDIX 2

"WE ARE PERHAPS BROTHERS"

"WE ARE PERHAPS BROTHERS"

This speech was given by Chief Seattle before the Assembly of the Tribes, in 1854.

The Great Father in Washington has told us of his wish to buy our land.

The Great Father has told us of his friendship and of his goodwill. He is very generous because we know that he has little need of our friendship in return.

However, we shall consider his offer, because we know that if we do not sell, the White man will come with his guns and take our land.

But how can you buy or sell the sky, the warmth of the earth? For us it is a strange idea!

If we are not the owners of the coolness of the air, nor of the sheen of the water, then how can you buy it from us?

The smallest bit of this land is sacred to my people. Each shining pine needle, each sandy shoal, each wisp of fog in the dark wood, each clearing, the buzzing of the insects, all of this is sacred to the memory and the life of my people. The sap that runs in the trees bears the memories of the red man.

The White man's dead, when they walk among the stars, forget their native land. Our dead never forget the beauty of this land, because she is the mother of the red man; we belong to this land as it belongs to us.

The sweet-smelling flowers are our sisters, the elk, the horse, the great eagle are our brothers; the crests of the mountains, the essences of the prairies, the poney's warm body, and man himself, all belong to the same family.

Thus, when he asks to buy our land, the Great Father in Washington asks much of us.

The Great Father has assured us that he would set aside a corner of it for us, where we could live in comfort, with our children, and that he would be our father, and we his children.

So we will consider your offer to buy our land, but it will not be easy because for us, this land is sacred.

The glimmering water of the streams and of the rivers is not merely water; it is the blood of our ancestors. If we sell our land to you, you will have to remember that it is sacred, and you will have to teach this to your children and show them that each ghostly reflection in the clear water of the lakes tells the story and the memories of my people. The murmur of the brook is the voice of my father's father.

The rivers are our brothers; they quench our thirst. The rivers carry our canoes and nourish our children. If we sell our land to you, you must remember that the rivers are our brothers and yours, and you must teach it to your children, and from now on you must show them the kindness you would show a brother.

The red man has always retreated before the white man, as the mountain mist retreats before the rising sun. But the ashes of our fathers are sacred. Their graves are on sacred ground; thus, these hills, these trees, this bit of land are sacred in our eyes. We know that the White man does not understand our thoughts. For him, one bit of land is the same as any other because he is the stranger who comes in the night to plunder the land for his needs. The earth is not his brother but rather his enemy, and when he has conquered it, he goes on his way. He leaves behind the graves of his fathers and does not care.

You must teach your children that the land beneath their feet is made of the ashes of our forefathers. So that they might respect it, tell your children that the land is rich with the life of our people. Teach your children what we teach our children, that the land is our mother. Everything that happens to the land happens to the sons of the land. When men spit on the land, they spit on themselves.

We know this: the land does not belong to man, it is man who belongs to the land. We know this: all things are joined like the blood that joins the same family. All things are joined.

Everything that happens to the land happens to the sons of the land. Man has not woven the web of life, he is but a thread of that web. Everything he does to the web, he does to himself.

But we will consider your offer to go to the reservation that you have put aside for my people. We will live by ourselves and in peace. What does it matter where we will spend the rest of our days? Our children have seen their fathers humbled by defeat. Our Warriors have known shame; after the defeat, they waste their days in idleness and sully their bodies with soft foods and strong drink. What does it matter where we will spend the rest of our days? They are not many. A few more hours, a few more winters, and there will be nothing left of the children of the great tribes who used to live on this land, or who still roam in the woods in small numbers; none will be there to shed tears on the graves of a people once so powerful, so full of hope as ours. But why cry for the end of my people? Tribes are made of men, no more. Men come and go, like the waves of the sea.

Even the White man, whose God walks with him and speaks to him as a friend with a friend, cannot escape the common fate. Perhaps we are brothers after all, we shall see. But we know one thing which the White man may discover one day: our God is the same God. You might think today that you own Him as you would like to own our land, but you cannot. He is the God of men, and his compassion is the same for the red man as for the White man.

The land is precious in His eyes, and he who wounds the land fills its creator with contempt. The White People shall pass also, and perhaps before the other tribes. Continue to sully your beds and, one fine evening, you will choke on your own refuse.

But in your loss, you will burn with dazzling fire, lit by the power of the God who brought you to this land and who, for reasons known to Him, gave you power over this land and over the red man. This fate is for us a mystery; we do not understand, when the buffalo are all slaughtered, the wild horses all tamed, when the secret reaches of the forests are heavy with the smell of many men, the look of the ripening hills is ruined by the wires that talk.

Where is the thicket? Gone. Where is the eagle? He is no more. What does it mean to say good-bye to the nimble poney and to the hunt? It is the end of living and the beginning of survival.

So we will consider your offer to buy our land. And if we accept, it will be to make very certain of receiving this reservation which you have promised us. There, perhaps, we will be able to end the brief days we have left to live in the manner that we wish. And when the last red man will have gone from this land, and that his memory shall be nothing but the shadow of a cloud gliding over the prairie, these shores and these rivers will still shelter the spirits of my people. Because they love this land as the newborn loves the heartbeat of its mother. Thus, if we sell our land to you, love it as we have loved it. Care for it as we have cared for it.

Keep in mind the memory of this country, as it is in the moment that you take it. And with all your might, with all your mind, with all your heart, preserve it for your children, and love it as God loves us all.

We know one thing: our God is the same God. He loves this land. The White man himself cannot escape the common fate. WE ARE PERHAPS BROTHERS. We shall see.

CHRONOLOGY OF EVENTS

1957

NOVEMBER 9. Birth of Ronald Cross in Brooklyn, New York.

1969

The Cross family moves to Kahnawake.

1990

MARCH 11. Oka: The Mohawks erect a barricade on a side road that leads to Route 344 in order to protest against the expansion of the golf course which would destroy the Pines of Oka, their ancestral lands, and the Cemetery of their ancestors. Jean Ouellette, the mayor of Oka, obtains an injunction forcing the Mohawks to dismantle their barricades. The Mohawks refuse.

APRIL 13. Ronald Cross is found guilty of assaulting a police officer. He is fined $250.

JULY 11. In an armed assault, the Sûreté du Québec charges the Oka barricade, which is protected by the Mohawk Warrior Society. SQ Corporal Marcel Lemay, 31 years old, is killed.

• The SQ surrounds the barricades at Oka and at Kahnawake.

JULY 12. The Quebec Minister of Indian Affairs, John Ciaccia, comes to Oka in an attempt to reestablish order. The Mohawks demand the departure of the SQ. The Minister replies that the SQ will leave if the Mohawks hand over their weapons and dismantle the barricades.

• The federal government claims the dispute is a provincial matter.

• The Mohawks continue fortifying their barricades and building bunkers.

• The Kahnawake Mohawks block the Mercier Bridge. The White population around the Bridge must now use the Champlain Bridge, a detour of many hours.

• The White population becomes hostile and Indians are burnt in effigy.

JULY 18. Meeting in Kahnawake of the 200 Native chiefs who support the Mohawks.

JULY 21. The official negotiations between the Quebec government and the Mohawks end.

AUGUST 6. The Warrior codenamed "Major" appears at the home of a veterinarian, Dr. Réjean Mongeon, and asks him if he can camp out in his stable.

AUGUST 12. Prime Minister Mulroney sends a mediator. He consents to lend the Canadian Army to the province of Quebec.

AUGUST 14. Arrival of the Canadian Army: 2,500 soldiers.

AUGUST 11-20. The Mohawks break off the talks, seeing the Canadian Army's arrival as a provocation, a means of intimidation. Some people claim the police force has lost control of the situation.

AUGUST 26. "Major" disappears from the Mongeon farm. Celebration in the stable. Roger Lazore says they are having a party.

AUGUST 28. Press conference. Prime Minister Mulroney supports Quebec's Premier, Robert Bourassa.

• Native women, children and elderly people try to flee from the reservation and are stoned by Whites.

AUGUST 31. The veterinarian Mongeon returns home and notices that his house has been vandalized. Everything has been turned upside down. He chases off the Warriors.

• Francis Jacobs and Ronnie Bonspille leave Oka, both to become SQ informers. Francis Jacobs betrays Ronald Cross to the SQ.

SEPTEMBER 1. The soldiers of the Royal 22nd Regiment close in on the Mohawk barricades.

• Francis Jacobs and his son Cory are assaulted by Ronald Cross, Gordon Lazore and Maurice Binette.

• Famous face-to-face encounter between Private Patrick Cloutier and a Warrior.

SEPTEMBER 2. *La Presse*: "The Warriors Have Obtained Secret Safe Passage."

SEPTEMBER 26. End of the Oka uprising. Arrest of the Warriors, including Ronald Cross.

1991

MARCH 15. Ronald "Lasagna" Cross and Gordon "Noriega" Lazore are released on bail.

MARCH 18. The Ministère Public appeals the bail release.

MARCH 28. The trial of the three Warriors—Ronald Cross, Gordon Lazore and Roger Lazore—held in Saint-Jérôme, begins. 85 accusations in all.

• Everything is adjourned till April 8, 1991, and it is mentioned that the Crown prosecutor intends to address the Court in French during the entire trial of these three anglophones.

APRIL 15. The Honourable Mr. Justice Benjamin Greenberg of Quebec's Superior Court renders his decision in favour of the Crown prosecutor. He refuses to conduct a trial in English.

MAY 11. An incident on the Kahnawake reservation: A Peacekeeper is assaulted. In this affair, three criminal accusations are made against Ronald Cross in Longueuil's Palais de Justice.

MAY 25. Marriage of Ronald Cross and Nadine Montour.

JULY 5. Ronald Cross does not appear at the Saint-Jérôme courthouse.

SEPTEMBER 17. Opening of the first inquest into the death of Corporal Marcel Lemay.

NOVEMBER 12. Inquiry with witnesses at the Longueuil Palais de Justice into the incident with the Peacekeepers that took place on May 11, 1991.

DECEMBER 5. Birth of Jerry Cross, son of Ronald Cross and Nadine Montour.

1992

JANUARY 8. Ronald Cross does not appear at his trial in Saint-Jérôme. Warrants for his arrest are issued.

JANUARY 9. During the night, Ronald Cross is arrested by the SQ in a Ville LaSalle apartment. He is brought back to the Saint-Jérôme courthouse the same day.

JANUARY 22. The trial of the three Warriors ends. Ronald Cross and Gordon Lazore are found guilty of some of the accusations made against them: Cross is found guilty of seventeen counts, and Lazore of five.

FEBRUARY 19. The Warriors are sentenced.

FEBRUARY 20. Request for appeal by the lawyers of Ronald Cross and Gordon Lazore.

JULY 3. Montreal's Palais de Justice: The thirty-nine other Mohawks are acquitted.

NOVEMBER. Mr. Richard Masson is mandated to be the Counsellor for the Coroner.

1993

JANUARY 20. Second inquest into the death of Corporal Lemay begins.

NOVEMBER 10. The SQ moves to stop the inquest, then changes its strategy. The SQ withdraws its request, with the result that the Superior Court has never had to make a judgement on it.

1994

FEBRUARY. The SQ prepares to request another suspension of the inquest. The request is presented before the Judge on February 12

• The Judgement delivered on February 25 rules to continue the inquest.

MARCH 15. Ronald Cross is called as a witness at the inquest.

BIBLIOGRAPHY

Amnesty International: Human Rights Violations Against Indigenous Peoples of the Americas. March 1992.

Andrews, Kristin. "The Oka Inquest: In the Shadow of the Pines." *The McGill Daily* 8 Apr. 1993: 8-9.

Berton, Pierre. *The Invasion of Canada*. 2 Vol. Toronto: McClelland & Stewart.

Boileau, Gilles. *Oka, terre indienne*. Éditions du Méridien.

Boisseau, Natalie. In *Maîtres* 2.7 (Sept. 1990): 11-26.

De Celles, Alfred D. *Papineau*. Beauchemin, 1905.

Christophe Colomb. Hachette, Jacques Heers.

Coleman, John. "Canada's Civil War" *Soldier of Fortune* Dec. 1990: 38-47.

Cortez. Éditions Hachette, Collection Génies et réalité.

Le Courrier Médical, Médecine Historique au Canada: Médecins de Nouvelle-France. Johanne Lepage.

L'épopée des Peaux-Rouges. Favre, Jean Pictet.

Farrow, E. P. *Psychanalysez-vous vous-même*. Éditions Poche Select.

Floriot, René. *Les erreurs judiciaires*. Éditions Flammarion.

Gauthier, Josée. "Rémi Savard et les 'Étrangers venus d'ici'," *Les Diplômés* printemps 1992. Published by L'Université de Montréal.

Geddes, Carol. "Une enfance autochtone." *Madame au foyer* Oct. 1990: 103-14.

Horn, Kahn-Tineta. *Mohawk Warriors Three: The Trial of Lasagna, Noriega & 20-20*. Kahnawake: Owera Books, 1994.

Jetté-Soucy, Nicole. *L'Homme délogé*. Éditions Le Beffroi.

Kandell, Jonathan. *La capital*. New York: Random House.

Lamarche, Jacques. *L'été des Mohawks*. Éditions Stanké.

Longeval, René. *Si j'ai tort*. Éditions d'Alcrena.

Maclaine, Craig, & Michael Baxendale. *This Land is Our Land: The Mohawk Revolt at Oka*. n.d.

Maclean's 103.32 (6 Aug. 1990).

Mesrine, Jacques. *L'instinct de mort*. Éditions J. C. Lattès.

Morrisseau, Miles. "Natives don't pay taxes? It's a myth." Report for Southam News.

Nations autochtones. Gouvernement du Québec.

Newcomb, Steve. "Papal Revocation Would Recognize Historic Wrongs of 'Discovery' Bull." *Indian Country Today* 18 (Aug. 1993): A6-7.

Nos racines. Tomes 1 & 2. Éditions Transmo.

O'Neil, Jean. *Oka*. Les Éditions du Ginkgo.

Pepin, André. "The Warriors Obtain Secret Safe Passage." *La Presse* 2 Sept. 1990.

Plummer, Dorothy, & Mary Mar. Article in *The Bridge*. Concordia University, Nov. 1992.

La Presse 23 Apr. 1992.

Richardson, Boyce. "Healing Time in Native Canada." *Readers' Digest*. [n.d.]: 67-72, 131-140.

Rumilly, R. *Papineau et son temps*. Tomes 1 & 2. Éditions Fides, 1977.

Sévigny, Colonel Pierre. *Face à l'ennemi: Mémoires du Colonel Sévigny*. Forthcoming. St. Lambert: Les Éditions Sedes, 1994.

Sioui, Georges E. *Pour une auto-histoire amérindienne*. Laval: Les Presses de l'Université Laval.

Tessier, Mgr Albert. *Neuve France*. Éditions du Bien Public.

Terre indienne. Autrement, Le chemin des larmes.

Vergès, Jacques. *Je défends Barbie*. Éditions Jean Picollec.

Wright, Ronald. *Stolen Continents*: *The "New World" Through Indian Eyes*. Toronto: Penguin Books, 1992.